THE NEXT 200 YEARS

BOOKS BY HERMAN KAHN

On Thermonuclear War
Thinking About the Unthinkable
On Escalation: Metaphors and Scenarios
The Year 2000: A Framework for Speculation
(with Anthony J. Wiener)
Can We Win in Vietnam?
(with members of the Hudson Institute Staff)
Why ABM? (with members of the Hudson Institute Staff)
The Emerging Japanese Superstate
Things to Come (with B. Bruce-Briggs)
The Future of the Corporation (ed.)

THE NEXT

A Scenario for

200 YEARS

America and the World

by Herman Kahn, William Brown
and Leon Martel

with the assistance of the Staff of the Hudson Institute

William Morrow and Company, Inc.
New York   *1976*

Copyright © 1976 by Hudson Institute

All rights reserved. No part of this book may be reproduced or utilized in any form or by any means, electronic or mechanical, including photocopying, recording or by any information storage and retrieval system, without permission in writing from the Publisher. Inquiries should be addressed to William Morrow and Company, Inc., 105 Madison Ave., New York, N. Y. 10016.

Printed in the United States of America.

10   77

Library of Congress Cataloging in Publication Data

Kahn, Herman (date)
Brown, William, Martel, Leon
    The next 200 years.

    Bibliography: p.
    Includes index.
    1. Economic history—1945-   —Addresses, essays, lectures.
2. Economic forecasting—Addresses, essays, lectures.   3. Technology and civilization—Addresses, essays, lectures.   4. United States—Economic conditions—1971-   I. Brown, William, joint author.   II. Martel, Leon, joint author.   III. Title.
HC59.K32   330.9′04   76-5425
ISBN 0-688-03029-7
ISBN 0-688-08029-4 pbk.

Preface

THIS SHORT BOOK is a partial report of work in progress at Hudson Institute on the crucial issues of population growth, economic development, energy, raw materials, food and the environment, which currently are the focus of attention for governments, academic institutions, private corporations, news media and concerned citizens all over the world.* While we do not ignore the short and medium terms, our focus in this book is on the long term—and we consider most of the immediate and medium-term issues that do arise as transitional phenomena. Rather than trying to solve the practical problems raised by these issues or even to predict the actual course of events, we have written a scenario for America and the world for the next 200 years which puts these issues in a new perspective. This scenario does, however, demonstrate that there are, in principle, solutions.

* This work originated in research initially undertaken for The Mitre Corporation Symposium on Energy, Resources and Environment (ERE), held on November 8–9, 1971, in McLean, Virginia. Subsequent presentations were made at the First General Conference, Phase II, of Hudson's Corporate Environment Study, January 9–14, 1972, in Venice, Italy, and The Mitre Corporation ERE Symposium of April 14, 1972, in McLean. Studies currently in progress at Hudson are expected to yield three additional books which will supplement and complement this volume. One will deal with the new environment for development; a second will focus on the next decade (1977–86); and the third will continue our examination of development and the prospects for mankind.

The American Bicentennial provides a unique opportunity to make such an examination, for it is a propitious occasion to assess where we have been, what the current situation is and where we are likely to go. There is an inherent human interest in seeing oneself, one's nation, one's time in the perspective of what has passed, and there is an equal interest in investigating the future—and these interests are enhanced at a time of historical commemoration. It is our hope that the thought and ideas growing out of this investigation will influence current public policy both directly and indirectly, and thus have an enduring impact.

Often contemporary issues are not fully understood until they have become history and can be seen in a historical context. To some degree futurology can furnish such a context now by giving us an artificial vantage point from which to look backward; examined in this long-term perspective, current issues look quite different and can be better comprehended. Even if the actual future turns out to deviate from the one projected, the exercise will prove worthwhile for the new insights it provides.

Such an effort seems particularly appropriate today, at a time when much popular and widespread discussion indicates that the prospects for mankind are very dim. We will not attempt here to rebut this view systematically (others, in addition to ourselves, have already undertaken that task in general and in detail). But we will try to depict a contrary scenario, one that if not correct in all of its particulars is still, we believe, much more likely to occur or to be relatively representative of what does occur.

Aside from the doomsday literature, we find little in the current discussions that looks much farther ahead than 10 or 20 years. We will try here to adopt the perspective of our grandchildren and our great grandchildren and represent—however inadequately—their interests and their needs. Mankind is now operating on such a grand scale that many current activities and programs raise issues that—at least conceptually—can be dealt with only in a much longer time frame. There is an obligation for all—but especially for the most advanced nation on earth—to define the problems of our future and suggest the means for dealing with them. In effect we are suggesting that both public and private institutions try to act as an early warning system and as a lobby for the medium- and long-term future; for we believe, to rephrase Santayana, that those who neglect the future risk losing it.

We have deliberately kept this report of work in progress as brief and nontechnical as possible. This means that our evidence is often more suggestive and heuristic than sufficient, that our arguments are foreshortened and that our conclusions will sometimes appear to be didactic and dogmatic. There may also be errors of both commission and omission. These we will attempt to deal with through further analysis and revision arising out of the program of specialized studies we currently have under way.

Beyond this we offer no apologies. We are trying to ex- amine some very important but for the most part basically simple issues. Our interest is as much in opening discussion as in closing it, in asking questions as in answering them, in raising issues as in settling them. However, we do speculate on solutions and conclusions as far as our courage and judgment will allow us to.

We frequently find that what is well known is poorly understood, and what is taken for granted is taken without thought. We also disagree with much of the thinking and discussion in academic, intellectual and literary establish- ments today. Therefore, for both the common and academic wisdom we offer uncommon analysis. The exercise may please some, jar others and perhaps upset more than a few. But we are confident that it will open a new perspective on the issues we discuss. For America and the world—in this anni- versary year—we could hardly ask more or offer less.

Herman Kahn
William Brown
Leon Martel

Croton-on-Hudson, New York
January, 1976

Acknowledgments

WE WOULD LIKE first to express our gratitude to those who have contributed generously to the research that has made this book possible: Community Funds, Inc., through T. Roland Berner; William B. O'Boyle; Raytheon Company; Henry Salvatori; Scaife Family Charitable Trusts; and the Alex C. Walker Educational and Charitable Foundation.

At Hudson Institute the authors have been most notably aided in their work by the research and analysis of the following staff members: Paul Bracken, Marylin Chou, Mary Esbenshade, Patrick Gunkel and David Harmon. In addition, special thanks are owed to our two 1975 Summer Interns: Owen Astrachan and Felicia Candela. We would also like to acknowledge our debt to Robert Panero, whose valued insights are sprinkled throughout this volume; to Marvin Gustavson for his contributions to Chapters III and VII; to Charles A. Zraket, Richard S. Greeley and Robert Pikul of the Mitre Corporation, who assisted us with Chapters VI and VII; and to Uno Svedin, who did research and analysis in support of Chapter VII.

We are all in agreement that this book has benefited greatly, both in form and substance, from the fine editorial hand of Arnold Dolin, and the expert editorial work of Ernest E. Schneider of the Hudson staff. We also want to express our appreciation to Ruth Ann Crow, who has drawn the graphics, and to our Librarian, Mildred Schneck, and her assistant, Ruth Paul, who have located numerous references, tracked down elusive citations and helped prepare our list of selected readings.

Our greatest thanks go to Maud Bonnell, Elaine Shelah and Josee Laventhol, each of whom has labored long and diligently to translate our often disparate and rambling thoughts into cogent manuscript. We would like to acknowledge also the tireless efforts of Vivian Hildebrandt, who has supervised typing of the manuscript, ably assisted by Kathleen Dymes, Louise Horton, Ann E. Marsek, Rose Marie Martin, Betty McRobbie, Mary Mitchell, Maureen Pritchard and Carolann Roussel.

To the distinguished members of our Prospects for Mankind Advisory Board,* we would like to express our appreciation for reading and commenting on earlier versions or portions of the manuscript. Particularly, we would like to express our gratitude for written comments on the first chapter by William W Kellogg, Senior Scientist of the National Center for Atmospheric Research, and Paul Weidlinger, of Weidlinger Associates. We also want to acknowledge our debt to those before us who have written about the postindustrial society and its implications, especially to the outstanding works of Daniel Bell, Colin Clark and Peter F. Drucker.

These, and many others who have assisted our work and encouraged our efforts, merit our gratitude for helping make this a better book, but we alone bear full responsibility for what finally meets the reader's eyes.

* A list of the members of this Board appears at the end of the book.

Contents

Tables

Figures

THE NEXT 200 YEARS

I

Introduction: Putting Growth in Perspective

THE SCENARIO PRESENTED, elaborated and tested in this book can be summarized with the general statement that 200 years ago almost everywhere human beings were comparatively few, poor and at the mercy of the forces of nature, and 200 years from now, we expect, almost everywhere they will be numerous, rich and in control of the forces of nature. The 400-year period will thus have been as dramatic and important in the history of mankind as was the 10,000-year period that preceded it, a span of time that saw the agricultural revolution spread around the world, giving way finally to the birth of the Industrial Revolution. At the midway mark in the 400-year period we have just seen in the most advanced countries the initial emergence of superindustrial economies (where enterprises are extraordinarily large, encompassing and pervasive forces in both the physical and societal environments), to be followed soon by postindustrial economies (where the task of producing the necessities of life has become trivially easy because of technological advancement and economic development). We expect that almost all countries eventually will develop the characteristics of super- and postindustrial societies.*

* It would be well to establish definitions of key words like "economy," "institutions," "culture" and "society" at the outset. We distinguish among them as follows: "economy" denotes economic and technological activity; "institutions" the laws and organizations; "culture" the style, values, national character and attitudes; and "society" refers to the whole.

THE CURRENT MALAISE

For the past several years many concerned, intelligent people have developed strongly pessimistic feelings about the evolution of economic, technological and industrial development. At first these feelings focused on glaring—and often growing—disparities in material well-being, not only between rich and poor nations, but within the rich nations themselves. More recently, rising concern about pollution and the possible exhaustion of many natural resources has increased the already serious doubts about the continuation of this "disproportionate" consumption—doubts often expressed as questions about the moral right of the rich to use up so many "nonrenewable" or scarce resources and often at prices that are considered unfairly low.

On the other hand, concern is also growing about the possibility of a new economic order in which resource-rich nations of the Third World would combine in cartels to set high commodity prices. By thus preempting for themselves much of the surplus available in the production process, they might permanently diminish the prosperity of the wealthy nations and make life intolerable for the resource-poor nations or those unable to join a cartel.

Added to these feelings is a pervasive loss of confidence in the ability of national leaders in almost all developed countries to deal with the problems that beset the world today. Domestic political scandal and a decade of futile combat in Southeast Asia have eroded the leading position of the United States in international affairs; worldwide inflation, accompanied by a major downturn in economic growth, has called into question the international economic institutions created in the wake of World War II. Bureaucracies have proliferated everywhere, while the services they offer have often declined as the number and cost of personnel have mounted alarmingly. To many it seems that the resources of the productive and fortunate are being increasingly drained without the lot of the less productive and less fortunate being measurably improved. Widely publicized ferment, agitation and so-called "liberation" movements among young people, women, and minority groups have signaled to some the imminence of possible revolution. French President Giscard d'Estaing's remark that "we can see that practically all these curves are leading us to disaster" * accurately encapsulates this current mood of malaise.

Indeed, a consensus is emerging among many scholars and journalists that a turning point has been reached in world history, one that portends either a much more disciplined and austere—even bleak—future for mankind, or a dramatic and revolutionary change in domestic and international society, or perhaps both. These observers argue that contemporary trends—and the increasing threats that appear to accompany them—rule out any realistic possibility, through current or even reformed institutions, of continued worldwide economic development. Indeed, they tend to view further development as endangering the prospects for mankind, and they conclude that technological, economic, political and moral imperatives require a basic change in the emphasis of mankind's activities—from seeking growth to slowing growth, from affluence to austerity, from conspicuous consumption by the few to equitable distribution of a limited and finite product among all.

THE HUDSON STUDY AND THE AMERICAN BICENTENNIAL

The Hudson Institute has been engaged for some time in the first phase of a major attempt to examine and analyze these issues in world development, and our preliminary findings suggest that the views described above may be based to a large extent on a misreading of certain current realities and their implications for the future. In fact, while Hudson's

---

* In press meeting, Paris, October 24, 1974, Press and Information Service, French Embassy, Washington, D.C.

examination of these problems in historical perspective does reveal serious and potentially disastrous future possibilities, it also shows that many of them are more the growing pains of success (often accentuated by ill-timed bursts of mismanagement as well as the needlessly dire prophecies of doomsayers) than the inevitable precursors of doom.

In our view, the application of a modicum of intelligence and good management in dealing with current problems can enable economic growth to continue for a considerable period of time, to the benefit, rather than the detriment, of mankind. We argue that without such growth the disparities among nations so regretted today would probably never be overcome, that "no growth" would consign the poor to indefinite poverty and increase the present tensions between "haves" and "have-nots." Nevertheless, we do not expect economic growth to continue indefinitely; instead, its recent exponential rate will probably slow gradually to a low or zero rate. Our differences with those who advocate limits to growth deal less with the likelihood of this change than with the reasons for it.

As part of our study we have developed two perspectives on the future which many might judge to be optimistic but which we consider quite realistic. (While events may not follow either of these two perspectives, we do think they provide good ways to examine current trends.) One perspective, which we call "earth-centered," assumes that for the next 200 years the vast majority of the human population will continue to inhabit the earth and that extraterrestrial activity will be limited to exploration and modest levels of exploitation. While important, these space activities will not significantly affect human population growth rates, nor will they entail radical shifts in the rate of growth of gross world product (GWP). Our second perspective, styled "space-bound," assumes a much more vigorous effort in extraterrestrial activities early in the 21st century, including the eventual establishment of large autonomous colonies in space involved in the processing of raw materials, the production of energy and the manufacture of durable goods—both for indigenous consumption and as exports back to earth or to other solar-system colonies. Such developments would involve substantial migration from earth and could eventually create very new and different patterns of population and product growth, all quite beyond any projections made from a basically earth-centered perspective.

For the purposes of this book—to present a plausible scenario for a "growth" world that leads not to disaster but to prosperity and plenty—we have focused on our first perspective. By doing so we are making what is in effect an *a fortiori* argument, asserting that the transition we foresee (and the resolution of many current problems) can be accomplished by what is available to us here on earth, in terms of both living space and resources. It is possible that our second perspective will turn out to be closer to reality, and if so, then it is clear that the growth projections of our 200-year scenario will be more than fulfilled. Thus, although personally we are somewhat more inclined toward the second perspective, it is on the first that our case rests. It should be noted that even if the second perspective turned out to be more difficult to achieve than we now believe, the fulfillment of the first perspective, with its enormous development and technological advancement, would create a potential for the allocation of resources to space that could contribute to the eventual successful development of the second perspective.

Figure 1 sums up our first perspective (with parenthetical remarks indicating plausible events in space associated with our second perspective). Here we argue that the growth first of population and later of GWP will approximate a flattened S-shaped, or logistical, curve, passing from an earlier era of slow growth through the present period of exponential growth to a final leveling-off.* (If we were to focus on our second perspective, we would argue that a new S-shaped curve may start sometime in the 21st century, representing the colonizing

* The current year is depicted as the inflection point of the curve, at once both its moment of maximum growth and therefore the beginning of slower growth. In reality, following current UN data and projections, we expect to witness the inflection point in rate of population growth during the period 1976 to 1980; for reasons to be explained in the following chapter, we believe that the inflection point in rate of growth of GWP will lag about a decade behind that of population. While both predictions are far from certain, the second one is much less certain than the first.

Figure 1. The Great Transition.

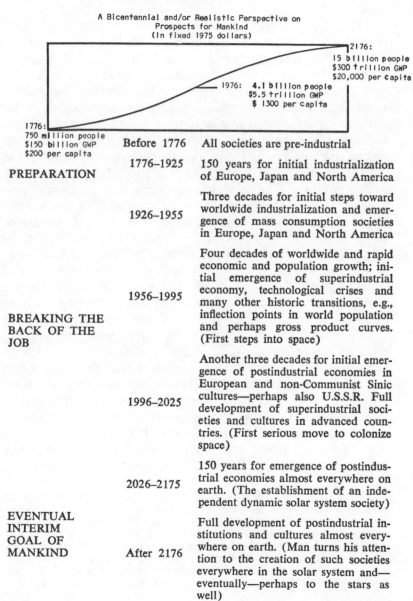

A Bicentennial and/or Realistic Perspective on
Prospects for Mankind
(In fixed 1975 dollars)

2176:
15 billion people
$300 trillion GWP
$20,000 per capita

1976: 4.1 billion people
$5.5 trillion GWP
$ 1300 per capita

1776:
750 million people
$150 billion GWP
$200 per capita

	Before 1776	All societies are pre-industrial
PREPARATION	1776–1925	150 years for initial industrialization of Europe, Japan and North America
	1926–1955	Three decades for initial steps toward worldwide industrialization and emergence of mass consumption societies in Europe, Japan and North America
BREAKING THE BACK OF THE JOB	1956–1995	Four decades of worldwide and rapid economic and population growth; initial emergence of superindustrial economy, technological crises and many other historic transitions, e.g., inflection points in world population and perhaps gross product curves. (First steps into space)
	1996–2025	Another three decades for initial emergence of postindustrial economies in European and non-Communist Sinic cultures—perhaps also U.S.S.R. Full development of superindustrial societies and cultures in advanced countries. (First serious move to colonize space)
	2026–2175	150 years for emergence of postindustrial economies almost everywhere on earth. (The establishment of an independent dynamic solar system society)
EVENTUAL INTERIM GOAL OF MANKIND	After 2176	Full development of postindustrial institutions and cultures almost everywhere on earth. (Man turns his attention to the creation of such societies everywhere in the solar system and—eventually—perhaps to the stars as well)

of the solar system and eventually generating growth rates that we would not even try to estimate; perhaps later, when this transition was near completion, yet another curve would begin, representing the colonization of interstellar space, a task that may be as open-ended as the galaxy, or for that matter the universe.)

The earth-centered perspective assumes that the world population flattens out at least for a while at 15 billion people, give or take a factor of two (that is, a range of 7.5 to 30 billion); the per capita product * at $20,000, give or take a factor of three; and the GWP at about $300 trillion, give or take a factor of five. The possible ranges of variability are, of course, larger than those given, but we find the above quite plausible.

If our basic assumptions are correct, then the metaphor of exponential growth during the next century will be increasingly misleading. Moreover, assertions that an impending dramatic collision with physical limits will force a choice between a policy leading inevitably to catastrophe and one of no-growth (or even a forced low-growth) are, in our view, based on highly implausible assumptions. Indeed, Hudson projections based on current trends point to the conclusion that growth is likely to continue for many generations, though at gradually decreasing rates, which we expect to result more from a slowing pace of demand than from increasing difficulties in obtaining physical supplies. According to this

---

* We have chosen to use "gross product" and "per capita product" as basic variables, despite much current criticism and even disillusionment with these concepts. There are many problems associated with the concept of GNP defined as the total amount of goods and services produced, but some of the criticism is not relevant. It is certainly true that it does not *necessarily* measure welfare, progress, quality of life, true wealth, power, strength or desirability, but then it is not supposed to. Nor does the fact that many consumer expenditures can be thought of as operating costs and not income change the utility of the concept.

In any event, for our purposes here, we have adopted the simple, common-sense and largely reasonable approach that dollars tend to measure opportunity costs and that gross product tends to measure the total heft of the economy and indicate the limits of what can or cannot be done with the resources of any particular economy.

It should also be noted that, except where otherwise indicated, all dollar figures are in fixed, constant 1975 equivalents, with inflation discounted.

analysis, the gradual leveling-off tendency will be a social consequence of the proliferation of such factors as modernization, literacy, urbanization, affluence, safety, good health and birth control, and governmental and private policies reflecting changing values and priorities (accompanied by the increasing desire of vested interests to protect their status quo from external pressures for expansion). Although the possibilities of overcrowding, famine, resource scarcity, pollution and poverty cannot be dismissed, they should be seen as temporary or regional phenomena that society must deal with rather than as the inevitable fate of man. In this context, one of our main concerns is that beliefs and attitudes that create resistance to economic growth will impede the resolution of our current problems and perhaps even lead to the kind of disasters we all want to prevent—that they will become, in effect, self-fulfilling prophecies.

America's first 200 years have both mirrored and driven the age of industrialization. The year of the start of American independence, 1776, also witnessed the publication of Adam Smith's *Wealth of Nations;* it is therefore a convenient benchmark for the beginning of the Industrial Revolution. These two revolutions marked the onset of a unique era in world history: It was the Industrial Revolution that spurred unprecedented productivity and economic growth, and it was America that came to play the leading role in that development. It thus seems both fitting and opportune that the American Bicentennial should almost coincide with the turning point in what can be mankind's great transition to a world which, without being a utopia, can create both the opportunity and the foundation for an environment of relative peace and prosperity for nearly everyone, and hopefully one of relative joy and fulfillment as well.

FOUR CHARACTERISTIC VIEWS OF TWO BASIC IMAGES OF THE EARTH-CENTERED PERSPECTIVE

There are two basic and totally different images (or models) of the earth-centered perspective, which we have labeled the *neo-Malthusian* and the *technology-and-growth* positions. The first is a modern version of the analysis of the 19th-century English economist Thomas Malthus, who argued that population would eventually grow faster than food supply, thus implying that starvation would soon become mankind's perennial lot, at least for the poor.* The opposite image stems from the premise that in the next 100 years material needs can be met so easily in the currently developed world that the more advanced nations will develop superindustrial and then postindustrial economies, and that the rest of the world will soon follow. Obviously these two basic images encompass a range of differing views and concepts, so to represent them fairly and without exaggeration, we have developed two detailed views for each of the two models—one of which in each case is a relatively extreme position, the other a moderate one. Thus, the neo-Malthusian model includes the views of a strong neo-Malthusian and a moderate neo-Malthusian (that is, a guarded pessimist); and for the contrasting model, we describe the positions taken by a moderate (or guarded optimist) and an enthusiastic advocate of technology and economic growth. Both of the moderate positions argue that we can expect serious problems in energy shortfalls, resource scarcities and food distribution. Both also raise the real possibility of cataclysmic or irreversible environmental damage. But both hold open the possibility (in one case barely and

* Scholarly integrity and concern for the somewhat maligned memory of Malthus compel us to note that this best-known conclusion of his was an early view which he tempered and amended in his later work. We are grateful to Roger Revelle for pointing this out to us.

Table 1. Four Views of the Earth-Centered Perspective.

A. Convinced Neo-Malthusian	B. Guarded Pessimist	C. Guarded Optimist	D. Technology-and-Growth Enthusiast
1. BASIC WORLD MODEL			
Finite pie. Most global nonrenewable resources can be estimated accurately enough (within a factor of 5) to demonstrate the reality of the running-out phenomenon. Whatever amounts of these resources are consumed will forever be denied to others. Current estimates show we will be running out of many critical resources in the next 50 years. The existing remainder of the pie must be shared more fairly among the nations of the world and between this generation and those to follow. Because the pie shrinks over time, any economic growth that makes the rich richer can only make the poor poorer.	*Uncertain pie.* The future supply and value of both old and new materials are necessarily uncertain. Past projections of the future availability of materials usually have been gross underestimates. One can concede this could happen again, but current estimates seem relatively reliable. Current exponential growth clearly risks an early exhaustion of some critical materials. Prudence requires immediate conservation of remaining resources. Excessive conservation poses small risks while excessive consumption would be tragic.	*Growing pie.* Past technological and economic progress suggests that increasing current production is likely to increase further the potential for greater production and that progress in one region encourages similar developments everywhere. Thus as the rich get richer, the poor also benefit. Higher consumption in the developed world tends to benefit all countries. Excessive caution tends to maintain excessive poverty. Some caution is necessary in selected areas, but both the "least risk" and the "best bet" paths require continued and rapid technological and economic development.	*Unlimited pie.* The important resources are capital, technology and educated people. The greater these resources, the greater the potential for even more. There is no persuasive evidence that any meaningful limits to growth are in sight—or are desirable —except for population growth in some LDC's. If any very long-term limits set by a "finite earth" really exist, they can be offset by the vast extraterrestrial resources and areas that will become available soon. Man has always risen to the occasion and will do so in the future despite dire predictions from the perennial doomsayers who have always been scandalously wrong.
2. TECHNOLOGY AND CAPITAL			
Largely illusory or counterproductive. Proposed techno-	*Mostly diminishing returns.* Generally, despite many ex-	*Required for progress.* Despite some dangers, only new tech-	*Solves almost all problems.* Some current problems have

logical solutions to problems of pollution or scarce resources are shortsighted illusions that only compound the difficulties. Even on a moderate scale this approach would only further deplete crucial resources while avoiding the real problems and prolonging the poverty of the LDC's. Any future economic development should be restricted to the Third World and should include some transfer of existing capital assets from the overdeveloped nations. A completely new approach is needed for the long term.

ceptions, the future will bring diminishing marginal returns from new investments, and the effort required for economic gains will increase dramatically. The technology, capital equipment and other efforts required to obtain minerals and food in increasingly marginal situations will accelerate the approaching exhaustion of many resources and substantially increase pollution and shortages— possibly to lethal levels. Until practical solutions to these problems have appeared, we must turn away from technology and investment.

nology and capital investment can increase production; protect and improve the environment; hold down the cost of energy, minerals and food; provide economic surpluses with which to improve living standards in the LDC's; and prepare prudently for any potential unexpected catastrophes. We must be alert for problems resulting from inadequately understood innovations, inappropriate growth and/or natural causes. However, we should proceed with energy and confidence even while exercising great caution and constantly reassessing future risks and benefits.

resulted from careless application of technology and investment, but none without a remedy. It is not paradoxical that technology which caused problems can also solve them —it only requires mankind's attention and desire. There is little doubt that sufficient land and resources exist for continual progress on earth. Most current problems are the result of too little technology and capital, not too much. In any case man's desire for expansion into new frontiers will lead eventually to the colonization of the solar system and effectively unlimited *lebensraum*.

3. MANAGEMENT AND DECISION-MAKING

Failure is almost certain. The complexities, rigidities and ideological differences among nations and their institutions make it inconceivable that present human organizations, even with computer assistance, could sufficiently comprehend and effectively act to solve our most important problems. A

Likely failure. The rapidity of change, growing complexity and increasing conflicting interests make effective management of resources, control of pollution and resolution of social conflicts too difficult. Some slowdown and simplification of issues are imperative —even if they require drastic

Moderately successful. Systematic internalization of current external costs and normal economic mechanisms can make most private organizations adequately responsive to most problems. A practical degree of public regulation and a low degree of international cooperation can

Not a serious problem. We flatter ourselves that current issues are more important and difficult than ever. Actually there is usually nothing very special happening. Mankind always has faced difficult and dangerous problems and poor solutions resulted in high costs. Sometimes there is even a Dar-

Table 1. (continued)

A. Convinced Neo-Malthusian	B. Guarded Pessimist	C. Guarded Optimist	D. Technology-and-Growth Enthusiast
drastic redesign is needed to circumvent the thrust toward bigness, to permit much more local and decentralized decision-making, and to live and work on a manageable human scale. More emphasis is needed on the community and regional level—much less on big business, big government and big organizations generally.	actions. If we don't reform voluntarily, more painful political and economic changes may be imposed on us by the catastrophic events made inevitable by failure to act soon. (Note that there is a wide range of attitudes here toward central planning and local decision-making, but almost all of them mistrust the current "unfree market.")	handle the rest, if somewhat awkwardly. Outstanding management is rare but usually not essential as most institutions learn from experience—if often slowly and painfully. (But good management can reduce the number and intensity of painful experiences.) Except for wars, shocks as great as the oil shock and other 1973–74 experiences are rare, and yet existing systems reacted adequately—and survived.	winian selection—the successes surviving and the failures disappearing. Progress has made the stakes today less dramatic. Modern communication and information systems and sophisticated organizations provide a capability for rapid adjustments to reality whenever changes are required and government interference is not counterproductive.

4. RESOURCES

A. Convinced Neo-Malthusian	B. Guarded Pessimist	C. Guarded Optimist	D. Technology-and-Growth Enthusiast
Steady depletion. Mankind is steadily, and often rapidly, depleting the earth's potential resources for foods, fuels and minerals, and overwhelming its capability to absorb or recycle pollutants. Catastrophic results for some of these resources may be postponed until the 21st century, but food, energy and some	*Continual difficulties.* The basic problem of limited resources may be insoluble. Even when sufficient resources exist, politics, incompetent management, poor planning and slow responses make effective solutions difficult under conditions of exponentially increasing demand. Where resources are becoming	*Generally sufficient.* Given slow but steady technological and economic progress and an ultimate world population below 30 billion, it should be feasible to attain economic living standards markedly better than current ones. With rapid progress and good management generally, even higher economic levels and an out-	*Economics and technology can provide superb solutions.* The earth is essentially bountiful in all of the important resources. Sudden large price fluctuations tend to be "self-correcting" within a few years although they can be misinterpreted as basic shortages (as in 1973–74). Near-term prices are certainly important, but we have

minerals already appear to be critically short for the near term. All signs point to catastrophe for the medium- and long-term future.

5. CURRENT GROWTH

Carcinogenic. Current population and economic production are akin to a spreading cancer. They are already more than the earth can sustain in a steady state. Future economic or population growth will hasten and increase the magnitude of the future tragedy. The current demand for continued economic growth and the likelihood of a greatly increased world population only imply a steady worsening of the present extremely dangerous conditions.

scarce and unrelenting demands for growth are coupled with incompetence, intolerable pressures are generated and disaster becomes probable. A more cautious approach to growth seems clearly desirable.

Large potential for disaster. Even if roughly current levels of production could be indefinitely sustained, continued exponential growth in population and production eventually must lead to exhausted resources and hazardous pollution. Few positive human values would be served by continued mindless growth. We must learn that demand is not need. Unless drastic voluntary reforms limit future growth, catastrophes stemming from limited resources and high pollution levels are likely to make these reforms mandatory before long.

standing quality of life become possible. Economic success enhances national capabilities to resolve specialized resource issues as they arise. However, the tendency toward cartels coupled with political conflicts could create occasional short-term problems in maintaining adequate supplies at reasonable prices.

Probable transition to stability. Although current projections are uncertain, social and cultural forces inherent in both developing and affluent societies appear likely to limit the world population to about three times the current level and average per capita production to about two or three times the current U.S. level. There seems to be more than enough energy, resources and space for most populations, assuming that a relatively small number of people put forth the necessary efforts and others do not interfere.

often lived with short-term problems. Trust in the economics of the market system, confidence in emerging technological solutions and a little patience will remedy the current resource issues just as they have in the past.

Desirable and healthy. No obvious limits are apparent. Even with current technological potential, growth (except perhaps in a few of the poorest nations) is and will be purely a matter of human choice, not of natural limitations. Problems always exist, but solutions always emerge—often as a result of the dynamism of growth. We do not know man's ultimate fate, but truly fantastic economic and technological capabilities are likely to be included as both a means and an end (e.g., they probably include self-reproducing automation and space colonization in the next century).

Table 1. (continued)

A. Convinced Neo-Malthusian	B. Guarded Pessimist	C. Guarded Optimist	D. Technology-and-Growth Enthusiast

6. INNOVATION AND DISCOVERY

A. Convinced Neo-Malthusian	B. Guarded Pessimist	C. Guarded Optimist	D. Technology-and-Growth Enthusiast
A trap. New discoveries of resources, new technologies and new projects may postpone the immediate need for drastic actions, but not for long. Such postponement will make eventual collapse earlier and more severe. Prudence demands immediate restraint, cutbacks and a basic change in values and objectives. The time for short-run palliatives is past.	*Increasingly ineffective.* The basic solution is to increasingly limit demands, not to encourage a desperate search for new inventions that might suffice temporarily but would exacerbate long-run problems by increasing environmental damage and depletion of resources, while encouraging current growth and deferring hard decisions. Although technological solutions may buy some time, it has become increasingly important to use this time constructively and avoid the undue economic expansion that new discoveries encourage.	*Usually effective.* New resources, new technology and economic growth often produce new problems, but they still do solve current problems, improve efficiency and upgrade the quality of life. Also, they increase the toughness and flexibility of the economy and society (i.e., provide insurance against bad luck or incompetency). With good management, they also can help to reduce population growth, conserve expensive minerals, improve nutrition within the poorer countries and generally improve future prospects.	*Mankind's greatest hope.* New and improving technologies (agronomy, electronics, genetics, power generation and distribution, information processing, etc.) aided by fortuitous discoveries (e.g., ocean nodules) further man's potential for solving current perceived problems and for creating an affluent and exciting world. Man is now entering the most creative and expansive period of his history. These trends will soon allow mankind to become the "master" of the solar system.

7. INCOME GAPS AND POVERTY

A. Convinced Neo-Malthusian	B. Guarded Pessimist	C. Guarded Optimist	D. Technology-and-Growth Enthusiast
Destined to tragic conclusions. The major consequences of industrialization and economic growth have been to enrich the few while exploiting and impoverishing the many. The gap between rich and poor as well as the total misery in the world are at all-time highs—	*Increasing and threatening.* Income gaps have been increasing and may lead to dangerous responses. A drastic decrease in income among the poor may even be likely soon. Worldwide class warfare may emerge following a series of desperate political crises.	*Declining absolute poverty.* Worldwide, the threat of absolute poverty (i.e., possible large-scale famine) is likely soon to be forever abolished. Some income gaps may increase during the next century, but some will decrease. Generally, incomes of both rich	*A misformulated problem.* Western civilization required about 200 years to change from general poverty to general affluence. Because of their success and continuing advances in technology, many of the current LDC's will be able to make a similar transi-

and growing. Meanwhile natural resources, the heritage of the poor countries, are being consumed by the rich, thereby denying the poor any real hope for better living conditions—even temporarily.

These are not only possible but may be imminent as a consequence of the gaps and the exploitation of the mineral resources of the LDC's. A more equitable income distribution has become a most urgent matter.

and poor will increase. Both the gaps and improving technology will tend to accelerate development in poor countries. Attempts to force a rapid equalization of income would guarantee only failure and tragic consequences.

tion within 50 years. All countries can be expected to become wealthy within the next 200 years. Any lesser scenario would be unreasonable or simply an expression of some exceedingly bad luck and/or bad management. The gap is a false issue possibly conjured up by neurotic guilt.

8. INDUSTRIAL DEVELOPMENT

A disaster. Further industrialization of the Third World would be disastrous, and further growth of the developed world even worse. The rich nations should halt industrial growth and share their present wealth with the poor. The poor nations should husband their precious natural resources, selling some of them only at prices much higher than those prevailing today.

A step backward. The LDC's should avoid the mistakes of the developed nations. They should instead seek smaller, more human and more community-oriented enterprises appropriate to their needs. They would be better off preserving their cultural, environmental and ecological values than entering headlong into destructive polluting industrialization, sacrificing thereby both their current values and any long-term potential for a peaceful world.

Should continue. Industrialization of the LDC's should and probably will continue. The rich nations will probably help with technical assistance, but would be unlikely to share their output to the extent of serious deprivation. Also the natural resources of the LDC's are at most of limited benefit even to those richly endowed. Their only real hope for affluence lies in economic development.

Necessary for wealth and progress. During the last 200 years progress has been identified mostly with technological innovation and economic development. Despite the current outcries, this view is and will be substantially correct. All those who wish to, can and should share in the benefits offered by modern civilization.

9. QUALITY OF LIFE

Ruined. Through excessive growth, mankind has become the most destructive species in history and may yet increase the extent of this damage

In conflict with much growth. Continued economic development or population growth might well mean further deterioration of the environment,

More gains than losses. If environmental protection, health, safety and other considerations are neglected, growth would be accompanied

A meaningless phrase and issue. Disgruntled or unhappy people often oppose real progress for romantic, class, selfish or other reasons. They

Table 1. (continued)

A. Convinced Neo-Malthusian	B. Guarded Pessimist	C. Guarded Optimist	D. Technology-and-Growth Enthusiast
manyfold. Indeed, a point of no return may have been passed already, mostly because of the persistent and growing potential for nuclear warfare. In any event, the values that lead toward a satisfying and wholesome life have already been largely destroyed in the developed nations.	overcrowding, suburban sprawl and a society suitable more for machines than human beings. Priorities must change; market demand is not the same as need; GNP is not wealth, high technology not the same as a good life; automation and appliances do not necessarily increase human happiness.	by an unnecessary destruction of important values. However, much of what some elites claim to be destructive others consider constructive (e.g., a pipeline). With adequate internalization of the appropriate costs (by society's criteria), complaints from unhappy factions might still be loud or visible but would be generally inappropriate.	are not representative of the nation and need not be taken at face value. In a changing world, some elites may not benefit much or may even lose somewhat. But most people would benefit and gain expectations for an even better future.

10. LONG-RANGE OUTLOOK

A. Convinced Neo-Malthusian	B. Guarded Pessimist	C. Guarded Optimist	D. Technology-and-Growth Enthusiast
Bleak and desperate. Unless revolutionary changes are soon made, the 21st century will see the greatest catastrophe of history resulting from large-scale damage to the environment and to the ecology of many areas. Billions will die of hunger, pollution and/or wars over shrinking resources. Other billions will have to be oppressed by harsh authoritarian governments. Grave and even draconian measures are justified *now* to alleviate the extent and intensity of future collapse.	*Contingent disaster.* Although it is not possible to predict which disaster is most imminent, many possibilities exist even if we are careful and prudent today. Unless we take drastic actions soon, mankind may be overwhelmed by climate changes, destruction of ocean ecology, excessive pollution or other disasters. Society must not challenge the environment and ecology so recklessly any more. We must also manage our resources and population more prudently—at least after the next disaster, if not before.	*Contingent success.* The 21st century is likely to bring a worldwide postindustrial economy in which most problems of poverty will be largely solved or alleviated. Most misery will derive from the anxieties and ambiguities of relative wealth and luxury. Some suffering and damage will mark the historical transition to a materially abundant life, but the ultimate prospect is far superior to a world of poverty and scarcity.	*High optimism and confidence.* We cannot know mankind's ultimate goals, but they include a solar civilization and a utopian notion for the quality of life on earth. The potentialities of modern technology and economic progress are just beginning to be visualized. Dangers exist, but they always have and always will. There is no need for faint heart. Man should face the future boldly and openly because the future is his to determine—and to enjoy.

in the other relatively clearly) that with technological progress, wise policies, competent management and good luck, mankind can deal with these problems and survive into a future where, at the least, opportunity is not foreclosed and disaster is not foreordained. The guarded optimist's view goes even further, holding that we may still avert ultimate disaster even if the policies are not so wise, management not so competent and luck not so good, but the worse the policies, management and luck, the greater the potential for tragedy along the way and even for final cataclysm.

These four views, as they relate to ten different issues, are summarized in Table 1. Columns A and B list the typical neo-Malthusian concerns about the limited potential of the earth and the likelihood of greatly diminishing returns on future investments, rapid depletion of resources and uncontrolled exponential or cancerous population growth. In this image, innovation and discovery are seen as traps and further industrial development is expected to hasten the approaching disaster; growth of either the population or the economy is considered antithetical to a high quality of life. In short, the long-term outlook is grim. The two views of the technology-and-growth model, listed in columns C and D, argue that because of the evolution of knowledge and technology, resources are increasing rather than fixed; more technology and more capital are vital; decision-making will probably rise to the occasion, despite some incompetency or bad luck; enough resources will be available at reasonable costs so that reasonable rates of growth can be achieved; current exponential population growth will make a natural transition to stability; innovative discoveries will yield great improvements; and although absolute income differences could increase for a while, current levels of absolute poverty will decrease almost everywhere (the rich will not get richer while the poor get poorer, but both will become richer). Thus, in this view, all things considered, the long-range outlook is quite good.

In this study we are more interested in the differences between B and C than in the gross differences between A and D, even though B and C come rather close to merging on some issues. Current advocates of column B (formerly closer to A) originally emphasized the sheer physical impossibility of the earth's supporting 10 or 20 billion people and often stated this claim in an extreme form. Today many of them take a relatively moderate position, but one still strongly colored by their past beliefs. Rather interestingly, many of the followers of these less extreme advocates have not shifted with them and talk as if those they support still hold A rather than B beliefs.

B and C advocates represent two of many possible middle positions. They project that in some places and at some time there will be too many people for available food supplies and that considerable suffering will result, but in the long term they see the rate of population growth slowing and world population eventually stabilizing—but for different reasons. The B position is remarkably close to the C position, but it tends to emphasize conscious and drastic efforts to reduce demand as the basic method of solution rather than major efforts to increase supply. Indeed, B advocates argue that unless there are very intense and dramatic programs to cut demand and limit it permanently, the situation will turn out much as anticipated in column A. Those who favor C, on the other hand, see the situation as rather close to the view in column D. However, they also believe that there are both more natural limitations to demand and more dangers in growth than the D people might concede. The C people also depict some few resources as fixed, limited and nonrenewable, but they argue that the growth of knowledge and technology will normally make available—though not always without problems and difficulties—new sources and substitutes. Acknowledging that there will be incompetency and bad luck, causing serious problems, they doubt that these will be fatal. They visualize much more demand than A and B believe can be tolerated, but not so much more that it could not be met, even if it required expanding supply capabilities somewhat.

In the last several years, the neo-Malthusian attitudes outlined in columns A and B have gained great influence. Not too many years ago—not more than a decade—most educated Americans would have placed themselves in column C, leaning toward D. Today they tend to be in column B and leaning toward A, and many unreservedly support that column's full neo-Malthusian conclusions. It has become increasingly fashionable, especially among intellectuals at prestige universities and among spokesmen in the most respected newspapers and journals as well as on television, to attack economic growth, capitalism, industrialization, the consumer society and related values. Casual references are made to our vanishing resources, the end of the "energy joyride," our increasingly "suicidal" pollution, our "self-destructive materialism," the poverty of our emotional and aesthetic lives, the disease of "consumeritis" and the need to "kick the energy habit." The United States is usually singled out as the prime culprit in this indictment: It has only one-sixteenth of the world's population, yet with incredible selfishness and shortsightedness, it has been allocating to its own use about one-third of the world's nonrenewable resources.

We believe that the movement toward column A—propelled by a combination of compassion and guilt for the plight of the world's poor and the coincidental occurrence of worldwide crises in the supply of food and energy—has gone too far. Spurred now by well-publicized studies, it has acquired a momentum of its own which, if continued, will only deepen the malaise it depicts and make longer and more difficult the recovery that is required. We believe that plausible and realistic scenarios can be written consonant with a view that sees the world moving from column C toward column D. We argue that there is both need and opportunity for growth, and that because America and the rest of the nations of the developed world *do* use resources so intensely, there will be stimulation, not depression, for the economies of the less-developed countries. In fact, as we will discuss in the next chapter, the clearest moral and political argument for further growth in the developed world (and against artificial and forced limitation) is that it aids the poor both within and outside the developed countries.

Despite the confident tone of these last few pages and some of our earlier discussion, we would like to stress that in no sense do we wish to play down the importance of the issues raised by the neo-Malthusians or to assert that there are no serious problems. While we generally tend to be optimistic about many of them, we recognize that very unpleasant situations can arise—possibilities which must be dealt with competently and responsibly. We also believe not only that this can be done, but that in many cases it already is being done. Finally, we feel that even though the costs and risks are great, the effort to achieve a postindustrial society is on balance a worthwhile one; and further, that priorities which emphasize technological advancement and economic growth, but with prudence and care, are likely to be acceptable and largely beneficial.

Thus our disagreement with advocates of the limits-to-growth positions sometimes is that they raise false, nonexistent or misformulated issues; equally often, perhaps, they pose as being basically insoluble real problems for which we believe rather straightforward and practical solutions can be found in most cases. In fact, it is one of the main purposes of this volume to set out at least *a fortiori* solutions to many of these "insoluble" problems. In our view, the more intractable and basic difficulties usually lie much less in the nature of things than in recent or current policies, in unnecessarily poor administration or sometimes in just plain bad luck. Most important of all, if successful programs are devised to deal with old problems, then inevitably new problems are uncovered and new goals are set; to those who take the initial success for granted, it may then seem as if nothing has been accomplished.

WATERSHEDS OF HISTORY

The two great watersheds of human history (excepting religious events) have been the agricultural revolution, which started in the Middle East's Fertile Crescent some 10,000 years ago, and the Industrial Revolution, which began in Holland and England about 200 years ago. In much the same way that the agricultural revolution spread around the world, the Industrial Revolution has been spreading and causing a permanent change in the quality of human life. However, instead of lasting 10,000 years, this second diffusion process is likely to be largely completed within a total span of about 400 years, or roughly by the late 22nd century. What we call the superindustrial and postindustrial economies will be emerging during the late 20th and early 21st centuries, to be followed eventually by corresponding changes in institutions and culture until a new and appropriate society has been developed.*

In order to characterize the nature of these changes, it is useful to distinguish four kinds of economic activities: primary, secondary, tertiary and quaternary.†

Primary economic activities are extractive—principally agriculture, mining, forestry and fishing. One can think of the corresponding society and culture as being organized to "play games with and against nature" and for protection against "barbarian" invaders and raiders; in such a society the ratio of rural to urban dwellers is in the range of twenty to one, with the former supporting the latter by some kind of primary activity.

Secondary economic activities have to do with construction and manufacturing. The corresponding society and culture, primarily urban, are organized mainly to "play games with and against materials, as well as against nature," and the other major activity tends to be organized warfare, both offensive and defensive.

Initially the emerging postindustrial economy will be characterized by a service economy, emphasizing what are called *tertiary* economic activities—services that support primary and secondary activities, such as transportation, insurance, finance, management, many governmental activities, much education and training. Nature becomes a relatively control-

---

* Various authors have developed and expanded notions of postindustrial economy, institutions and culture. Preeminent among these in the depth and sophistication of their analyses are Daniel Bell's *The Post-Industrial Society: A Venture in Social Forecasting* (New York: Basic Books, 1973) and, with a very different manner and emphasis, Peter Drucker's *The Age of Discontinuity* (New York: Harper & Row, 1969).

† The terms "primary," "secondary" and "tertiary" were first used in this sense by Colin Clark, Research Fellow at Monash University, Melbourne, Australia. "Quaternary" is used at Hudson Institute to describe the postindustrial era activities.

lable variable and constraints set by materials become less and less important as technology and affluence increase. This results in a society and culture, probably more suburban than urban, whose major activity is "games with and against organizations," and which is characterized by a structural society which emphasizes organizational and professional pluralism in the distribution of power and prestige. Knowledge rather than experience becomes the major asset and there is an increasing problem of "educated incapacity." * Wars no longer "pay" and the recourse to large-scale organized violence becomes restricted generally to defensive situations or attempts to preserve some aspect of the status quo.

Eventually, in the 21st century, we should expect a transition to a different kind of service economy, to what we term a *quaternary,* or truly postindustrial, economy. Here the primary, secondary and tertiary activities will constitute only a small part of human endeavors; more and more people will do things for their own sake, and even more than today ends will become more important than means. Indeed there will be a tendency to choose means which are also ends, and at the same time in many situations the distinction between ends and means will gradually disappear. This attitude is also often found in a primary or pre-industrial society, and there are, in fact, great similarities between our view of a likely post-industrial society and many pre-industrial societies. This quaternary society can be characterized as emphasizing people "playing games with and against themselves, with and against others, and with and against communities." We hope that the emphasis will be more on "with" than "against," but both will be clearly possible. At first sight the problem of war appears anomalous in this context, but there may well be possibilities for both offense and defense; there will certainly be issues of the use and control of violence. The major quaternary activities—often constituting what we now more or less consider leisure activities—could include the following:

---

* By "educated incapacity" we mean an *acquired or learned inability to understand or see a problem,* much less a solution. Increasingly, the more expert, or at least the more educated, a person is, the more likely he is to be affected by this.

Ritualistic and aesthetic activities (perhaps creating special structures and environments), including the evoking of images or feelings of splendor, pride, pomp, awe, and communal, ethnic, religious or national unity or identity; oneness with nature and the universe, and various "explorations in inner space."

The creation of taboos, totems, demanding religions, traditions, and customs; arbitrary pressures, constraints and demands; moral and social equivalents of war; some other pressures and risks, including those involved with some of the more bizarre forms of "discretionary behavior."

Reading, writing, painting, acting, composing, musicianship, arts and crafts—particularly if done for their own sake.

Tourism, games, contests, rituals, exhibitions and performances.

Gourmet cooking and eating, an aristocratic and formal style of life, epicurean and family values (including visiting, entertaining and "togetherness").

Hunting, fishing, hiking, camping, boating.

Acquisition and exercise of nonvocational skills.

Improving property (noneconomically motivated), such as by gardening, upkeep, interior decorating and the use of home-made artifacts.

Conversation, discussion, debating and politicking.

Many other cultural and social activities.

Most welfare and social security functions.

Other "recreation," including the search for change, broadening experiences, adventure, excitement and amusement.

Many public works and public projects (e.g., some space activities, some underseas exploration, most protection or improvement of the environment, monumental architecture).

The transition to a society principally engaged in quaternary activities—a transition likely to be well under way in the next century—will mark the third great watershed of human history. Future ages will undoubtedly look back at what happened in these four centuries of economic development and technological advancement as mankind's most effective and pervasive transformation—from a world basically inhospitable to its few dwellers to one fully commanded by its expanded multitudes.

Of course there will be problems. Some of them are likely to be: wishful thinking, illusion, decadence, educated incapacity and a kind of violence-prone boredom. Furthermore, we suspect that, even if the society were to work as we outline in this image of the future, many of our readers will be somewhat unhappy with the prospect and wonder whether mankind really wishes to "stagnate" in such a total quaternary society. We believe that at least for a time most people would generally enjoy this postindustrial society, but there would be many who would not. For them it simply would not be exciting and challenging enough; indeed, it might be rather boring for many ambitious, advancement- and achievement-oriented people (though there will be fewer such people). We rather suspect that space will be the major focus for many of these people, and that the existence of such a frontier—as a locus of dynamism, initiative and entrepreneurship—will be very healthy for the quaternary society that is developing on earth.

None of this should be taken as denigrating the possibilities that actual income and resources from space could be important to the earth, that space could generate many economically and technologically profitable activities, and that exploitation of space could serve as a major positive economic and technological influence on our earth-centered perspective. But our point is that mankind will seek to explore and exploit space not just for its economic and technological reasons, but because it will be seen as a psychological and moral frontier. There will always be some for whom even the most utopian society on earth will be an empty or inadequate achievement; for many of these, space will not be the last frontier, it will simply be the next frontier. Thus the evolution of a postindustrial society on earth need not be the end of man's future, but a beginning—a base from which to start the journey across yet another great watershed in human history.

We believe that many well-intentioned people are being distracted from mankind's real future problems and possibilities by issues that appear central today but are in fact largely temporal, peripheral or badly formulated. We are presenting here a scenario for America and the world that sees the dominant issues of today—population, economic growth, energy, raw materials, food and pollution—as basically solvable or resolvable in the near- and medium-term future, transitory issues of a transitory era, the problems of a time between world penury and world prosperity.*

We further suggest that many fashionable concerns of the day encourage the self-defeating belief that our present problems are either hopeless or that efforts to solve them by expanding supply will only make them worse. We, of course, believe that available skill, sound management and sensible policies can transform most of these issues into memories, and that by coping with them sucessfully mankind will gain the incentive and the morale needed to face the real issues of tomorrow. All the problems will not be solved or avoided, but the human costs involved in getting from here to there can be significantly reduced, and every aspect of the trip can be facilitated. And the prospect of doing all this should help to alleviate many current problems of morale and commitment, of direction and purpose.

---

* See the Appendix, where we contrast these issues with what we consider the *real,* and basically uncertain, issues of the future.

II

Turning Points in the Growth
of Population and Product

A BASIC ASSUMPTION underlying our 400-year earth-centered scenario is that the rates of world population and of economic growth are now close to their historic highs and will soon begin to slow until finally, roughly 100–200 years from now, they will level off in a more or less natural and comfortable way. Such an evolution obviously must have a very different impact upon the prospects for mankind from that of the scenarios currently forecast by many advocates of the limits-to-growth position, who often assume that growth rates will be exponential until limited by physical barriers. Some of these advocates have argued that exponential rates would not only exhaust the earth's resources but produce—after a number of doublings—a population covering the planet's surface and expanding away from it into space. But in any perspective there must eventually be limits to population growth which obviously must occur long before such growth would result in a compounding calamity of scarcity, famine, pollution and accompanying social disorder.

Our perspective, consequently, foresees a gradual slowing —in percentages but not necessarily in absolute terms—of these rates in a world of growing prosperity, which may be the main reason for the reduction. That is, a reduced or leveled off demand rather than inadequate supply will drive the transition. In our view, the resources of the earth will be more than sufficient—with a wide margin of safety—to sustain, for an indefinite period of time and at high living standards, the levels of population and economic growth we project. In this chapter we will present evidence and analysis, first, for a turning point in the rate of world population growth, perhaps during the American Bicentennial year, and second, and less convincingly (but we believe still persuasively), for a relatively early turning point in the rate of world economic growth, perhaps in a decade or two.

POPULATION IN PERSPECTIVE

The picture of world population growth that exists today in the minds of most informed persons resembles the one shown in Figure 2—that is, with population rapidly accelerating from the beginning of the Industrial Revolution to the present, where exponential rates would have it doubling in less than 35 years. With this curve rising ever more steeply, it seems clear that history's course can lead only to disaster.

Figure 3 presents a sharply different perspective. In the diagram on the left, three 60-year population growth-rate curves are illustrated, each of which reaches a maximum within the next few years. The slowest of these (A) is based on the United Nations Population Bureau's "medium" variant projection; the second (B) assumes higher rates and is used in many of our "surprise-free" projections; * and the third (C), with still higher rates, is used in some of our *a fortiori* projections.†

Seen in this perspective, the problem of exponential population growth appears almost to be solving itself. There can,

---

* The "surprise-free" projection is one that assumes innovation and progress that would not be surprising in the light of past trends and current developments—that is, it is based on extrapolations of current or emerging tendencies and expectations.

† The *a fortiori* projection used here is one that is mostly based on current—or near current—technology and avoids the assumption of great future improvements like those that have characterized past historical experience.

Figure 2.   Population Growth—1750 to Present

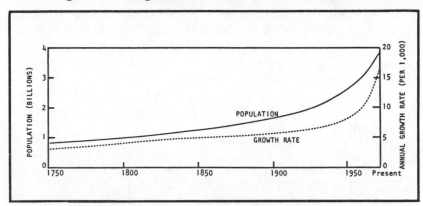

SOURCE: Adapted from Ansley J. Coale, "The History of the Human Population," *Scientific American*, September 1974, p. 42.

Figure 3.   Rate of Growth of World Population

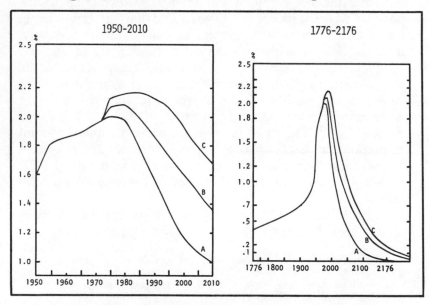

A...UN MEDIUM/HUDSON LOW
B...HUDSON MEDIUM (SURPRISE-FREE)
C...HUDSON HIGH (*A FORTIORI*)

Figure 4. Population Growth Rate in Long-Term Historical Perspective

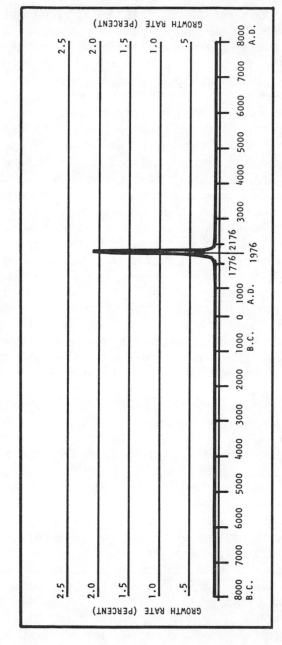

SOURCE: Adapted from Ronald Freeman and Bernard Berelson, "The Human Population," *Scientific American*, September 1974, pp. 36–37.

of course, be no certainty that these projections will prove to be accurate, for we have only the available data and demographic theory on which to rely. But these constitute a historical basis for forecasts and strongly suggest that fears of a population explosion should disappear within the next half-century. By then, if these projections are reasonably correct —and we have deliberately avoided centering our argument on the most optimistic of these (A)—the population worries and alarmist exhortations of the 1960's and 1970's may well be recorded as an amusing episode in human history.

The diagram on the right in Figure 3 extends population growth rates to plot a forecast for our 400-year transition scenario. This time frame shows even more clearly the rapid rise in the population growth rate and its anticipated fall; and when one looks backward from 2176, the temporary nature of the current population phenomenon becomes very obvious.

Finally, in Figure 4 we present a much longer time perspective on population growth—16,000 years—in which current rates of growth appear as a momentary spike, or blip, in an otherwise smooth line. It is, of course, a blip that has created a vast change in the nature of the world, and it appears especially meaningful to us since we are probably living at its very apex. The clear message of this last perspective is that despite —or perhaps because of—the anticipated twentyfold increase in world population over the 1776–2176 period, any expectations of exponential population growth continuing over appreciable periods of time can only be a delusion, at best a rather naive extrapolation of an unusual human experience into the indefinite future without a real understanding of the dynamic forces involved. To those who cry out that this exponential growth must stop, the answer is that it does in fact appear to be stopping now, and not for reasons associated with desperate physical limitations to growth. Therefore, except for some particular problems in certain geographic areas, our attention can be more profitably placed on the attending social changes, the time scale of the process and the special problems raised along the way.

We would like to add one further point that could carry the problem of population growth quite literally into another realm and which may strike many as fanciful or even absurd.

It is our strong feeling that we may have oversimplified the discussion by ignoring potential future technological developments that could provide new solutions as well as encourage new cycles of growth. One such development—which seems entirely feasible during the next century—is the construction of ocean-based facilities, especially very large, partially submerged, *floating* industry-oriented complexes. Current studies and some actual construction indicate that these structures can be substantially less expensive than comparable land installations when the ratio of volume to area is sufficiently large. (Some major savings occur because the structures are invulnerable to earthquakes and high winds.) With modular designs, such structures could be made quite large—approaching the size of a small city.* We can only guess at the impact of such a development, but we do know that the useful area that oceans can provide for such ventures is large and often strategically situated.

Another likely development to be considered is the previously discussed possibility of migration to outer space. Speculation on such activity is still greeted by most observers as the stuff of far-out fantasy; yet within the past two years a growing number of serious scholarly studies have not only asserted a technical feasibility for colonization in space but have also indicated an economic viability as well.† Were such an event to begin and be successfully maintained, it could conceivably lead to a massive migration over a century or more and, as with major migrations of the past, initiate a new—and desired—cycle of population growth.

These are only two of numerous possibilities; technological progress is such that within 50 years many more will be thought of that simply would not be taken seriously at this time. Their total effect on future population growth can only be guessed. Instead of the desire for more living and working

---

* John P. Craven, "The City and the Sea" (Honolulu: University of Hawaii, Marine Programs, rev. February 12, 1975).

† For example, Gerald K. O'Neill, "The Colonization of Space," *Physics Today*, September 1974, pp. 32–40; Krafft A. Ehricke, *Exoindustrial Productivity: the Extraterrestrial Imperative of Our Time* (El Segundo, Calif.: North American Space Operations, Rockwell International Corporation, May 1975); and T. A. Heppenheimer, "R&D Requirements for Initial Space Colonization," *Astronautics and Aeronautics*, December 1975.

space, an unknown potential for a better quality of life may turn out to be the major incentive for the creation of such "new worlds" in oceanic and/or outer space. In the past such an incentive has been powerful and a spur to population growth. However, none of this plays an important role in the considerations of this chapter, though it may be exactly such developments that will dominate the real future.

It should be noted that there is plenty of room in almost all countries for everybody to have a suburban lifestyle. For example, in such places as Holland, Bermuda or Westchester County (all of which are considered almost ideal areas in which to live) we find that population densities range between 1,000 and 2,000 per square mile. This means that in 10 percent of the United States we have enough room for from 300 to 600 million people, and thus we have 90 percent of the land left over for recreation, agriculture, industry and various other purposes. This conclusion even applies to the more populated countries in Asia, where the population densities are not unduly high (about 500 per square mile in India).

We also believe that the comparison of the results of experiments with high-density caged rats to modern urban life is completely misleading; the real issue is not one of raw population density but of floor space and a structured community. Cities of the future will not be as crowded as were those of the ancient world, where people lived clustered within protective walls.

THE DEMOGRAPHIC TRANSITION

The anticipated reduction in the rate of worldwide population growth is best explained by referring to what is known as the "demographic transition," which we do not consider a hard-and-fast theory but a description of historical experience, replete with exceptions, anomalies and occasional reverses. For our purposes it depicts the change that has occurred, and that seems likely to occur in the future, in population growth rates during the successive stages from pre-industrial to post-industrial society.

In the pre-industrial stage annual birth rates were about 40 per thousand, a rate determined largely by the maximum number of children that could be born under prevailing local conditions. There were undoubtedly wide fluctuations in local populations as death rates were affected by sporadic calamities (wars, famines, plagues, floods and other natural accidents), but overall these kept pace with birth rates, permitting only a slow, almost imperceptible rate of population growth.

Then, as the process of economic and technological development gathered momentum, following the onset of industrialization, productivity increased and food distribution was regularized—reducing famines and famine-induced disease—and more resources were devoted to improvements in public health and safety. The consequent decline in death rates—with birth rates remaining high—caused a rapidly increasing population. As industrialization matured in the developed nations, a third stage was reached when parents began to have fewer and fewer children, prompted by the reduced value of children as economic assets combined with the increased cost of rearing them and the erosion of traditional religious and social pressures for large families. The result, coexistent with a leveling of the death rate, was a decreasing rate of population growth. Finally, as we move into the super- and postindustrial stages, birth and death rates have both been leveling off, and eventually we will again reach an equilibrium in population, similar to that of the pre-industrial stage. However we still expect short-term fluctuations in birth rates triggered by transitory events such as wars, depressions or unusual prosperity.

Many demographers and economists now believe that this transition will occur, or is even now occurring, in the less developed countries just as it has in every country of the developed world, and that the process is in fact accelerating. Historical evidence seems to support this conclusion that the demographic transition is compressing. The time required for the transition to very low growth rates in Western Europe and North America was 150 years (1775–1925), for the Soviet Union it was 40 years (1910–50), and for Japan it was only 25 years (1935–60). The most recent estimates show a definite decline in crude birth rates in the 1960's for 15 developing nations and a probable decline for eight more. Since these figures represent all major world regions except sub-Saharan Africa, it is possible that the 1960's marked the beginning of a worldwide decline in the fertility of developing nations.

None of the above implies that a continued drop in world population rates is inevitable, but our "surprise-free" projection is that the world's population is on the verge of passing through the inflection point of its growth and that in 200 years it will total approximately 15 billion, give or take a factor of two. Nonetheless, for the purposes of this book—setting forth a scenario showing the feasibility of high standards of living in a future world with a large population—we could have projected a population of 30 billion, retained the earth-centered perspective and still made our case. In order to demonstrate the enormous leeway we believe will be available to a population as large as 15 billion, we now set forth our explanation of why we expect most of the world's developing nations to achieve rapid and sustained economic growth.

ECONOMIC GROWTH, YESTERDAY AND TODAY

In the nations of Western Europe and North America, where industrialization began, economic growth was a slow and extended process of acquiring capital, resources, learning and technology. The activities involved in moving from invention to application, and then on to investment and finally to return spanned decades. In the United States, for example, it took about 200 years to go from $250 to about $7,000 in per capita GNP; the process went much faster in Japan, but still it took more than a century to go from about $100 to about $4,000. Today we would expect the process to go much more rapidly in many of the developing nations, the central reason for this being the existence of the gap between the developed and the developing that many deplore as the source and cause of underdevelopment. In the following pages we will describe 10 forces that will aid this growth, each unique to the developing nations and each taking advantage of the gap between them and the developed nations.

But before going on to examine these positive factors, we must first note that there are many aspects of the current world environment that do not facilitate development—that is, ways in which the developed nations might actually impede or even reverse progress in the developing nations. Some of them are: excessive destruction or damage to indigenous social structures, morale or traditional beliefs and character; the generation of excessive expectations; harmful or excessive exploitation by foreigners; political and social unrest and other strains caused by the foreign presence itself; misplaced benevolence; and harmful fashions or ideologies.

Probably most important among these are the many effects that can result from the impact of two cultures on each other —particularly when one of the cultures is more modern and powerful, or at least is judged to have many features that seem worth adopting. The impacted culture can develop a rather severe inferiority complex or other pathology. Many experts once considered this desirable in that they saw the goal of development as the breaking apart of the old society and the rebuilding of a new society more or less along Western lines. But this view has generally been replaced by the belief that there should be mutual adaptation. The Japanese, and to some degree the Chinese, have shown us that it is often very worthwhile to save much of the old society, to attempt to reform, modify and adapt the new techniques, technologies and institutions so as to fit them into the existing framework— and, of course, vice versa. It now seems likely that each society that successfully modernizes will find its own way to industrialization and then eventually to a post-industrial society. Thus this process may be analogous to the perspective common to Asian religions in which there are "many mountains up to God and many roads up each mountain."

Keeping in mind these problems posed by the West for the developing world, let us return now to our examination of the 10 forces we see as making possible an acceleration of economic growth in most of the underdeveloped nations.

1. *Availability of capital, markets and technology*

We begin with the Middle East as the most spectacular example. There may be more than a trillion barrels of recoverable oil buried beneath the sands and waters of the Middle East, particularly around the Persian Gulf. Civilized people have lived there for almost 10,000 years, yet this treasure was practically unused until quite recently. At current prices (roughly $12 a barrel), the nominal value of Middle East oil is $12 trillion, or twice the total real tangible wealth of the United States. This is misleading, though, since the oil is buried and mostly not available—or usable—for a long time to come. For a fairer comparison, one can think of the oil as generating an income stream of about $50–$100 billion per year over the long term. If this is discounted between 5 and 10 percent a year, it implies a total present value between $1 trillion and $4 trillion, or, roughly speaking, about a third of the real tangible U.S. wealth.

What created this wealth? First, of course, it was nature; second, and almost more important, it was the fact that the developed countries of the world were not only eager to buy and use this oil, but were able and willing to furnish the wealth, capital and technology necessary to find and exploit it. The Middle East countries had to be able to strike a bargain for their share of the income, and it is true that for many years they got relatively little ("relatively little" here means about $5–$10 billion a year).

With full credit to nature and to the governments and people of the Middle East, we think it fair to say that it was the existence of the developed nations that made most of the difference between the value of that oil 50 years ago and its value today. Of course the developed world did not create this wealth in the Middle East out of altruism. Nevertheless, the fact is that the industrialized world needs huge amounts of raw materials and other products and has the capital, technology and institutions necessary to help utilize almost every kind of resource in the developing world. Therefore, almost anywhere in the world, if a country has anything usable at all—from a minimally decent labor force to almost any kind of minerals or tourist attractions—these resources can usually be identified and then exploited to the mutual benefit of the host country and outside countries. There is often an initial need for help from outsiders, but even then, within a decade or two (if appropriate policies are in effect), indigenous personnel can take over the day-to-day operations, become first professional workers, then managers and finally owner/operators. Further development can then generally be carried through with largely indigenous means, or at least with the host nation and/or its nationals in control. It is also worth noting that even if the task of development has to be shared for a while with outsiders, which may often include transnational companies, this mutual effort usually involves less cost and in some cases even less exploitation than would have occurred with any comparable process in the past.

We are not, of course, arguing that the West can create anywhere else in the world the kind of overnight rags-to-riches story that the Middle East has seen. What we are saying is that analogous, though more limited, events are going to occur in many developing nations, and we can already cite the examples of Malaysia and Indonesia with tin and rubber, and Zambia and Chile with copper. At first this will involve mostly the so-called "coping" nations (those which have developed useful resources and have been able to utilize the income from them to accelerate their per capita economic growth), but eventually even many of the noncoping will be more or less pulled forward because of the gap between them and the more developed nations—and because of the reduced competition from the now relatively developed coping nations.

2. *Export of labor*

From 1960 onward, Spanish emigration grew rapidly and in the late 1960's reached an annual level of around 100,000—representing 10 percent of the entire labor force. Most of these were "guest laborers" in other European nations (that is, migrant workers). Not only did they send home substantial earnings, but they also saved money, most of which they brought back when they returned to Spain. They also picked up important skills while away. This process by itself has been sufficient to greatly facilitate development, not only in Spain but in all of southern Europe from Portugal to Turkey, in some parts of North Africa, in much of Latin America, to some degree in South Korea and to a lesser extent in Taiwan. It may soon be an even more important factor in some of these nations and also could occur in many other parts of the world; in fact, it might be very important to try to stimulate wider participation in the future on both sides, by both the senders and receivers of laborers.

One conclusion of our present studies is that, once the current recession is over, a pressing problem of the next decade or two will be an enormous labor shortage in the developed world, particularly in jobs that can usually be found at the bottom of the socioeconomic ladder. Citizens in the developed countries no longer wish to perform these tasks since they have many better opportunities. This labor shortage will coexist with an even larger labor surplus in the developing world. It is of course difficult to bring these two needs together, because many countries—for clearly stated reasons—do not wish to follow a policy of relatively unrestricted migration. Therefore, we are not likely to see an acceleration of the movement of the late 1960's and early 1970's, when there were perhaps 12 million legal and illegal guest laborers in Europe, and perhaps 3 million illegal Latin American immigrants in the United States. But it ought to be possible to organize a systematic movement of temporary labor, combined perhaps with some kind of education or training, in which workers will be exported from the Third World to developed nations, where they will reside for periods varying from six months to three years and then return to their own country with capital and skills. In order to ensure their return, it might be possible to have the host government pay part of the earnings after the guest laborer returns home. Potential problems with labor unions might be alleviated if the guest laborers contributed modestly to union dues or even to the pension programs, ensuring that indigenous union members would gain from the use of migrant labor (both might even be employer contributions). Many might call this indentured labor or exploitation, but not the laborers themselves, who would be able to earn perhaps 10 times the wages in their own countries (where many are grateful to have any kind of job at all) and to pick up useful skills and experience as well.

There is, of course, the problem of the poor in the host country. In some countries, particularly the United States, there is some competition for these jobs at the bottom of the economic ladder (particularly at times—like the present and recent past—of persisting unemployment). It would be wrong to introduce this process too early and on too large a scale; but in many more homogeneous countries this problem hardly exists at all.

3. *Import of export-oriented industry*

Many European businessmen (and some Americans), rather than use guest laborers, have found it more desirable to move their labor-intensive factories to a developing country and use its indigenous labor. In many ways this is both less expensive and more convenient than moving the labor to the work. Of course, an important condition is the belief that the financial and political milieu is, and will remain, stable. It is rather interesting that this movement has spread to Eastern Europe, often via the mechanism of the joint enterprise, as well as elsewhere in the world. The most spectacular examples have been the Japanese in Taiwan and South Korea, and, to a lesser but still important degree, the United States in both East and Southeast Asia; and Mexico has the so-called "border industries," which—often at distances many miles from the border—can import parts and materials from the United States and re-export finished products, paying U.S. import tax only on the value added by the Mexican factories.

If this kind of opportunity can be made more generally available, it will probably do more to expedite development and increase the standard of living in both the developed and the developing nations than almost any other single program we know of. To be sure, such a program must be designed with care and carried through with some intelligence and flexibility to prevent either excessive dislocation or excessive dependence in both the developed and the less-developed worlds. There would have to be, on the one hand, protection of certain important industries and hedging against activities, like those of the Organization of Petroleum Exporting Countries (OPEC), perceived as "hostile" and, on the other hand, protection against instability and excessive influence. For example, it would not be in the interest of the United States to "export" 90 percent of its steel and automobile industries, an unlikely but possible outcome if this process were allowed to continue for decades without controls. However, the gradual export of about a third of these industries would probably be viable.

4. *Tourism*

Two decades ago tourists traveling to Spain numbered about 5 million a year. Today Spain receives about 35 million foreign visitors a year (about 10 percent more than its population), who spend on the average about $100 each. Most countries do not have that many tourists, but in some the amount spent by each tends to be higher. In Spain's case the $3.5 billion it derives from this source is sufficient almost by itself to guarantee successful development. Tourism also plays an important role in Portugal, Greece, Mexico, South Korea, Taiwan, Hong Kong, Italy, much of Southeast Asia, North Africa and many parts of Latin America. In fact, in many of the coping countries tourism is doubling every two or three years and soon may reach quite high numbers.

It seems reasonable to assume that by the end of the century tourism will be one of the largest industries in the world, if not the largest. As closely as we can estimate, it should continue its current tendency to increase by 10 to 20 percent a year until about the year 2000, when the familiar S-shaped curve might start operating here also.

It is easy to see why this should be so. People seem to have an almost insatiable desire to travel; and for increasing numbers the money and time available for travel have been growing, while the facilities for traveling have become more convenient and less expensive. Today few American tourists would find themselves dominated by cost or time considerations in choosing between a trip from New York to Seattle and one from New York to Copenhagen. This attitude may eventually be held by tens of millions of people for almost any place on earth. While much of this recreational traveling will go from developed countries to developed countries—or, increasingly, from developing to developed—in enough cases the main recipient of the income will be the coping countries. Being host to hordes of tourists is not necessarily a pleasant way to facilitate economic development, but for those who wish to develop rapidly, or even slowly, many sacrifices may be required, of which playing host to tourists could be one of the least onerous.

5. Technology transfer

Until about the time of World War I, it was almost impossible to transfer moderately complicated technologies to other than Western European and North American countries, Japan or Russia. One reason for this was that because the technology itself was both complicated and unreliable, its maintenance and operation were prohibitively difficult and expensive, even in those settings where the technology transfer was superficially successful. Today many kinds of industrial and scientific technology are very easily transferred. For instance, almost every growing country of any size either has a steel mill with the capacity of at least a million tons a year or expects to get one soon.

One of the most startling examples of the new technology is the rapid growth and proliferation of hand-held calculators and computers. The most advanced of these—priced well under $1,000 and getting cheaper all the time—are fully programmable, with 10 computation-capable memories and a capacity for 100 orders. Indeed, in many important ways these computers are as capable as machines that less than two decades ago would have occupied 2,000–5,000 feet of floor space, cost over $1 million and required a staff of 5 to 10 persons to operate. Today more and more advanced technology is available to every country in the world. Each nation can now buy this technology, install it and expect reasonable operation for many years without extraordinary effort or training. The products are not restricted to producer goods but also include many kinds of consumer goods which can make life happier, more convenient and healthier—transistor radios, television sets, other appliances, home telephones, antibiotics and X-ray machines.

But perhaps most important, we now know how to transfer highly productive agricultural technology. It is true that in many cases it is not possible to transfer such technology directly from the developed world to a specific developing country. Indigenous research must first create the various inputs needed for local agriculture, and the country must also construct adequate infrastructure and institutions. At the same time we do have the ability to design the necessary programs, at least for most circumstances and places.

6. *Availability of useful examples, institutions and individuals*

In some ways the most important achievement of the Western nations was to blaze the trail of development. Now, however, much more has been done. There are so many developed countries today, providing a wide range of examples of how to do it—and even more countries that provide examples of how not to do it. There are also many institutions facilitating growth in the developing countries. Some have asked why the developed world does not make greater use of those institutions and knowledge, and the most obvious answer is that most exchanges already occur quite efficiently and effectively at the private level, mainly through schools, journals, books, sheer visibility, actual work experience, and various other contacts and experiences. Most problems that do exist, with the exceptions noted later, are with the students, not the teachers—though clearly the teachers could do much more, and to an increasing extent many of the academic and international organizations seem to be teaching wrong or irrelevant lessons.

To some degree, if a developing country lacks sufficient indigenous skills or organizations, it can hire them or persuade the developed world to supply them. This is very useful, particularly if it is recognized as a temporary or interim arrangement. Sometimes the pride of the developing country or of individuals there impedes such arrangements, particularly if the outside assistance comes not from an industrialized nation but from another Third World country. Yet often the most suitable and appropriate help can come from another nation at about the same level, or one just a little more advanced than the country being aided. Sometimes special arrangements can be made to make this kind of aid acceptable—especially if it is a commercial arrangement, which is indeed one of the great virtues of commercial arrangements.

7. Importation of "pollution" and "menial" activities

It is common today to sneer at the concept of shifting polluting and annoying activities to the developing world, as if it were unfair or even immoral to do so—a particularly reprehensible exploitation of the Third World. Practical people understand that this is not so. The poor and the untrained have always done the dirtier and less pleasant work, and this is true among countries as well as within them. In fact, one of the main opportunities for the poor and the untrained is to undertake those activities which the affluent and well-trained no longer wish to do for themselves or can no longer find local people willing to do.

Of course one must be reasonable. We do not expect poor and untrained people to accept risky or unhealthy occupations, and there is no reason why a country should do the same—for example, no country should be willing to import dangerous kinds of heavy-metal pollution, at least not under normal circumstances. On the other hand, some erosion of clean air and pure water standards is almost inevitable if there is going to be rapid development. But since many new anti-pollution technologies are now readily available, the sacrifices that may be made here are going to be much less than those already experienced by the developed countries. There is no particular reason why one should look askance at this process or feel in any way uncomfortable about it. In much of the Third World, the greatest pollution is poverty, and it is worth making very great sacrifices indeed to reduce that blight rapidly and effectively.

8. *Import substitution*

Often the various industries in the developing nations buy many of their inputs—of both labor and materials—from abroad at least initially, and this can result in real aggravation in the host country. In addition, the host country must pay a price that is a drain on its foreign exchange when it imports products for indigenous use. However, once these markets have been established, it is frequently an easy matter for the importing country's suppliers and manufacturers (and manpower) to compete effectively with the overseas exporter. Sometimes this competition is greatly aided by government acts that encourage or force purchases from local suppliers and/or the hiring of indigenous labor. These regulations can be justified by the argument that it takes time to develop one's own production facilities and skill and that such encouragement and protection by the government help to reduce the time needed. But this argument can be pushed too far. Often industries or individuals protected by their governments are simply not able to develop a competitive capability, and the country is thus saddled with expensive supplies (or labor) which actually slow down development rather than facilitate it.

While it is easy to see the benefit of such encouragement, it is difficult for people to envisage or measure the many activities that have been discouraged because of the existence of such a program; often the second consideration swamps the first, but the activity that failed to materialize because it was discouraged is not represented by any lobby or interest group —or even noticed.

One way to prevent excesses in this direction is to assist a local project solely through a tariff (or special tax on foreign labor) rather than using quotas or other compulsory measures. It is thus possible to measure clearly the advantage being given to the local supplier (or indigenous labor), and furthermore, if he cannot "make it" behind the shield offered by a high tariff (or tax), the country is not saddled by ridiculously high-cost and/or low-quality goods (or labor). If the outsider can manage to meet the local competition, even though it is protected by a tariff, he probably deserves to get the business, not so much as a moral or ethical issue but for the greater good of the country imposing the tariff.

9. *Existence of a high order of external stability*

We have already mentioned the fact that the Middle East is probably worth at least several trillion dollars. Rather remarkably, considering past history, it appears that if the various OPEC nations behave reasonably well, they are likely to be allowed to enjoy their wealth more or less undisturbed for some time, perhaps forever. True, some of them are spending billions of dollars for national defense, but in many cases they are more concerned about each other or internal security than they are about the outside world.

What we have here is actually an unprecedented situation in world affairs. Let's look at the example of Libya, which currently enjoys an income of $7.5 billion a year from oil exports. While it is now estimated to have only 21 billion barrels of oil (worth, at current prices, about $250 billion), if properly explored it would probably soon yield much larger reserves. Despite the fact that Libya has acted provocatively and irresponsibly in supporting a number of extremist groups— Arab and non-Arab—we would hazard a guess that Libya is quite safe from attack, although it has been estimated that a very small number of battalions of moderately well-trained and equipped Western troops could probably take over the country. The neighboring Egyptians, who could certainly make good use of the revenues from Libya's oil, have sufficient military power, and in many ways the rulers of Libya have gone to considerable trouble to antagonize the Egyptian leaders. Still it would appear that Libya is reasonably safe from an Egyptian or other army's attack and subsequent occupation and annexation.

It is true that there is continuing interference in the internal affairs of many developing nations—including much subversion and corruption by developed countries—and that other difficulties are created as by-products of this "cold war." However, in comparison with any earlier period, the developing nations are relatively safe from military threats by the developed world (and in most cases from their neighbors as well). Even vulnerable countries can now go to rather remarkable lengths in provoking the industrialized world and still feel a rather high degree of safety. The most extreme case in recent history was, of course, the Vietnam War. The tonnage of bombs dropped was larger than in World War II, but the extraordinary amounts of explosives were handled with considerably more restraint. There was nothing in North Vietnam remotely like the damage done to Rotterdam or Hamburg—and the vital canals were safe from all but accidental bombing.

Some years ago Costa Rica disbanded its army (though not its police force), arguing that its security was not dependent on having such a force. While few countries would do likewise, it is still true that for most nations, particularly many of the less developed countries, the burden of providing for the national defense has never before represented such a small portion of the national economic and human effort.

10. *Foreign aid*

This factor is placed at the end of the list because for the most part foreign aid seems likely to play a relatively small role in the future, even smaller than it has in the past. We say this because unless foreign aid becomes a much larger and more productive force than expected, the nine other factors will tend to make its role relatively small. There is also a counterproductive aspect of foreign aid in that it is often given not to help the poor nation but to salve the conscience of the rich donor nation.

Aid motivated by this kind of guilt can result in the misformulation of issues and attitudes on the part of the donor that force or influence the receiving country into counterproductive programs (for example, furnishing social services it cannot afford or trying to develop much more uniformly than is practical). This is not to say that attempts to make development more uniform or increase social services are always wrong; but it is quite easy for a wealthy country to overestimate needs and to suggest a new emphasis that can turn out to be self-defeating for the developing country. The example of New York City is revealing. One could argue that almost all of its programs were perfectly reasonable; the city is rich and could afford substantial social services, welfare and many other burdens. The problem is that New York did not make selections but chose to pursue all programs simultaneously— a course no city can afford today. The same is often true of poor developing countries: They must choose very carefully among available goals and options.

We hope we have now made plausible our belief that the coping poor nations will soon grow more wealthy. The mix of economic forces varies in different countries, but the overall direction is the same—toward rapid economic growth by taking advantage of the gap between the developing and the developed nations.* We do not necessarily expect that the

---

* It is interesting in this connection to reread Karl Marx, who fully understood how effectively the capitalist system had spread as a result of its very dynamic nature; except for the personal hostility that shows through, his description is vivid and apt:

The bourgeoisie . . . has accomplished wonders far surpassing Egyptian pyramids, Roman aqueducts and Gothic cathedrals. . . .
The bourgeoisie has through its exploitation of the world market

noncoping poor will grow economically as rapidly in the near future, though this could happen; but we do believe that as the coping nations become rich then their present place in the industrial hierarchy will be taken by the currently noncoping. This is roughly analogous to the situation in New York City, where Puerto Ricans have taken over many jobs given up by Blacks, who in turn had taken over jobs earlier held by other immigrant groups.

We therefore argue that by the year 2000 perhaps a quarter of mankind will live in emerging postindustrial societies and more than two-thirds will have passed the level of $1,000 per capita. By the end of the 21st century almost all societies should have a GNP per capita greater than $2,000

---

given a cosmopolitan character to production and consumption in every country. To the great chagrin of reactionaries, it has drawn from under the feet of industry the national ground on which it stood. All old-established national industries have been destroyed or are daily being destroyed. They are dislodged by new industries, whose introduction becomes a life and death question for all civilized nations, by industries that no longer work up indigenous raw materials, but raw materials drawn from the remotest zones; industries whose products are consumed, not only at home, but in every quarter of the globe. In place of the old wants, satisfied by the products of the country, we find new wants requiring for their satisfaction the products of distant lands and climates. In place of the old local and national seclusion and self-sufficiency, we have intercourse in every direction, universal interdependence of nations. . . .

The bourgeoisie, by the rapid improvement of all instruments of production, by the immensely facilitated means of communication, draws all, even the most backward, nations into civilization. The cheap prices of its commodities are the heavy artillery with which it batters down all Chinese walls, with which it forces the underdeveloped nations' intensely obstinate hatred of foreigners to capitulate. It compels all nations on pain of extinction to adopt the bourgeois mode of production; it compels them to introduce what it calls civilization into their midst, i.e., to become bourgeois themselves. In one word, it creates a world in its own image. . . .

The bourgeoisie, during its rule of scarcely one hundred years, has created more massive and more colossal productive forces than have all preceding generations together. Subjection of nature's forces to man, machinery, application of chemistry to industry and agriculture, steam navigation, railways, electric telegraphs, clearing of whole continents for cultivation, canalization of rivers, whole populations conjured out of the ground—what earlier century had even a presentiment that such productive forces slumbered in the lap of social labor?

Karl Marx and Friedrich Engels, *The Communist Manifesto* (New York: Washington Square Press, 1964), pp. 62–66.

and be entering some form of postindustrial culture. The task is not to see that these societies proceed along the same path as Europe, North America and Japan, but rather that each should find its own way. However, even in the year 2100 there may be large income gaps. Today per capita GNP ranges from about $100 to $10,000, and it would not at all surprise us if the range at the end of the 21st century were still rather large, perhaps from a basic minimum of a few thousand dollars to a maximum of 10 to 20 times greater. As far as we can tell, arithmetic differences (as opposed to ratios) in per capita product will generally increase for the next 100 years, with (of course) many exceptions. But this should not be disastrous either morally or politically since there are very few peasants, workers or even businessmen in developing nations who care much about gaps (whether arithmetic or geometric), no matter how much intellectuals, academics and some businessmen may profess to. The major objective of most people is to increase their own safety and improve their own standard of living and their own capabilities. When they make comparisons, it is usually with others at their socioeconomic level or with those who have recently been at their own or a lower level.

THE ECONOMIC TRANSITION

Now let us look at the other side of the coin. Why is it that we do not expect the developed world—and the coping and noncoping nations, once they have developed—to continue growing at high rates more or less indefinitely? Those who take a limits-to-growth position tend to argue very strongly that there are limits to supply, that available sources of energy, raw materials and food will run out, and that this exhaustion—along with overwhelming pollution—will inhibit and eventually halt further economic growth. While some of this may occur, we believe that because of the flexibility of modern economies and the huge surplus of land, energy and resources available, the limitations set by scarcity should not usually prove dominant. We emphasize instead the demand side of the equation. We argue that once worldwide development has essentially been completed, economic growth rates will slow and finally many economies will achieve a more or less steady state. There are, we believe, several reasons—together cumulative and accelerating—why this is likely to happen.

First, since we project that the rate of population growth will slow and that eventually total world population will reach a more or less fixed number, it is clear that there is an implied upper limit on economic growth. Still, without additional dampening effects, economic growth might continue at a rapid rate for a long time. We believe that our additional points below show what some of these dampening effects will be.

We see as a second reason for the slowing down of economic growth in some developed nations the diminishing returns from increasingly costly factors of production (often known as the Ricardo effect*). This will be especially true for fixed factors, land in desirable locations being the best example. But we believe it will also be true for variable factors in which economies from scale, advanced technology, innovation, design and substitution no longer will be able to reduce costs proportionate to the investment made in them. Increased investment, technological progress and other innovations so often reverse this effect that we do not believe it will ever be a dominating factor for society's prospects—unless none of these developments takes place.

Third, we believe that with the advance into the super-industrial era there is likely to be a diminution in the marginal utility of wealth and production. With insurance, social security and welfare for all, there will be protection against most of the vagaries of life, and this should produce a shift in priorities and values. Something like this has already been seen in the upper middle-class of Japan and what we call the "Atlantic-Protestant culture" area (Scandinavia, Holland, England, the United States, Canada and Australia), where there is a growing denial of the importance of wealth. While the "flower children" of the 1960's have faded, the fact remains

---

* From the studies of David Ricardo, the early 19th-century English economist.

that a change has occurred and our culture has taken some steps away from the work and advancement ethic and probably will not return to anything like its earlier state.

Fourth, and closely related to this third reason, is that many vested interests exist which oppose either growth itself or the changes accompanying growth—an opposition that need not be unworthy or self-serving. It seems likely that there will be an increasing desire to leave things as they are, for as people get richer they tend to be satisfied with their quality of life, with the status quo. As the number and the influence of people who want to change their standard of living or raise their status decrease, the balance of political and economic forces will change. At the moment this shows up most dramatically in the phenomenon we call "localism"—the tendency of people in a community to halt its further development (as in Aspen, Colorado) or to prevent the incursion of new industry even though it might bring jobs and supply important needs (as in Durham, New Hampshire, where plans to locate a refinery were successfully resisted by upper-income residents). This phenomenon will surely increase and prove an important check to the economic growth of affluent societies. In general, economic and technical efficiency will be given much less weight as first the new affluent values and then the similar postindustrial values gain in strength and pervasiveness.

It should be noted that in many countries, at something like $1,000–$2,000 per capita, the upper middle class tends to fare worse as the country as a whole does better. In other words, while the standard of living is improving, the quality of life may be deteriorating for some groups. For example, if one compares upper-middle-class people in southern Europe, East Asia or much of Latin America with those living in Scandinavia or the United States, one finds that the former live in larger houses (construction costs are very low), often have the traditional three live-in servants (cook, maid and gardener), have a certain status and various perquisites, and can satisfy many desires that simply cannot be served in the Scandinavian or North American context. (The noted economist Joseph Schumpeter once said, "One good maid is worth

Table 2. U.S. Shares of Employment and GNP by Sector, Selected Years and Projected to 1985 (in current dollars)

Sector[a]	1929 Empl.	1929 GNP	1945 Empl.	1945 GNP	1955 Empl.	1955 GNP	1965 Empl.	1965 GNP	1972 Empl.	1972 GNP	1985 Empl.	1985 GNP
Primary	27.6%	16.6%	19.2%	12.3%	11.1%	8.1%	6.7%	5.7%	4.8%	4.8%	2.4%	3.0%
Secondary	29.2	35.9	34.0	36.9	31.7	42.0	30.2	39.9	27.8	37.4	26.6	36.9
Services	43.2	46.3	46.8	50.6	57.1	51.8	63.2	54.8	67.5	56.4	71.0	59.8

[a] Sectors are comprised as follows:

Primary: Agriculture, forestry, fisheries and mining

Secondary: Contract construction and manufacturing

Services: Transportation, communication and public utilities, wholesale and retail trade, finance, insurance and real estate, services and government

SOURCES: U.S. Department of Commerce, Bureau of the Census, *Statistical Abstract of the United States: 1966*, 87th ed. (Washington: U.S. Government Printing Office, 1966); U.S. Department of Commerce, Bureau of the Census, *Statistical Abstract of the United States: 1974*, 95th ed. (Washington: U.S. Government Printing Office, 1974); and U.S. Department of Labor, *The U.S. Economy in 1985* (Washington: U.S. Government Printing Office, 1974). Because of rounding, not all percentage totals equal 100.

a household full of appliances," and this is still true). We believe that one of the major reasons for the objections to growth by the elites arises directly out of this class interest, but we find it difficult now to judge just how important this particular class interest will be in slowing down growth.

Finally, we believe that economic growth in the super- and postindustrial eras will slow and stabilize—at least as far as the use of physical resources is concerned—because of the nature of the growth process itself. This is best explained by thinking of production as divided into the four sectors or types of activities previously described: primary (extractive), secondary (industrial), tertiary (services to primary and secondary) and quaternary (services for their own sake). As nations grow economically, the characteristic pattern of change these sectors have experienced (in terms of labor participation and shares of total product) is somewhat as follows: in the pre-industrial era the primary sector (largely agriculture) is paramount, there is some secondary activity (mostly construction) and almost no tertiary and quaternary activity. During industrialization the primary sector's share grows smaller relative to that of the secondary, which enlarges rapidly. The service sectors also grow, especially in the superindustrial stage, when their rate of growth outpaces that of the secondary sector. Finally, in the postindustrial era, the primary and secondary sectors' shares of total product will be very small compared to those of the tertiary and especially the quaternary, which we estimate will have the largest share of both labor participation and total product. (Trends in this direction in the United States are shown in Table 2, which presents recent and projected changes in the percentage of persons employed by sector, and sector shares by GNP.)

It is clear from Table 2 that it takes fewer and fewer people in the primary and secondary sectors to supply all of the goods we need. It is precisely this increase in the productivity of the primary and secondary sectors that drives growth initially. Later it is the transfer from low-paid jobs in the primary and secondary to high-paid (or productive) jobs in the tertiary and quaternary that drives growth. When these two are used up, many economists believe that the future increases in productivity will be small. Actually, there are some activities of the tertiary sector (trade and banking, for example) that have had, and are still likely to have, enormous increases in productivity. But we believe that the eventual dominance of relatively nonproductive quaternary activities—combined with the other reasons set forth above—will ensure the transition to a postindustrial era of slowing and finally stabilized economic growth.

GNP PER CAPITA—THE TRANSITIONS COMBINED

If we now combine the 200-year projection of population growth rates with our examination of economic growth in the developing and developed nations, we can arrive at our surprise-free projection of gross national product per capita for the world as a whole and its current economic groupings. Such a projection is illuminating for it provides us with a yardstick for measuring individual economic well-being throughout the period of our 400-year scenario. Consider, for example, the perfectly reasonable(but clearly not certain) expectation that India will grow by an average of 2.3 percent a year in per capita income between now and the year 2176, and therefore by then should have a per capita income 100 times its present income, or about $10,000. (Even a mere 1 percent growth per year would result in a per capita income of $750.) Such a projection makes clear that the issue is probably not whether India will develop, but how rapidly and with how much difficulty. In this context it is instructive to note that it took the United States 200 years to rise from about $250 per capita to $7,000 per capita (in constant 1975 prices) and that India may easily do as well or even better. In this perspective the future of India—beset today with agonizing political and economic problems, and a fitting subject for Cassandra-type prophecies—looks very different indeed.

In making our projection we have divided the nations of the world into four economic groups, based on their current development and income. The first group comprises the world's developed nations, including the industrial nations of Western and Eastern Europe, North America, certain countries of the British Commonwealth (Australia, New Zealand and the white portion of South Africa), Japan, Israel and the wealthy Persian Gulf countries. The second group consists of China, North Korea and the four nations of the former Indochina. The third is the group we call the coping nations—those with annual per capita incomes over $400, or those which are resource-rich though not necessarily industrialized, or those which are growing at the rate of more than 5 percent a year. The fourth group, the noncoping, corresponds roughly to the International Monetary Fund's designation of "Most Seriously Affected," nations that all have per capita incomes below $400 and generally suffer from adverse terms of trade (their imports cost more than their exports earn). In all cases, the noncoping had a projected balance-of-payments deficit for 1974 and 1975 not smaller than 5 percent of imports. (These criteria for grouping nations, of course, will not hold true for each nation for the entire 400-year scenario, but for simplicity we will keep the membership of each group fixed, to show what has happened and will happen to these groups as they are now structured.)

Our projections for these four groups of nations are set forth in Figure 5, within the framework of our previously projected growth by 2176 to a world population of 15 billion people with a $300 trillion GWP, yielding $20,000 per capita. In this projection it is the developed nations that continue to drive economic growth, though their rates do slow down at a faster rate than that of the rest of the world. The coping nations start below the average GWP but grow quickly and pass through it early in the 21st century; communist Asia achieves the world average somewhat later, then stays close to it; and the noncoping nations, starting much later, undergo their maximum growth only late in the next century.

One consequence of this surprise-free projection is that the current 100–1 ratio of per capita product between the wealthiest 10 percent and the poorest 20 percent of the world population could shrink to about 5–1 after 200 years, give or take

Figure 5.   Gross World Product Per Capita, 1776–2176

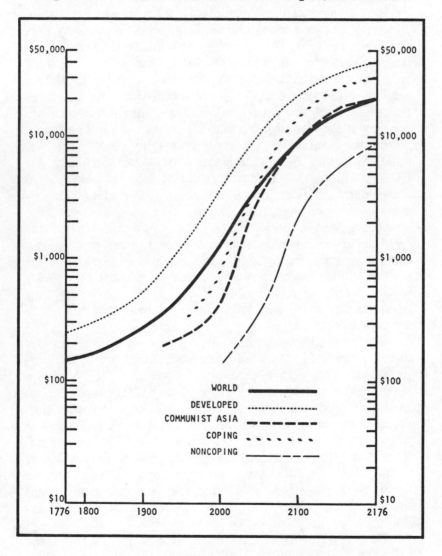

a factor of two or three. If, however, our projection is incorrect and, for example, many of the developing countries continue to grow in population with much less economic growth than projected, then a similar 100-1 ratio might persist. But even in this case we would expect their absolute standard of living to reach or exceed that of lower European standards today (for example, Spain or Greece). Although many people presently believe that only relative income is important, we think that this view is clearly in error. For a struggling nation to move from $100 to $1,000 in per capita product removes it from desperate poverty to current lower-middle-class standards, a much more impressive and important change than an increase in a developed country from $1,000 to $10,000 per capita, equivalent there to a move from largely lower-middle to largely upper-middle-class standards.

Certainly one of the most important implications of our projection is that it would be very difficult to construct a plausible scenario that inevitably leads to famine or other extreme hazards great enough to cause a major world tragedy in which a large portion of the population is lost. We do not deny that many tragedies can result from various deprivations associated with poverty, but we are asserting that over the longer term—that is, within 200 years—the likely economic outcome is not between poverty and desperate poverty as some pessimists have suggested, but rather between failure and success, in which "failure" means an annual per capita product of $500 to $2,000 for the poorer countries and "moderate success" means a range of $3,000 to $10,000.

III

Energy: Exhaustible to Inexhaustible

WHEN PRIMITIVE MAN learned how to make fire, he had discovered controllable energy, which then became a "servant" destined to perform an endless series of "miracles," beginning perhaps with simple cooking. This discovery may have been the single most vital factor which allowed mankind to develop modern civilization. Indeed early fuels also enabled man to find new and more abundant sources of energy in ever-increasing amounts; thus he progressed from wood to coal to petroleum to hydro- and thermoelectric power, and most recently to nuclear power. Because even these resources are somewhat limited, he is now prepared to utilize the best tools from the most recent technology in the development and exploitation of several new alternatives that are known to constitute essentially *eternal* sources, from which man should be able to extract as much energy as he is ever likely to require on earth.

The commercial tapping of these eternal energy sources may initially cost the consumer somewhat more (perhaps twice as much) per unit than currently, but in time the costs can only decrease in real terms. The real *cost* of energy supplies has almost always dropped over time; the *price* of energy, however, fluctuates around this general downtrend according to market conditions. Despite the activities of OPEC and the current pessimism about the extent of petroleum reserves, we believe that energy costs as a whole are very likely to continue the historical downward trend indefinitely.

The data required to support the above thesis about the long-term supplies and costs of energy are the heart of this chapter. We hope they are presented in sufficient quantity and are of sufficient quality to make clear to the reader just how we were able to justify our optimistic conclusion.

There is certainly no question that mankind's future well-being is intimately linked to the prospects for an abundant supply of energy at reasonable prices. The recent fuel crisis spread concern throughout the world that energy supplies were short, and would remain so for a long time, quite possibly worsening.

While understandable, this reaction was rather paradoxical. There was almost no substantive basis for it since there was no physical shortage of oil, only a cartel that succeeded in forcing at least a temporary increase in the price of the commodity it controlled. One effect of this action was to increase the rate at which new energy came on the market and to decrease the rate at which energy was used—that is, the cartel's moves actually decreased the possibility of future energy shortages.

There is general recognition that the oil crisis and subsequent events represented an energy watershed, but it was not a watershed from abundance to scarcity, or even from cheap to expensive, but rather from cheap to inexpensive. That is, many in the industrialized world will continue to drive large cars if they like them, live in big houses, overheat and over-air-condition their homes, expand suburban sprawl, use electric signs and street lighting lavishly, and continue other high-energy-consumption activities. But it also seems quite clear that more care will be exercised—that some will switch to smaller or more energy-efficient cars, homes will be better insulated, more efficient lighting, heating and cooling systems will come into use, and so on. Thus the functions that used energy so lavishly in the past will continue to be performed with relatively little change, but there will be considerable change and improvement in the efficiency of the means of performance.

While what happened was fairly straightforward, the historical significance of the OPEC embargo has been largely misread in public discussion. For 50 years oil had been eating into the market once supplied by coal because oil was cheaper and more convenient. As long as oil sells for less than $5 a barrel, it must largely displace coal; but once it goes to twice this price (or more), there should be a major shift to coal, and there is plenty of coal to last for a very long time indeed. It should be noted, however, that in fact the shift to coal has been slow, one reason being that it takes about 15-20 years to amortize major new coal investments if they include much infrastructure such as ports and railroads. It doesn't seem likely that oil prices will stay very high for more than 5 or 10 years, and possibly much less; they might easily return to something like $3-7 in the Persian Gulf long before the new coal infrastructure has been amortized. This kind of practical uncertainty can be very important in modifying the speed and effectiveness of an adjustment, but it has very little to do with the scarcity of resources. In fact, just the opposite is the case. If the oil in the Persian Gulf were to disappear over the next 10 years, the relatively immediate and obvious need for coal would dictate that the adjustment be made swiftly and effectively.

Perhaps the most important point to be made here is that despite the sudden quadrupling of the price of oil in 1973-74, it is clear that there will be an adequate adjustment to the new price well within a decade, even if it does stay high. No doubt the world will face many other economic shocks in the future, but surely few will be as great as that of the oil crisis. Even so, and while the adjustment has unquestionably been quite difficult, and almost catastrophic in some local areas, life and progress do continue. (The comment that the poor suffer much more from events like the oil shock than do the rich is so obvious that one hesitates to make it. Yet the fact that this is one of the best possible arguments for being rich, that it tends to insulate one from this kind of problem is one of those self-evident truths that often goes unrecognized.)

In an effort to keep energy costs within reasonable bounds over the next few decades, the industrialized world is now vigorously and simultaneously tackling the energy problem on many fronts. We expect this activity to continue until indigenous supplies and competitive sources are built up to a level where utilization of OPEC sources becomes a matter of preference rather than necessity; when this occurs, the price of fuels will be much closer to the marginal costs of production than they are today.

Conservation is obviously the quickest way to reduce dependence on foreign oil, unpalatable though it may be to people who have long enjoyed being able to use oil freely. The pressures have not been strong enough yet in most countries, and changes do not come about easily in deeply ingrained habits—nor should they necessarily occur, given current uncertainties. Indeed, the OPEC cartel can now produce about a third more oil than it can sell at current prices, and the margin is increasing. While the rest of the world is trying to assure access to energy supplies, OPEC's main impact will probably be on prices rather than availability. Although another oil embargo cannot be completely ruled out, this possibility appears somewhat less ominous as time passes, and the tactic is not likely to be effective when there are relatively large stocks and large excess production capability.

An appropriate near-term solution would probably involve some increase in petroleum inventories and stocks and, more importantly, a substantial increase in domestic and non-OPEC world production capacity over a reasonable time. But important as this is for today, it has little to do with the long-run future.

FUTURE DEMAND

Table 3 shows in condensed form our estimates of the amount of energy the world will need during the next 200 years, given our population and GWP projections.* This table

* For convenience, we have adopted a system used in the tables and throughout this chapter in which energy units are expressed in *quads* (q) or *quints* (Q). A quad represents a quadrillion (10^{15}) BTUs; a quint is a quintillion (10^{18}) BTUs. A billion barrels of oil contain about 6q (or .006 Q). Qe refers to quints of electrical energy.

Table 3. Estimates of World Energy Consumption
$(Q = 10^{18}$ BTU)

Year	Pop.[a] (Bil.)	GWP[a] ($ Tril.)	GWP/ CAP[a]	Eff.[b]	Annual Consumption	Cumulative Consumption (from 1975)
1975	4.0	5.2	1,300	1.00	.25 Q	—
1985	5.0	8.5	1,700	1.15	.35	3 Q
2000	6.6	17.2	2,600	1.4	.60	10
2025	9.3	52	5,600	2.0	1.2	30
2076	14.6	152	10,400	3.0	2.4	115
2126	15.0	228	15,200	3.5	3.2	240
2176	15.0	300	20,000	4.0	3.6	400

[a] Hudson Institute studies.
[b] Relative overall efficiency assumed for production, conversion and utilization of energy compared with 1975.

assumes that a new energy consciousness in the world, coupled with advancing technology, will gradually increase the efficiency of production, conversion and utilization of energy. Energy demand therefore increases less quickly than the GWP; after 200 years projected increase of energy demand is by a factor of 15, while the GWP is larger by a factor of almost 60. Note that this probably underestimates the likely reduction in use of energy because it ignores the shift to services and to much modern technology. We expect this increased efficiency to be motivated by economic considerations rather than by energy shortages as such. Nevertheless, total energy use may ultimately be limited by environmental considerations that cannot be foreseen today—for example, the long-range effects upon regional and global climate.

It is quite reasonable to ask how this huge projected global demand can be met without great concern about the wells running dry or the biosphere becoming excessively polluted. To respond, we will first look at the energy reserves and resources that are familiar and upon which we will depend most for the near and medium term; we will then examine new, alternative sources of fuel and power that might lead eventually to an energy system that would depend only upon more or less eternal sources.

FOSSIL FUELS

The world's known reserves and potentially recoverable resources of petroleum and natural gas are shown in Table 4,

Table 4. Resources of Principal Fossil Fuels
(Q = 10^{18} BTU)

	Proven Reserves		Potential Resources	
	U.S.	World	U.S.	World
Oil [a]	.3	3.7	2.9	14.4
Natural Gas [a]	.3	1.0	2.5	15.8
Coal (Incl. Lignite) [b]	15	95	30	170
Shale Oil [b]	12	19	150	2000
Tar Sands [c]	—	1.8	—	1.8
Total	27.6 Q	120 Q	185 Q	2200 Q
Years of World Consumption at Current Projections	48	102	120	~500

[a] Ford Foundation, The Energy Policy Project, *Exploring Energy Choices: A Preliminary Report* (Washington, 1974).

[b] D. A. Brobst and W. P. Pratt (eds.), U.S. Geological Survey, *U.S. Mineral Resources* (Washington: U.S. Government Printing Office, 1973).

[c] National Research Council, Committee on Resources and Man, *Resources and Man* (San Francisco: W. H. Freeman, 1969).

and Table 5 contains cost estimates for some fuels which can be extracted from coal, from oil shale and from tar sands. Allowing for the growth of energy demand estimated earlier, we conclude that the *proven reserves* of these five major fossil fuels (oil, natural gas, coal, shale oil and tar sands) alone could provide the world's total energy requirements for about 100 years, and only one-fifth of the *estimated potential re-*

Table 5.　Anticipated Initial Cost of Synthetic Fuels from Various Sources (Hudson Institute estimates)

	$/Million BTU
From Coal (Delivered Price)	.4 to 1.0
Syncrude (Synthetic Crude)	2.0 to 4.0
Syngas (Synthetic Gas)	3.5 to 5.0
Low/Intermediate BTU Gas	2.0 to 3.5
Shale Oil	2.0 to 5.0
Tar Sands: Syncrude	2.0 to 4.0

sources could provide for more than 200 years of the projected energy needs!

Hudson's estimates suggest that potential U.S. resources of oil, gas and coal are sufficient to supply the energy needs of this country for more than 150 years, given our projected GNP growth. Furthermore, once an effective process for the extraction of oil from shale is developed, the total available supply of fossil energy could be more than quadrupled.

In commercial practice, the chosen form of fuel is usually the most profitable one. For our purposes, it suffices to establish that, at various conversion prices (which appear in Table 5 to be tolerable), the preferred proportions of the solid, liquid or gaseous forms are a matter of choice. Within the decade or two needed to make the appropriate industrial changes, complete substitutability could be accomplished by absorbing the conversion costs.

The development of facilities for the conversion of coal to liquid and gaseous fuels and for the extraction of oil from shale and tar sands is now vigorously under way in many different programs in many countries.* At this time, there is little ques-

* We wish to make clear that the exact cost of commercial extraction of oil from shale is still quite uncertain. Except in a few of the best locations, this process may well not be competitive with other alternatives for decades. Thus, if most of the oil from shale could be extracted only at costs exceeding $25 per barrel, it might be a long time before it became a major commercial resource. However, the development of a relatively inexpensive *in situ* extraction process cannot be ruled out; it is now under active research and development by private companies and by government-sponsored efforts. Such a process might be quite inefficient initially, perhaps extracting only 20 percent or so of the potential fuel (although recent pilot-plant

tion about the ultimate technical feasibility of these processes; the real difficulties lie in their near-term economic viability, optimum rates of development, and associated environmental, land use and water allocation problems. We expect all of these concerns eventually to be resolved, but they will seriously affect the prices of the fuels produced and will probably dominate discussion of these potential energy sources for the balance of this century.

At a cost of $12 per barrel of crude oil (that is, $2 per million BTUs for all fossil fuels), current levels of energy usage would absorb about 10 percent of the GNP of the United States. Nevertheless, we believe that the world can successfully adjust to fuels at this price *if need be,* and particularly as it becomes more affluent and as energy is used more efficiently. Actually, however, we believe the price of oil has already peaked in real terms, or soon will.

Until the development of eternal power sources has been accomplished on a large commercial scale—which will probably occur by the middle of the next century, if not sooner—the world's best hope lies in the use of the solid fossil fuels, especially coal. They will be our best insurance against any unexpected serious reduction in estimates of the world's potential oil and natural gas resources (which alone, it is comforting to note, are sufficient to supply the world's energy requirements for about 50 years—see Tables 3 and 4). The only other major technology currently being developed commercially that is likely to have real impact upon energy supplies during the next 50 years or so is the nuclear fission reactor.

FISSION POWER

Until the last few years, nuclear fission was generally considered to offer the best hope for an escape from dependence

---

operations suggest that a 40–50 percent recovery rate is feasible). Even 20 percent might constitute a very useful *beginning,* however, considering the vastness of the resource base. Costs from such an *in situ* process are expected to be much less than that of the current retorting process.

upon fossil fuels. Recently, however, this form of nuclear energy has come under growing attack by consumer and environmental groups, abetted by adherents of the no-growth philosophy. Their major arguments merit some serious attention. They point out that in the event of a serious accident or sabotage, nuclear power plants might contaminate large areas with radioactivity, especially if deadly plutonium aerosols escaped from a damaged reactor. Furthermore, they argue that the problems of handling huge and ever-growing quantities of long-lived radioactive wastes, including plutonium, have not been satisfactorily solved. They also contend that reactors contain large quantities of fissionable materials from which nuclear explosives can be made, thereby creating an enormous potential for the proliferation of nuclear weapons, for the theft of fissionable materials and, perhaps most frightening, for the eventual control by terrorist groups of clandestine nuclear weapons.

The resolution of these issues is so much in doubt that there is serious possibility of a moratorium one day being placed upon the construction or use of nuclear energy plants, at least in the United States, but this need not seriously affect future growth possibilities. It is precisely because there are other alternatives available that a case of any kind can be made against nuclear power. We will not pursue this debate now, but an examination of the potential for nuclear power development should illuminate what it is that may have to be stretched out, postponed or given up.

The total free world's resources of yellowcake, uranium ore (U_3O_8), are generally taken to be about three times those of the United States. Even then, the available uranium can probably be considered no more than an interim supply unless (a) the breeder reactor becomes commercially feasible and politically acceptable, (b) the extraction of uranium from the sea becomes practical or (c) an efficient nuclear reactor becomes available.* It should be pointed out that the current (high) cost of uranium, about $20 per pound, translates to

---

* An advanced design of the Canadian heavy water reactor (CANDU) suggests a potential tenfold increase in fuel efficiency.

about 1 mill per kilowatt-hour of electricity (KWHe). If the price eventually rose to $100 per pound, the fuel would cost about 5 mills per KWHe, which still would not be large compared to today's cost of power production from conventional sources.

Without a much more efficient commercial reactor or an economically viable seawater-extraction technology, the electrical energy available through current technology, from uranium-235 burned in light water reactors (LWR's), may be between 5 and 15 Qe for the noncommunist countries. This represents a respectable amount of energy indeed—comparable, in fact, to that represented by the world's total oil resources (see Table 4). To the extent that LWR's participate in power production during the next several decades, they would certainly help to cushion possible uncertainties about future fossil fuel supplies. CANDU-type designs would increase the potential by a factor of almost 10. And in the not unlikely event that breeder reactors, advanced CANDU reactors or extraction of uranium from seawater or low-grade shales become practical and acceptable, the fission process could provide a very large part of the world's electric power for centuries.

THE TRANSITION TO LONG-TERM SOURCES

The world is at the beginning of a transition from fossil fuels as the primary energy sources to the phasing in of long-term alternatives—a transition we expect to be largely completed about 75 years from now. Thus by 2050, a major part of total energy supplies should be emanating from such eternal sources as solar, geothermal, fission and fusion reactor installations. By 2076, the U.S. Tricentennial year, we expect fossil fuels to be used principally as basic chemicals. During this transition period, the world is likely to lean increasingly on the solid fossil fuels (coal and shale), with nuclear power as a possible important adjunct. We anticipate that by the year 2000 coal, shale and lignite will be converted on a large scale to relatively clean-burning fluids, because of the convenience of handling as well as the need to reduce air pollution. Moreover, the price of imported fuels, at least in the United States, is apt to be kept relatively high by tariffs and quotas in order to protect domestic producers of synthetics. Present expectations are that various synthetic fluids from coal and oil shale will be commercially available in 10 to 15 years at costs equivalent to $5 to $20 a barrel (depending upon successes in *in situ* extraction and other developments). Variation between these extremes will depend upon such factors as the type of synthetic fuel, the price of coal, the distance of the user from the mines or conversion plants, and technological improvements over time.

While the political battles associated with nuclear fission are being resolved, coal and oil-shale mining are expanding, and commercial conversion facilities for them will be developed during the next quarter-century; meanwhile, the funding of research and development for the long-term renewable and/or essentially inexhaustible energy resources will also be growing quite dramatically. The main entrants in this race are solar, geothermal and fusion energy.

SOLAR ENERGY

Broadly defined, solar energy is available in a large number of forms. The sun's energy drives the wind, grows all the plants and warms the oceans, thereby enabling man, in principle, to extract energy from these sources as well as from the direct radiance itself. Even the fossil fuels are stored solar energy, technically speaking, as is hydroelectric power, and the vast energy of ocean currents and wave motions. We limit ourselves, however, to the six solar alternatives which now are most promising, discussed in the order in which they are expected to achieve substantial commercial production:

1. *Wind Electric Power—to be obtained from strategically placed arrays of large modern windmills.*

It may seem strange to go back to a power source which is thousands of years old. However, the new technology available for generating and storing power from windmills makes this an attractive and economical power source for regions where the wind blows rather steadily or at a higher than average speed, or both—for instance, the Texas Gulf coast, the Aleutian Islands, the Great Plains and the Eastern Seaboard of the United States. A U.S. government program is under way to determine the optimum locations and test various windmill systems. The current expectation is that the first commercial systems will be installed during the early 1980's, and the cost will probably be less than that of most current conventional sources (see Figure 6).

2. *Bio-Conversion (BC)—energy obtained by converting organic materials, especially wastes, to fuels or electric power.*

This is a catchall term for processes that can convert organic matter—including all organic wastes from cities, industry and agriculture—to fuels or power. Furthermore, selected crops or trees which are the most efficient converters of sunlight might be grown for their energy potential, or for dual purposes (for example, sugarcane for food and energy, hemp for fiber and energy).

Although the concept of growing crops for energy (hence, "energy farms") is in an early stage of investigation, various processes for the conversion of dry organic wastes into energy are reasonably well developed. With economic credit for the cost of waste collection and disposal (required in any event), several BC alternatives are expected to become commercially feasible before 1980. These include: (a) the direct burning

Figure 6. Projected Cost Ranges for Several Types of Solar Energy

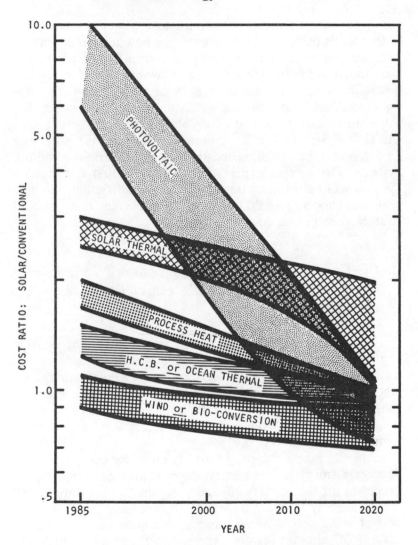

SOURCE: Adapted from data given by the Mitre Corporation/Batelle Columbus Laboratories; Report MTR-6513, December 1973.

of wastes as a fuel; (b) pyrolysis, the conversion of organic material to oil and gas through heating in an oxygen-free atmosphere; and (c) hydrogenation or chemical reduction, which, through the use of a heat and pressure process, can convert most organic materials to oil and/or gas. Many other promising BC alternatives will be evaluated during the next decade.

3. *The heating and cooling of buildings by the direct use of solar radiation as a heat source (HCB).*

This is probably the best-known form of solar energy. The concept is as ancient as civilization, but has been less than completely satisfactory because of the intermittent nature of sunlight. At present a substantial research and development program is being devoted to this process, which some experts predict will become standard in new structures in the United States during the next decade or two. Indeed, some solar systems for homes are already on the market and many large corporations are studying HCB's commercial potential.

At current energy prices, HCB systems are considered to be competitive in some parts of the country—particularly, of course, in those regions with more than the average amount of sunshine. If the price of fossil energy climbs further and the technology of HCB improves, the incentives to install these systems in new structures, or even to retrofit existing ones with them, can be expected to grow rapidly.

4. *Photovoltaic Power (PVP)—the conversion of sunlight by solar cells to obtain direct-current electricity.*

As a consequence of the use of silicon solar cells on space vehicles, this technology is now one of the promising approaches for utilizing solar energy. Because current solar cells are too costly for commercial use by a factor of about 500, a big effort is under way to produce them inexpensively. Several developments already suggest that this goal could be met before the end of this century, and possibly much sooner.

One advantage of the PVP approach is that it directly converts sunlight into electricity at an efficiency that is expected to be about 20 percent of the total incoming radiation. Sophisticated designs may be able to use much of the remaining 80 percent for heating or cooling, or perhaps for generating solar thermal power (STP). Estimates of the PVP potential are enormous: It might conceivably supply the world's total energy needs at prices comparable to or less than those of today's conventional sources. (Figure 6 shows the projected economic viability.)

5. *Ocean thermal power—electric power derived from the sun-warmed surface waters of the ocean.*

This method offers an inexhaustible and huge potential for electric power. Within about 1,000 miles of the equator the upper layers of the ocean are about 35 degrees Fahrenheit warmer than the deeper waters. This temperature difference in principle permits floating (or shore-based) generators to operate continuously, extracting electrical power at a practical efficiency of perhaps 2–3 percent, about one-third of that theoretically possible. If these systems become economically competitive (the "fuel" is free), they would be able, eventually, to produce more electric power than the world would need 200 years from now.

The Energy Resource Development Administration (ERDA) is sponsoring a research program to test this approach, with pilot plants now under construction. Although preliminary engineering estimates suggest that competitive power appears feasible, the development to prove its validity will clearly require another 10 to 20 years.

6. *Solar Thermal Power (STP)—the direct conversion of solar radiation to heat, probably in the form of steam, to drive electric power generators.*

Solar radiation is easily converted to heat, merely by allowing it to strike a blackened surface. Again a major problem is created by the intermittent nature of sunshine, and several technical problems must also be solved before even the sunniest desert areas could be used for STP installations. Efficient methods must be developed for the installation and maintenance of solar collectors over very large areas. Ways must be found to heat and transport hot water or steam efficiently from the collectors to central power plants. And relatively inexpensive energy storage systems large enough to keep power plants operating when sunshine is not available will be needed.

If these rather formidable problems are overcome, STP alone would be capable of supplying all of man's future power needs. At a 10 percent overall conversion efficiency, 1 percent of the world's land area used for STP could provide the world's total energy needs in the year 2000. While the subject is controversial, conservative estimates suggest that STP will not become commercially competitive until well into the next century, if then (see Figure 6), but many think it will be much earlier. However, technical breakthroughs or the use of hybrid systems (for example, combining STP with PVP and/or the commercial use of "waste" heat) could affect the economics considerably.

One oversimplified image of a future world energy economy visualizes a large part, perhaps one-third, of the Sahara Desert being devoted to solar power production. Theoretically, at 20 percent efficiency such a system could produce about 4 Qe per year, which is enough to supply the projected world needs 200 years from now. The energy presumably would be transported to the principal consumers in the form of clean-burning, pollution-free hydrogen.

We are not suggesting that this system would be desirable; on the contrary, even with hybrid design it would probably be relatively expensive and entail other potential disutilities. Nevertheless, we want to stress that this one alternative could meet all of the world's energy needs with almost no pollution, and although it is economically problematical now, the cost will probably become tolerable during the 22nd century. Thus this hypothetical system constitutes an *a fortiori* argument for the future availability of sufficient nonpolluting energy.

GEOTHERMAL ENERGY

The heat contained within the earth is so enormous that in principle it could be tapped to produce more than 1 billion Qe. Moreover, more heat is constantly being generated within the earth by radioactive decay processes. Although most of this heat is presently too deep for commercial exploitation, the amount within reach is large and should increase rapidly during the next several decades as drilling technology improves.

The upper layer of the earth's crust is sufficiently irregular that, over geological ages, many "hot spots" have been created that are within current drilling range (about 25,000 feet); some are only a few thousand feet from the surface. These hot spots are often hundreds of square miles in area and probably of great or even unlimited depth. A few of them, probably much less than 10 percent, contain strata of porous rock filled with hot water, some of them so hot that the water they contain exists as high-pressure steam. (One such region is the site of the well-known California Geysers.) Geothermal reservoirs are customarily classified as vapor-dominated (dry steam), liquid-dominated (hot water), hot-dry-rock and the magma itself, the molten rock beneath the earth's crust. In addition, many geopressurized zones have been found (mainly along the Gulf coast of the United States) in which hot water mixed with methane and other gases is trapped at very high pressures, but the water temperature is generally not sufficiently high to produce much steam.

Rough estimates of the amount of energy available from some of these resources indicate that, although the more desirable dry steam formations may be quite scarce, liquid-dominated reservoirs in the United States alone probably have a much greater energy content than the total estimated petroleum and natural gas resources of the world. The really large geothermal reservoirs, however, are those classified as hot-dry-rock; in the United States, the amount of energy of this type available within 30,000 feet of the surface has been estimated as sufficient to produce 4,000 Qe, and might be even 10 times more.* Thus a geothermal resource base exists in the United States which, without our having to use the magma itself, is theoretically sufficient to provide the entire world's energy needs for far more than the next 200 years.

Current cost estimates for producing geothermal power from the hydrothermal reservoirs suggest that it may become one of the least expensive sources of power, but early estimates of this kind are often overoptimistic. Since almost no interest has previously been shown in this option (except for the scarce dry steam fields—and even the Geysers, the only commercial U.S. project, has only been operating since 1960), the technology required for each kind of reservoir must be developed from scratch. Although Federal funds for research and development in this area have expanded rapidly, the fiscal 1976 budget request was still less than $30 million. Nevertheless, the appeal of the geothermal potential is rapidly spreading, and we believe it may well be the first of the eternal sources to achieve large-scale power production—though we concede great uncertainties.

Indeed, estimates of the rate at which geothermal resources might be developed have varied widely. Although most have been conservative, at least one prestigious group of experts (the W. J. Hickel Conference on Geothermal Energy in 1972, sponsored by the University of Alaska †) were surprisingly

* A. H. Ewing, "Stimulation of Geothermal Systems," in P. Kruger and C. Otte (eds.), *Geothermal Energy* (Stanford: Stanford University Press, 1973), pp. 217–22.

† See the Conference's *Special Report* (Fairbanks: University of Alaska, 1973).

optimistic. Practical results will depend upon such basic factors as the difficulty of the problems encountered, funding for research and development, and exploration. In addition, favorable Federal policies for leasing prospective geothermal areas and for providing reasonable economic incentives during the early development period will be needed. Also the exploration companies will need assistance in making appropriate arrangements with electric power producers (the latter operate as a regulated monopoly and there is little tradition or experience in forming such associations). Until these institutional factors are resolved, progress will be difficult and uncertain. But if there is genuine merit in the concept, there is probably more than enough time to phase in this enormous resource well before fossil fuels become very scarce.

What are some of the disadvantages of geothermal energy? For one, the best U.S. geothermal reservoirs known are located in Western states, often far away from major population centers. This creates a potentially serious transmission problem —except to the extent that major power users would gravitate to the regions. Second, the area required for each geothermal field may be very large, perhaps 100,000 acres or more. Although this would preclude many types of residential or commercial development within such areas, it should not excessively hamper agricultural or industrial development since the wells generally would be spaced far apart. The connecting pipelines would require little acreage and could be buried if necessary. Third, as is true for every new energy development, there will be some environmental problems, varying in different locations and of magnitudes not easily assessed at this time. Nevertheless, those who have examined these potential problems have tended to conclude that they would be much less difficult than those associated with coal or oil-shale mining and conversion, and that, where needed, solutions are available or can be made within current technology at reasonable cost.* Finally, and most important, we have little idea today of the many possible problems and associated costs that can arise during development of this resource.

* R. G. Bowen, "Environmental Impact of Geothermal Development," in Kruger and Otte, *Geothermal Energy,* pp. 197–216; also Joseph Barnea, "Geothermal Power," *Scientific American,* January 1972, pp. 70–77.

NUCLEAR FUSION

The search for a means to control fusion began shortly after nuclear fission began to be considered as a commercial competitor with conventional power. The technical difficulties that must be overcome have been numerous and complex, but many observers believe fusion research is on the verge of demonstrating technical feasibility. The possibility now exists of achieving commercially viable fusion power in each of three distinctly different approaches, known technically as closed toroidal machines, open magnetic wells and laser implosion systems. In each case, first-generation designs are based on the so-called D-T (deuterium-tritium) reaction, which requires a minimum temperature of about 100 million degrees to start the fusion process. Once started, the reaction becomes enormously energetic in terms of the energy-mass relationship. The fusion of one pound of a D-T mixture releases about the same amount of energy as fissioning three pounds of U-235, the energy equivalent of about 10,000 tons of coal.

The consensus among scientists today is that the commercial feasibility of one of the magnetic fusion systems (probably the TOKAMAK, based on a Soviet design) is likely to be established by the early 1990's. A practical laser fusion process is not apt to become operational before early in the next century. Which of the successful alternatives proves to be commercially competitive over the long term is still an open question, and there is actually no assurance that any will be commercially competitive; as always, the uncertainties are simply too great.

The principal advantages of fusion over fission reactors are that: (1) the associated radioactive hazards are anticipated to be smaller by several orders of magnitude; (2) the threat of a runaway process or explosion does not exist; and (3) the inherent temptation for theft or sabotage would be much smaller. In other words, nearly all of the grim scenarios conjured up in connection with fission reactors disappear, or are very much reduced, with nuclear fusion. Although it does present some risk of tritium leakage, this potential danger not only can be minimized by reactor design, but can be continuously monitored. Fortunately, tritium is one of the mildest radioactive isotopes, but it must be treated with great caution because of the relatively high quantities involved (about two pounds per day for a 1,000-megawatt plant). One problem with fusion reactors is that they could become a source of cheap neutrons—a possibility with many implications for arms-control negotiations, since in principle these neutrons can be used to make explosives for nuclear weapons. It is possible to imagine circumstances in which this could create worse problems than those from the current reactor program —although the scenarios involved might not appear to be very probable.

ENERGY SYSTEMS OF THE 22ND CENTURY

Two developments are likely to occur during the next 100 to 200 years which will prepare the way for what we think will emerge as a more or less steady state in energy production and distribution, regardless of which long-term energy sources become commercially dominant.

There is little debate about the first—that most of the energy produced on a large scale will be in the form of electric power. Thus, most present concepts for major long-term energy sources (solar, geothermal, fusion) are based upon electric power production at central plants.

The second major development is the prospective use of hydrogen as both a basic fuel to replace natural gas and as part of a general system to convert, store and/or transmit electric energy over long distances. For energy storage and the long-distance transmission and distribution of energy— especially from desert solar power "farms," ocean-based generators or geothermal power centers—it might be practical to convert the generated power into hydrogen which could easily be piped to the distribution centers. At these centers the hydrogen could either be reconverted to electricity by fuel cells (which are expected to become 80–90 percent efficient after 50–100 years of research and development), or it could be used directly as a fuel for commercial, industrial or transportation purposes.*

Hydrogen can be stored as a pressurized gas in underground caverns, above ground as a liquid (at very low temperatures) or as a solid in the form of hydrides, compounds formed by the diffusion of hydrogen gas into metals. As a gas it can flow through pipeline distribution systems cheaply, much as natural gas does today. As a liquid it can be stored above ground in bulk, perhaps in 10-million-gallon tanks. As a hydride it would constitute a source of hydrogen gas, which could be used as a portable tank of fuel in conjunction with either large engines for mass transportation or smaller ones for personal motor vehicles. With relatively nonpolluting electric power from any of the eternal sources and clean-burning hydrogen in an intermediate role between power plant and consumer, the overall impact on the environment—especially on air pollution—could clearly be minimized.†

Although hydrogen seems likely to play a major role in the future as a form of energy transport and storage, other processes may also be useful, at least during the transition period, and in certain locations may be preferable for reasons of efficiency or safety. Here we note only two possibilities, the first of which, flywheels (wheels that can store energy through the speed of their rotation), looks very promising. The second, batteries and fuel cells, represents one of the main candidates for widespread use in the 21st century.

Flywheels: It appears to be feasible to construct flywheels of almost any needed size that would be efficient converters (93–95 percent) in first storing and then releasing electric

---

* In producing hydrogen from electricity, the theoretical maximum efficiency is about 120 percent, the extra energy coming from the environment. In practice, prototypes have reached 85 percent, and 100 percent is deemed a reasonable goal for future commercial operations.

† The only pollutants from burning hydrogen in air are the nitrogen oxides. Even these would be much less than the amounts released in using gasoline in an auto engine, however. In an external-combustion mode, these oxides can be eliminated almost completely by using lean mixtures, especially with catalytic burners, or by burning with pure oxygen.

power. Moreover, the kinetic energy of rotation is readily converted to alternating electric power, an important feature. Theoretical analysis has shown that flywheels made of modern materials may be able to store energy at densities comparable to or better than the most promising batteries. Furthermore, they could absorb or deliver electric power at rates as fast as or faster than almost any competitive system. But the engineering is at an early state of development, and a decade or more may pass before this potential can be reliably estimated.

Batteries and fuel cells: Some of the many batteries being developed today look quite promising. Within a decade or two, a battery-operated electric auto might even become competitive with today's vehicles, at least for driving ranges up to 200 miles. An electric automobile would be pollution-free, and would probably be more energy-efficient than the internal-combustion engine (even after allowing for conversion losses in obtaining the electric power from a fossil fuel source). It almost certainly would be much quieter and require less maintenance. Also, because of their efficiency in DC electric systems, batteries could be used for electric energy storage in conjunction, for example, with photovoltaic systems installed either at large central power plants or in individual structures.

A fuel cell (which may be considered a hybrid battery *) with about 40 percent conversion efficiency is expected to enter power production on a substantial scale within about five years. Unlike steam-powered generators, which are efficient only in large sizes operating at design capacity, fuel cells can be made large or small and their efficiency in operation is essentially independent of the loading. Thus they may avoid most of the distribution costs of electric power as well as provide pollution-free power and offer substantial opportunities for utilizing the "waste heat" effectively. As we proceed further toward electric and/or hydrogen-electric power systems, the electric conversion efficiency and potential for use of fuel cells can be expected to increase substantially.

---

* A battery stores electricity and delivers it on demand. A fuel cell creates the electricity from fuels such as natural gas or hydrogen. Like a battery, it also can be run in reverse—that is, electricity will create fuel.

EFFICIENT USE OF ENERGY

To an observer looking back from the 21st or 22nd century, today's use of energy will probably seem inefficient in many respects. In oil-fired electric power generation and transmission, for example, about 70 percent of the energy in the fuel is lost before the user receives the power. Autos generally deliver, as motive power, only about 10 percent of the energy in the original petroleum. Conservation advocates have frequently advised that buildings be better insulated; they also point out that most industrial processes are far from optimal in energy utilization. These inefficient systems have developed during recent decades when technology was in its infancy and energy has been relatively cheap, but future trends are apt to change this. Our projection (see Table 6) assumes that worldwide efficiency in energy extraction, conversion, transmission and utilization will improve overall by a factor of 4 during the next 200 years. For example, we expect that soon after the year 2000 improved methods of generating electricity from fossil fuels could provide an overall efficiency of about 60 percent, compared to today's 35–40 percent. The electric engine or other substitutes for today's internal-combustion engines could quickly double, and eventually more than triple, present automobile energy efficiencies. Better insulation and design of buildings could reduce heat-transfer losses by a factor of 2 or more. Electric-powered heat pumps, theoretically much more than 100 percent efficient, undoubtedly will be increasingly phased into the economy—especially as the efficiency of electric power production increases. Also, electric power transmission losses can be cut by 50 percent or more by use of properly shielded higher-voltage overhead lines, more modern underground systems and DC power. The current incandescent bulb will probably be replaced by other forms of lighting which will be 10 times more efficient.

Finally, we expect new power-generating systems to emerge that will utilize the waste heat which today is about

Table 6.   Summary of Global Energy Resources

Source	Long-Term Potential (Est.)	1st Commercial Feasibility (Est.)	Problem Areas [a]
Hydroelectric	.1 Qe/yr.	Current	C
Oil & Natural Gas	30 Q	Current	E
Tar Sands & Oil Shale	30–2,000 Q	1985	C,E
Coal & Lignite	200 Q	Current	E
U–235 (Free World)	15 Qe	Current	E
U–235 (Ocean)	3,000 Qe	Current	C,E
Uranium for Breeders	>100,000 Qe	1995	C,E
Li–6 (D–T Fusion Reactor)[b]	320 Q	1995–2005	C,E,T
Deuterium (D–D Fusion Reactor)	>1 billion Q	2020–50	C,E,T
Solar Radiation (1% of Surface Energy)	30 Q/yr.	1980–2000	C,T
Ocean Gradients	20 Qe/yr.	2000	C,T
Organic Conversion	1.2 Q/yr.	1975–90	C
Geothermal—Magma	>1 billion Q	?	C,E,T
Hot Dry Rock	>100,000 Qe	1990–95	C,E,T
Liquid-dominated	>1,000 Qe	1980–85	C,E
Dry Steam	1 Qe	Current	—

[a] C = cost, E = environment, T = technology.

[b] Li–6: The lithium isotope used to breed tritium in first-generation fusion reactors. World resources might be 10 times greater than shown.

two-thirds of the total energy input and is not only dissipated, but is also considered a pollutant. Large capital investments are therefore necessary to dispose of it in ways which are less environmentally disturbing; this solution is not only costly but often unaesthetic (cooling towers are an example). Waste heat, however, has many potentially useful applications. Although there has been little incentive for utilizing waste heat until recently, it has a demonstrated practicality depending, of course, upon such variables as design, season and location. Widespread commercial applications probably will not come rapidly, because they often require complex integration into new systems on a large scale—and retrofitting can be very costly. However, we expect that during the next 200 years heat sinks for waste energy will increasingly achieve a utilitarian role, thereby reducing society's overall energy requirements, and that eventually issues of large, polluting, "waste energy" projects will be viewed as a relic of the 20th century.

Table 6 offers an estimate of current major energy resources, as well as the potential capacity of new contributors to meet the world's future demands. As we compare Table 6 to Table 3, which projects the world's energy requirements, the prospects appear quite encouraging. Indeed, we expect that all but one of the sources listed in Table 6 * will be commercially feasible before 2050, and most of them by the year 2000. We can now only guess which of these alternatives will emerge as the principal commercial competitors; the eventual outcome will be a matter partly of institutional and environmental developments and partly of technological change.

We do not mean to imply that the path to abundant energy will be smooth. Future energy projects will tend to become increasingly immense, and costly mistakes may create serious temporary local or regional supply problems lasting perhaps 5 to 10 years, higher costs, rationing, brownouts and similar troubles. In retrospect, the developed world's present vulnerability to OPEC appears to be attributable to a mistake of this kind. We find it hard to visualize, however, that the effects of such a mistake in the future could last for as long as 20 years, and usually it will be for much less time; too many options for new supplies already exist and they will increase over time. Even with lead times of 5–10 years for major facilities, very large changes in production capacity can be made within 20 years. We therefore might characterize future energy systems as relatively inflexible within a decade, flexible over 20 years and potentially revolutionary within a half-century.

The basic message is this: Except for temporary fluctuations caused by bad luck or poor management, the world need not worry about energy shortages or costs in the future. And energy abundance is probably the world's best insurance that the entire human population (even 15–20 billion) can be well cared for, at least physically, during many centuries to come.

---

* The exception is geothermal energy directly from deep molten rock (magma).

IV

Raw Materials:
The End of the Beginning

MOST AMERICANS BELIEVE we are facing the prospect of a basic shortage of minerals in the world, according to a Harris poll taken in November 1975. A majority of the respondents to the poll (64 percent versus 29 percent) anticipated that a reduction in future living standards would result from continued "wasteful" consumption; they also believed (by 55 percent to 30 percent) that the *disparity* between the size of the U.S. population and its relatively high per capita consumption of minerals (about six times the world average) was harmful to the welfare of the rest of the world. As a consequence, 50 percent of those polled were concerned that a continuation of this trend would turn the rest of the world against the United States.

These views, which surely were not generally held 10 years ago, presumably were created and/or enhanced by the phenomenon of the limits-to-growth, or neo-Malthusian, movement, as well as by recent shortages. Among the more deleterious effects of some of the limits-to-growth concepts may be the sense of guilt or unworthiness they encourage in the industrialized world, and the sense of having been short-changed that they encourage in spokesmen for the developing countries. (For some, the initials GNP have increasingly been interpreted as representing "gross national pollution," and more and more references are made to the "effluent society" and "mindless growth" as though industrial production were worse than meaningless, as though it generated garbage rather than useful and desirable products.) Both attitudes are unhealthy, particularly since they are based largely on misformulations and misinformation, produce unnecessary confrontation and endless irrelevant rhetoric, and create an unfortunate diversion of attention from real issues. If the neo-Malthusian view of the world as a fixed pie were correct, if every non-renewable resource any nation used diminished the amount remaining for the rest of the world and future generations, then the world might properly be labeled as wicked and unjust. Under these circumstances, our encouragement of increased production and our attempts to facilitate the greater use of raw materials by all, including the rich of the current generation, could be considered "criminal." But, as already discussed, while the fixed-pie metaphor may be very persuasive to some people, our analysis finds it completely misleading. The major theme of this chapter is that there is an abundance of raw materials for future generations as well as the present one, and that the more man develops economically and technologically, the more there will be for all of humanity.

Generally speaking, while modern societies might *appear* to be quite vulnerable to a sudden severe shortage of energy or food, they have almost never been desperately vulnerable to shortages of raw materials. For example, even during wartime, when blockades cut off normal sources of supply and the manufacturing and construction industries were redirected to the needs of a wartime economy, civilians usually have managed to fulfill their vital needs surprisingly well for long periods of time (although there may have been annoyances in terms of their creature comforts, such as having to maintain their cars or houses a little longer, fix broken appliances more often, and repair frayed clothing or shoes). In this context it would be possible for a modern society to live for years, *if necessary,* with its existing structures and stocks of manufactured products.

This is not to say that the lack of adequate raw materials might not have an extraordinary effect on the business cycle, for it could easily mean the difference beween prosperity and depression, between winning and losing a war. It is only to say that mineral shortages are unlikely to have an immediate impact upon survival expectations. Not only is it a fundamental law of science that no elementary substance (except radioactive ones) can be used up, except for fuels in a modern society most of the resources that have been extracted from the earth generally exist above ground somewhere and thus can be reclaimed and recycled, provided only that sufficient energy is available. Indeed, given the potential of future technology to recycle, to conserve energy and materials, and to accomplish more with less resources, it does not appear unreasonable for the long-term future to imagine an expanding economy operating largely on recycled materials, should any become relatively scarce.

Finally, we should realize that, in principle, no industrial society can be dependent in the long run upon any single critical industrial mineral. This should be obvious because if such a mineral had never been discovered, industries would have developed around the minerals we did know about, and we would not be aware of our loss.* The only raw material that might cause one to question this statement even momentarily is iron because the widespread availability and utility of iron ore have led to our steel-based civilization. Obviously, every society becomes dependent upon its traditional raw materials and would find it difficult to make a relatively rapid change if a sudden unanticipated shortage appeared. But that is to take a short-term view.

Over the long term we have projected world population growth to 15 billion and GWP to $300 trillion by 2176, with an abundance of energy at roughly today's prices (or at least not more than triple). Under these circumstances the world's annual requirement for raw materials, if linear with GWP, would be about 60 times that of today (although a factor of 15 or less might be more reasonable because of the expected

---

* The noted economist Wilfred Beckerman is fond of pointing out that civilization has *failed* because his uncle forgot to invent "Beckermonium," just such a "critical" material, one that would now be dominating society if only his uncle had invented it (Wilfred Beckerman, *In Defense of Economic Growth* [London: Jonathan Cape, 1974]).

relative increase in services over production, the lower relative value of raw materials in a more highly technological society and the reduced requirement anticipated for maintenance and replacement). Yet even with a factor of 60, we would reject out of hand the notion that we could *run out* of any really critical material resource, one that would prevent the growth we envisage from actually occurring.

It is our view that very few important materials in the world—perhaps none—will become unduly scarce, although the distribution of the prime sources of many of them is so uneven that unless we are careful cartels might occasionally be able to extract higher prices than usual from consumers, thus causing local needs for conservation, substitution and redesign. (If the price set by a cartel has been high for decades, then there usually is not a problem because the user has not become excessively dependent.) Gold and silver are high-priced metals mostly because they are naturally scarce; consequently we used them less than we otherwise would and have never become dependent on them. For example, most electrical wire is made out of copper though silver would be better; and when the price of copper gets too high, as it occasionally has, aluminum can take its place for most present uses (although this does force adjustments that may be temporarily inconvenient). The same considerations apply to all metals—indeed, to almost all *materials*. Table 7 lists some

Table 7. Principal Substitutes for Materials

Material	*Principal Substitutes*
Aluminum ore (bauxite)	Kaolinite, dawsonite, alunite, anorthosite, nepheline syenite, saprolite, coal ash
Chromium	Nickel, molybdenum, vanadium
Cobalt	Nickel
Copper	Aluminum, plastics
Lead	Rubber, copper, plastics, tile, titanium, zinc
Molybdenum	Tungsten, vanadium
Tin	Aluminum, plastics
Tungsten	Molybdenum
Zinc	Aluminum, plastics

potential substitutes for metals in common use. It should be noted how frequently plastics appear. The increasing utility and versatility of plastics and other new materials (such as high-strength fibers and composites) reinforce the general argument, even though it may not need reinforcing.

In a hypothetical world in which all materials would be sold at approximately their marginal cost of extraction (or production), the possibility of any shortages because of exhaustion could be anticipated for decades and gradual adjustments made to avoid undue economic stresses. In the real world *sudden* or *very rapid* changes in supply or demand can occur and create temporary economic anguish. The rate of growth in GWP increased by about 40 percent during 1973 (and into 1974), and at the same time there was an unusual degree of inventory accumulation accompanied by considerable speculation in commodities. As a result, prices skyrocketed and the public was told that "everything was scarce" in 1974. But only a year later, "nothing was scarce." How easy it was for panic to take hold when the 1973–74 commodity price fluctuations followed the energy crisis. That "everything scarce" phenomenon quickly became a permanent theme about a growing resource dilemma of the world, even though many commodity and resource prices returned to "normal" levels after about a year. In any event, the possibility of mineral resources being depleted over the course of the next century or two needs to be examined carefully and thoughtfully if the argument that an expanding demand will soon exhaust the supplies of a finite earth is to be refuted.

THE LONG-TERM PERSPECTIVE FOR RESOURCES

In a recent work, one of the leading neo-Malthusians, Dennis Meadows, listed 19 principal mineral resources in use today, with estimates of their reserves and their potential resource base.* In each case it appeared that the mineral was "soon" to be exhausted if the projected worldwide growth in its use continued, with estimates ranging from a low of 6 years to a high of 154 years before exhaustion. Therefore, the inescapable conclusion, based on the data presented by Meadows, was that the world must reverse its economic growth tendencies.

Since our view of the future of mineral resources so directly contradicts that of Meadows and his colleagues, we find it necessary to explain the huge gulf between the two points of view. First, consider the three energy minerals—coal, oil and natural gas, the most important sources today. We have already analyzed alternative energy resources in some detail and found that with very little doubt we could expect essentially an eternal abundance of energy, the only requirements being that the sun keep shining and modest technological progress continue for a few years. But one would be forced to

* POTENTIAL EXHAUSTION OF SELECTED MINERALS.

Resources	Average Annual Growth in Use (%)	Years Remaining Low	High
Aluminum	6.4	33	49
Chromium	2.6	115	137
Coal	4.1	118	132
Cobalt	1.5	90	132
Copper	4.6	27	46
Gold	4.1	6	17
Iron	1.8	154	n.a.
Lead	2.0	28	119
Manganese	2.9	106	123
Mercury	2.6	19	44
Molybdenum	4.5	65	92
Natural gas	4.7	19	58
Nickel	3.4	50	75
Petroleum	3.9	23	43
Platinum	3.8	41	49
Silver	2.7	15	23
Tin	1.1	62	92
Tungsten	2.5	27	n.a.
Zinc	2.9	76	115

Adapted from Dennis L. Meadows *et al., Dynamics of Growth in a Finite World* (Cambridge, Mass.: Wright-Allen Press, 1974), pp. 372–73.

an opposite conclusion if Meadows' data were the sole source of information. We do not have the space to deal with each of the remaining 16 minerals he lists, but we will discuss aluminum, iron and mercury in some detail and the rest with more general observations.

Except for silicon (a semimetal), aluminum is the most abundant metal in the earth's crust, which contains about 8 percent aluminum, or roughly 2 million trillion tons. Can that much metal (or even .0001 percent of it) be used up in 49 years, the high side of Meadows' estimate? The resolution of the apparent confusion lies in Meadows' footnotes, where he explains that he has counted only the aluminum in *known reserves of bauxite*. In other words, if we ignore every possible source of aluminum except known high-grade bauxite deposits, we will come up with his numbers. Or will we? No, not even then. For even though he states in a footnote that unless otherwise specified he will use data from the 1973 U.S. Geological Survey document *U.S. Mineral Resources*, in the case of aluminum there is another footnote explaining that he has taken the estimate of aluminum reserves instead from the earlier U.S. Bureau of Mines report *Mineral Facts and Problems, 1970*, which happened to use a 1965 estimate that was less than half the one given in the 1973 document. Moreover, the later volume unambiguously asserts in a summary statement that ". . . the nation has virtually inexhaustible potential resources of aluminous materials other than bauxite," and it proceeds to describe 10 of them in illuminating detail —including the fact that one U.S. deposit of oil shale (250 square miles in surface area) contains 19 billion tons of the mineral *dawsonite* (about one-fifth pure aluminum) which is available as a by-product of extracting shale oil. This single small area contains more aluminum than Meadows' estimate for total known world reserves plus potential future resources.

As for iron, the world's most important metal, Meadows says that there may be reserves enough for only 154 years, and regarding potential resources says "no estimate available." This is true—sort of. The Geological Survey does assert, however, that "Because of the great amounts of identified iron-ore resources, no attempt is made to estimate quantities of hypothetical iron-ore resources beyond stating that they are enormous." * How could they be otherwise when iron constitutes about 6 percent of the earth's crust?

Mercury, like gold and silver, is relatively scarce—or perhaps it would be more accurate to say that it is hard to find. Therefore, if it continues to be used at increasing rates, there might be no more available after 44 years (Meadows' high-side estimate). How do we handle this problem, assuming that the estimate of supply is valid (although we will even question this later)? To answer, we look at the principal uses of mercury and consider the possibility of other solutions. The fact is that there are substitutes available for each of the major uses of mercury.† Indeed, some of the former uses are now banned because of the extremely poisonous nature of mercury compounds. While some of the suggested substitutes might be more expensive, up to 44 years are available to find better ones; if this fails, then the extra costs might have to be paid. But if some of the substitutions are successful, that would give more time to work on the others—and, indeed, more mercury might also be found.

It should also be pointed out that Meadows' estimate for mercury resources must be inaccurate since good data are simply not available. The Geological Survey report said: "At most mercury mines, no effort has been made to ascertain the ultimate reserve of the deposit in advance of exploitation, and at few mines is enough ore blocked out for more than one year of operation." ‡ Indeed, Meadows' estimate, given under the heading "Hypothetical plus Speculative Resources," is, as he states in a footnote, for "mercury recoverable at $1,000/flask"—that is, it is an estimate of low-grade *identified reserves* and does not include hypothetical or speculative resources at all.

The fact is that *known reserves* for most minerals tend not

---

* U.S. Geological Survey, *U.S. Mineral Resources* (1973), p. 304.

† H. E. Goeller and Alvin M. Weinberg, *The Age of Substitutability,* Eleventh Annual Foundation Lecture for presentation before the United Kingdom Science Policy Foundation Fifth International Symposium—"A Strategy for Resources"—Eindhoven, The Netherlands, September 18, 1975.

‡ *U.S. Mineral Resources,* p. 409.

to exceed a few decades of demand, for obvious economic reasons. We would not be surprised to learn, for example, that if the lead industry had proved reserves sufficient for 30 years at anticipated demand, it would be only *mildly* interested in searching for new reserves. Since anything found today probably could not be sold for 30 years or so, it would hardly be a fantastic investment opportunity. Indeed, great success by several companies in locating new reserves would put severe pressure on current prices. Consequently, if new lead mines are found in the next few years it is more likely to be a fortuitous discovery than the result of a concerted exploration for the mineral. Thus far, capital spending in the mining and primary metals industries has remained unchanged from 1967–68 levels, which would not suggest that any uncommon shortages in reserves are being felt by them.

World reserves of many minerals have actually grown so rapidly, as Table 8 shows, that if further exploration were encouraged it would be more for reasons of national security or fear of excessively high prices from foreign cartels than from a concern about fundamental shortages. If the estimated re-

Table 8. How "Known Reserves" Alter

Ore	Known Reserves in 1950 (1,000 Metric Tons)	Known Reserves in 1970 (1,000 Metric Tons)	Percentage Increase
Iron	19,000,000	251,000,000	1,321
Manganese	500,000	635,000	27
Chromite	100,000	775,000	675
Tungsten	1,903	1,328	—30
Copper	100,000	279,000	179
Lead	40,000	86,000	115
Zinc	70,000	113,000	61
Tin	6,000	6,600	10
Bauxite	1,400,000	5,300,000	279
Potash	5,000,000	118,000,000	2,360
Phosphates	26,000,000	1,178,000,000	4,430
Oil	75,000,000	455,000,000	507

SOURCE: Council on International Economic Policy, Executive Office of the President, *Special Report, Critical Imported Materials* (Washington, D.C.: U.S. Government Printing Office, December 1974).

coverable zinc resources are sufficient for at least 1,000 years at current demand rates, as they are, who would be interested in exploring for more now? On the other hand, if current ore reserves were down to 10 years or less, then the marketplace would reflect that condition with increased prices until new mines are opened and reserves are expanded to higher levels.

Because of these economic considerations, there is little reason for known reserves to exceed the expected demand by more than a few decades. It does happen occasionally but *not* because shortages have prompted a search for additional supplies. Thus, if we have stumbled upon coal reserves sufficient for more than 200 years and iron ore for more than 1,000, we can hardly expect private investors to be excited about a proposal to look for still more. As a result, those who make conservative predictions about the future availability of materials based upon such data naturally tend to underestimate future production capability. The literature is full of such predictions. As one example, the prestigious Paley Report of 1952 stated that by the mid-1970's U.S. copper production would not exceed 800,000 tons; in fact, it was 1.7 million tons in 1973. The report also said the *maximum* lead production would be 300,000 tons; yet it actually exceeded 600,000 tons.* This tendency to underestimate future production is so strong that similar mistakes are made over and over again, as Tables 8 and 9 vividly illustrate.

The tendency to confuse temporary shortages with permanent ones can be caused by various factors. For instance, a cartel, while it is successful, deliberately creates a shortage of supply sufficient to increase the price of its controlled commodity substantially. During the height of the cartel's success there is a tendency to believe that the induced shortage can become permanent. Historically most such cartels have failed.

---

* U.S. President's Materials Policy Commission, *Resources for Freedom* (Washington: U.S. Government Printing Office, 1952). For 1973 figures, see Statement of Simon D. Strauss, executive vice-president, American Smelting and Refining Company, "Global Scarcities in an Interdependent World," Hearings before Subcommittee on Foreign Economic Policy of the Committee on Foreign Affairs, Ninety-Third Congress, May 1974, p. 121.

Table 9. Oil Prophecies and Realities

Date	U.S. Oil Production Rate (billion bbls/yr)	Prophecy	Reality
1866	.005	Synthetics available if oil production should end (U.S. Revenue Commission)	In next 82 years the U.S. produced 37 billion bbls. with no need for synthetics
1885	.02	Little or no chance for oil in California (U.S. Geological Survey)	8 billion bbls. produced in California since that date with important new findings in 1948
1891	.05	Little or no chance for oil in Kansas or Texas (U.S. Geological Survey)	14 billion bbls. produced in these two states since 1891
1908	.18	Maximum future supply of 22.5 billion bbls. (officials of Geological Survey)	35 billion bbls. produced since 1908, with 26.8 billion reserve proven and available on January 1, 1949
1914	.27	Total future production only 5.7 billion bbls. (official of U.S. Bureau of Mines)	34 billion bbls. produced since 1914, or six times this prediction
1920	.45	U.S. needs foreign oil and synthetics: peak domestic production almost reached (Director of U.S. Geological Survey)	1948 U.S. production in excess of U.S. consumption and more than four times 1920 output
1931	.85	Must import as much foreign oil as possible to save domestic supply (Secretary of the Interior)	During next 8 years imports were discouraged and 14 billion bbls. were found in the U.S.
1939	1.3	U.S. oil supplies will last only 13 years (radio broadcasts by Interior Department)	New oil found since 1939 exceeds the 13 years' supply known at that time
1947	1.9	Sufficient oil cannot be found in United States (Chief of Petroleum Division, State Department)	4.3 billion bbls. found in 1948, the largest volume in history and twice our consumption

Table 9. (continued)

Date	U.S. Oil Production Rate (billion bbls/yr)	Prophecy	Reality
1949	2.0	End of U.S. oil supply almost in sight (Secretary of the Interior)	Petroleum industry demonstrated ability to increase U.S. production by more than a million bbls. daily in the next 5 years.

SOURCE: Presidential Energy Program, Hearings before the Subcommittee on Energy and Power of the Committee on Interstate and Foreign Commerce, House of Representatives. First session on the implications of the President's proposals in the Energy Independence Act of 1975. Serial No. 94–20, p. 643. (Washington: U.S. Government Printing Office, February 17, 18, 20, and 21, 1975.)

OPEC, which has had a phenomenal recent success, is now being tested by the economic reactions to the threat that it poses.* But the main point is that unless the cartel slows down

* In this connection, the following is presented as an amusing *a fortiori* scenario about possible developments with a copper cartel:

In response to certain events that occurred before January 1985 (the activities of an effective international copper cartel, depletion of American copper resources during the prior decade, and a doubling of demand for the metal after energy became cheap again and worldwide industrial growth boomed), the price of copper rose rapidly within several months from $1 to $10/lb. and hovered there after May 1985. The following facts were recorded:

1. The U.S. had "consumed" about 90 million tons of copper, most of which still existed in various forms within structures or equipment. As the value of scrap copper increased from .70 to $9/lb. during the 1985 price rise, metal dealers realized that existing U.S. copper was now worth about $1.7 trillion, an average of $6,000 per person!—almost equal in value to a third of the prior wealth of the country (estimated in 1984 at about $5 trillion). Needless to say, a rush developed to locate old brass beds, brass handles, copper pots, lamps, locks and all other copper scrap—and 65 billion pennies were suddenly worth a nickel each at the scrap dealer's.

2. Utility companies went into a crash program to substitute aluminum for copper in transmission lines, engineers began designing copperless heat exchangers, many radiant-heated floors and walls were ripped open to get the copper tubing, and plumbers were in great demand to replace copper pipes and tubing in homes and buildings.

research and exploration, technological progress and/or economic development, its actions will cause the resource to last longer than it otherwise would have.

NEAR-TERM IMPORT DEPENDENCE

The Third World, generally speaking, is poor, not rich, in the raw materials used by modern society. Most of the world's current known reserves of raw materials belong to

---

3. CBS News reported one engineer's calculation that copper could be profitably extracted from many of the above-average grades of igneous rock at a cost of about $4/lb. At $6/lb. profit from the copper, the higher-grade volcanic rock in the U.S. was now worth about $5/ton (net profit), and the engineer estimated the total value to be more than $1,000 trillion for rock within 100 feet of the surface. The next morning there was a stampede at every mining claims office in the world.

4. It was reported that people were lined up in long queues with barrels full of copper and brass artifacts at every scrapyard in the developed world, waiting for their turn to sell.

5. Before the year was up, nearly everything that had been made of copper had been redesigned to use other metals. Where used at all, copper was applied in only very thin films, as in electroplating.

6. It was on November 1 that quotations on copper futures first started to plummet, and they fell the limit every day for 38 days. By year's end copper was once again $1—a month later it was only .50/lb. Some of the new alternatives were found to have unanticipated advantages over the original copper construction, many substitute projects were already under way, and manufacturers were loath to risk using copper again.

7. The copper affair sent shock waves throughout world economies; some organizations went bankrupt, and many people who had bought copper futures at $8–10/lb. were ruined.

A number of conclusions can be drawn from this scenario:

1. Copper is a *renewable* resource. Mining and smelting just change it from a low-grade ore below ground to a very high-grade ore above.

2. The above-ground reserve is scattered but easily collectible—when the price is right.

3. There are now about 80 million tons of copper in the U.S.—above ground.

4. At about $4/lb. the amount of copper available from ores becomes essentially unlimited.

5. Nothing made in quantity from copper today is critical. The electrical and heat-conduction properties of copper are excellent, but substitutes are available and some may even be cheaper once the capital is invested.

6. The price of copper will be limited in the long-term future by the cost of mining it from lower-grade ores or extracting it from marine sources. Either source, if needed, is likely to come in at much less than $4/lb. throughout the next century.

the developed nations—80 percent in Canada, Australia, the United States, the Soviet Union and South Africa. But perhaps these reserves are "known" precisely because these countries' knowledge about their actual mineral resources is far more advanced than that of the Third World.

Although it is a major producer of raw materials, the United States depends upon imports of certain important metals or their ores—totally for cobalt, chromium and manganese, between 80 and 90 percent for tin and bauxite, and between 60 and 70 percent for nickel and zinc. All in all, however, the United States is extraordinarily well situated in terms of industrial raw materials. Although it is not self-sufficient, its dependence upon imported materials is much less than that of Western Europe or Japan, as Figure 7 shows.

Figure 7.   Import Dependence in Selected Industrial Raw Materials

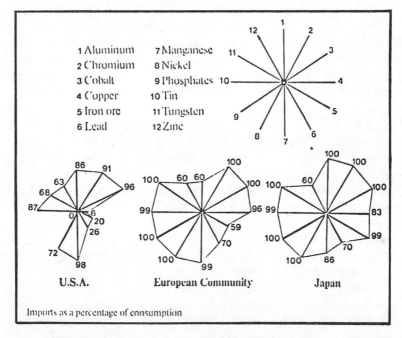

SOURCE: Hudson Research Europe, Ltd., *The Hudson Letter, A Special Report, Industrial Raw Materials: The Outlook* (Paris: *International Herald Tribune*, 1975).

How are these dependency figures to be interpreted? For the near term, the figures can be taken literally, but for the medium term or beyond, they tend to become meaningless— at least for the United States. Most ores or metals are imported because it is the cheapest way to obtain them. If the current import sources become exhausted or uneconomical for various reasons, then lower-grade ores can be mined elsewhere or other materials might be substituted to a significant extent. Given 10 years or more to anticipate a particular problem, it is hard to imagine a mineral that would cause a severe industrial crisis because of a constricting supply from present sources.

MUTUAL DEPENDENCE

If the producers of copper, cocoa, tin or any other commodity decide unilaterally to impose a large increase in the price of their product, usually there is no automatic corrective mechanism in the short run. In the medium run everything depends upon what action is taken by the buyers of the commodity and their governments. We have already seen examples of this in bauxite and phosphates: Jamaica recently increased its bauxite prices; Morocco, which produces the majority of the phosphate used in Europe, has increased its price by about three times. The first set of prices has remained firm and perhaps could be increased again; the second has already begun to fall dramatically. But neither of these actions should constitute any major threat to the industrialized countries, assuming that these countries formulate appropriate economic and technological policies. In both cases new investment is now being directed toward breaking the monopoly of the producers, though the effort has not gone very far yet.

Among commodity producers, the copper-producing countries have been successful recently in banding their interests together. CIPEC,* the producers' association formed

---

* Conseil Intergouvernmental des Pays Exportateurs de Cuivre.

by the main copper-producing nations—Chile, Zambia, Peru and Zaire—was modeled after OPEC in an attempt to maximize revenues from copper production. Since the amount of primary copper produced by these four countries, as a fraction of total primary copper production, is only about 10 percent less than the comparable figure for crude petroleum produced by the Arab members of OPEC plus Iran, there appeared to be a prima facie case for the success of such an association. But when the demand for commodities began to falter in 1974, the pressures from substitutes and recycling (and the dumping of Japanese stockpiles of copper) almost completely negated the cartel's program.

The fact is that the real prices of many important raw materials were about constant or declined between the early 1950's and 1971, as shown in Table 10. Where the revenues

Table 10. Metal Prices (¢/lb)

Year	Aluminum		Copper		Lead	
	Current Prices	Constant Prices	Current Prices	Constant Prices	Current Prices	Constant Prices
1946	14	14	13.8	13.8	8.1	8.1
1948	14.7	11.9	22	17.8	18	14.6
1950	16.7	13.5	21.2	17.2	13.3	10.8
1952	18.4	13.5	24.2	17.8	16.5	12.1
1954	20.2	14.5	29.7	21.3	14	10
1956	24	17.2	41.8	30	16	11.5
1958	24.8	16.8	25.8	17.4	12.1	8.2
1960	26	17.1	32	21.1	12	7.9
1962	23.9	15.4	30.6	19.8	9.6	6.2
1964	23.7	14.9	32	20.2	13.6	8.6
1966	24.5	14.7	36.2	21.8	15.1	9.1
1968	25.6	14.4	41.8	23.5	13.2	7.4
1970	28.7	14.4	57.7	29	15.6	7.8
1972	26.4	12.0	50.6	23	15.0	6.9
1974 (May)	31.5	13.0	130	53.5	32.5	13.4
1975 (Oct)	40	14.6	56	20.5	20	7.3

Base date for constant prices is 1946.

SOURCE: *Metal Statistics* (Frankfurt-on-Main: Metallgesellschaft Aktiengesellschaft, 1973), for current price data through 1972; *The New York Times* for 1974 and 1975 current price data.

of the producer countries increased over the period, it was principally through increasing volume and higher productivity. A recent study has also shown the trend of declining real commodity prices since 1900, noting the ratio of the price of some of the most important minerals to the price of labor in the United States. The examples of copper, iron, zinc, aluminum and crude petroleum are given in Table 11.

Table 11. Price of Minerals Relative to Average Cost of Labor

	1900	1920	1940	1950	1960	1970
Copper	785	226	121	99	82	100
Iron	620	287	144	112	120	100
Zinc	794	400	272	256	126	100
Aluminum	3,150	859	287	166	134	100
Crude Petroleum	1,034	726	198	213	135	100

Base: 1970 = 100

SOURCE: W. D. Nordhaus, "Resources as a Constraint on Growth," *American Economic Review,* May 1974.

This continuous decline in the cost of minerals relative to labor over the last 70 years came to a dramatic halt during 1973–74, when the commodity boom saw most raw material prices doubled or tripled, even without cartels. But then, in the recession in the major consuming countries during 1974–75, the majority of raw material prices fell, some by more than 50 percent.

We expect that in the medium term average prices will be somewhat above the depressed pre-1973 levels. Over the long term the fluctuations of the commodity cycle will undoubtedly continue, around a slowly changing trend line, which is much more likely to be downward- than upward-sloping.

FUTURE LONG-TERM WORLD DEMAND AND SUPPLIES

If we look at the principal metals used in the world (Table 12), we note that over 95 percent of the world demand is for

Table 12. Consumption of Major Industrial Metals Considered Inexhaustible (1968)

Clearly Inexhaustible	U.S.	World
Iron	85.70%	89.83%
Aluminum	8.22	4.47
Silicon	1.05	.71
Magnesium	.21	.09
Titanium	.02	.01
Subtotal	95.20%	95.11%
Probably Inexhaustible		
Copper	1.38	1.35
Zinc	1.23	.97
Manganese	1.19	1.76
Chromium	.50	.45
Lead	.25	.20
Nickel	.15	.09
Tin	.03	.03
Subtotal	~4.73%	~4.85%
Total	99.93%	~99.96%

SOURCE: Goeller and Weinberg (1975) derived these data from *Mineral Facts and Problems, 1970,* U.S. Bureau of Mines, Bulletin 650 (Washington: U.S. Government Printing Office, 1970).

five metals which are not exhaustible. The least abundant of these is titanium, which constitutes about 1 percent of the earth's crust and which eventually, as technology improves, may become one of the world's most important metals because of its light weight, strength and excellent corrosion resistance. We therefore need to be concerned only about the other 5 percent. Moreover, as we find after digging deeply enough into the specifics related to each of the next seven metals in Table 12 (including new discoveries, new sources, advancing technology and the potential for recycling, substitution and functional redesign), our future problem can be reduced at most to worrying only about the remaining ones (including mercury), which together constitute less than 0.1 percent of the total demand. There should be some relief in concluding that 99.9 percent of the probable future demand for metals (by weight) is clearly satisfiable at least for a world of 15 billion people and $300 trillion GWP—and that this conclusion does not depend upon using the considerable resources of outer space.

In examining data about "known reserves" or "ultimately recoverable resources," we are dealing with the technology of the immediate or near future. For our *a fortiori* argument, we only assume that the main changes that will take place in mining will involve equipment and techniques similar to those currently in use, exploiting lower grades of ore. In the 19th century, for instance, only copper ores containing 4 to 6 percent of copper were regarded as useful. At present, however, ores are worked with an ore content of as little as 0.4 percent. It is virtually certain that in 20 to 30 years ores with as little as 0.25 percent will be profitably exploited. Flotation methods of enriching polymetallic ores have been developed, and hydrometallurgical and other processing techniques make it possible to extract zinc, lead, silver, copper, nickel, cobalt and many other metals from low-grade ores. Until recently, for example, the mineral nepheline (about 20 percent aluminum) was considered to be of little or no value. Now a technique has been developed for extracting its aluminum content, and it has been reclassified as a valuable raw material. Indeed, as mentioned earlier, the U.S. Geological Survey now lists 10 major sources of aluminum other than bauxite. Technological advances of this type are certainly not uncommon and will clearly continue.

Certain other corridors of technical development seem to be opening. The first involves the possibility of extracting minerals at deeper levels of the earth than are worked today. At depths of more than 5 kilometers, some of the rock formations are thought to contain extremely large deposits of iron, manganese, chromium, cobalt, nickel, uranium, copper and gold. In order to get at these resources, very sophisticated scientific research and engineering design are necessary to develop instruments and equipment that can be used under extreme heat and pressure. Although intense research and development efforts are under way, it may not be until sometime after the year 2000 that this equipment has been evolved. That it will evolve seems almost certain. Whether or not it will be economical is less clear. But if other methods grow very costly, then this one would become more competitive.

A really big difference in both the near- and long-term futures seems likely to be caused by the mining of the ocean floor, which is already developing rapidly. Interest has been shown in this concept since the beginning of the 1960's and the basic technology for mining at depths from 10,000 to 15,000 feet now appears to be available. The manganese, nickel, cobalt, copper and other minerals that are found on the floor of the Pacific Ocean in iron-manganese nodules would, if brought to the surface, increase the supply of some items enormously. It is still too early to give accurate estimates of the amount of the nodules, but some experts have claimed that the Central Pacific alone could contain 1,600 billion tons. Table 13 shows estimates of the potential of these nodules (based on a 1,000-billion-ton total) and compares them with other resources. The lessons that will almost certainly be learned in this field in the next 5 or 10 years should result in substantial production from the seabed well before the end of this century; and this kind of mining will perhaps be especially attractive for nations such as Germany and Japan, which are currently have-nots from the point of view of natural resources, but are highly developed and organized in industrial research and production techniques

Table 13. Some Comparative Land and Sea Resources (tons)

	Land[a]	Ocean Nodules[b]	Sea Water[c]	Earth Crust[d]
Aluminum	3.6 billion	—	18 billion	80,000 trillion
Chromium	8.9 billion	—	80 million	110 trillion
Cobalt	11 million	3 billion	800 million	25 trillion
Copper	1.06 billion	3 billion	6 billion	63 trillion
Gold	50,000	—	8 million	3.5 billion
Iron	710 billion	130 billion	18 billion	58,000 trillion
Lead	1.8 billion	4 billion	60 million	12 trillion
Manganese	24 billion	160 billion	4 billion	1,300 trillion
Mercury	920,000	—	60 million	9 billion
Uranium	29 million[e]	—	6 billion	180 billion

[a] Dennis Meadows, *Dynamics of Growth in a Finite World.*

[b] Assumes 1 trillion tons recoverable ore. Uncertainties are large. But J. Mero estimates 1.6 trillion tons in the Pacific Ocean alone (John L. Mero, "Potential Economic Value of Ocean-Floor Manganese Nodule Deposits," in David R. Horn [ed.], *A Conference on Ferromanganese Deposits on the Ocean Floor* [Washington: The Office for the International Decade of Ocean Exploration, National Science Foundation, January 1972], p. 191).

[c] National Research Council, *Resources and Man* (San Francisco: W. H. Freeman, 1969).

[d] Upper layer only: 1 million trillion tons—about 4 percent of total (*U.S. Mineral Resources, 1973*).

[e] High estimate of U.S. resources at costs up to $100/lb.

Other long-term possibilities include extracting ores from seawater or processing higher-grade rocks. Calculations indicate that every cubic kilometer of seawater contains approximately 37.5 million tons of solids in solution or suspension. The major portion of this consists of sodium and chlorine, but there is also an enormous amount of magnesium and varying and relatively huge quantities of gold, cobalt, lead, mercury and many other minerals. A cubic kilometer of the earth's crust on average contains about 210 million tons of aluminum, 150 million tons of iron, 150,000 tons of chromium, 7,000 tons of uranium, 80,000 tons of copper, and so on. Table 13 compares the crustal and sea resources with Meadows' estimates for land resources.

Current scientific techniques already enable man to obtain some materials from the sea and from the ocean floor. Others will follow as incentives develop. For example, both the Japanese and the Germans have launched projects to extract uranium directly from seawater. In time the rocks and the ocean will constitute an essentially infinite resource base, although it is unlikely in view of the alternatives that average crustal rocks will ever be mined for mineral content.

The above would seem to most to be an optimistic scenario. We would characterize it as realistic, but because of the many potential advances it has left out, it may be a little pessimistic. After all, why is it optimistic to postulate: a growing rate of resource exploitation via conventional methods for the next few decades or so, accompanied toward the end of this century by a commercial mining of the ocean nodules; in the next century and after, deeper drilling into the earth for important concentrates; and ultimately, technologies for extraction of minerals from seawater and from ordinary but higher-grade rock, where needed? Such a flow of events is, of course, by no means certain. Nonetheless, all of it is more or less in the cards and only waiting to be revealed. The long-term outlook for minerals cannot be the limbo of resource exhaustion to which mankind has been condemned by neo-Malthusian groups.

V

Food: Supplying Demand

BECAUSE LARGE SECTIONS of the world, especially in the developing areas, appear crowded and on the verge of famine, most observers seem to feel that the gap between food demand and food supply must inevitably grow. But we argue that, as a direct consequence of available resources and improving technology, a more reasonable projection would be in the direction of an eventual abundance of food. Although this conclusion can be strongly supported by the evolving potential for food production, it rests in part on the expectation that relatively sensible policies and priorities will characterize future food production in many of the most seriously affected nations—and more important, that there will be enough economic growth so that even poorer groups can afford an adequate diet. We believe the potential is so great that even with moderate levels of bad luck and poor management, the new conditions should be achieved in the not too distant future.

During 1974, the year of the World Food Conference, prospects for sufficient nutritional food for the world's people were viewed most pessimistically. Factors that had contributed to this grim view were the two years of extensive droughts (1972 and 1974) in many countries, including the United

Note: Most of the material in this chapter is based on the research and analysis of David P. Harmon, Jr., and Marylin Chou.

States, and published statistics revealing the lowest world grain reserves in decades, coupled with the highest prices ever. The worst forebodings of the neo-Malthusians seemed to be confirmed.

Our assessment of this experience, however, is that from a historical perspective two years of bad weather should not be perceived as anything more than temporary bad luck. There is no reason why weather fluctuations and other agricultural hazards, which generally are unpredictable, should be interpreted as heralding a trend toward permanent scarcity. Indeed, during the spring of 1975, as a bumper world harvest appeared in the offing, the attention of most food-exporting countries shifted rapidly to problems associated with oversupply and falling prices. On the other hand, at the time of writing, it seems likely that the Soviet Union will have one of the worst shortfalls in history, which may put some pressure on food prices. It should be noted, though, that the Soviet shortfall does not imply any shortage of grain for human consumption, but mainly of feed stock of its farm animals and cattle.

The position we argue is that, except for the occasional regional fluctuations caused by natural disaster, inappropriate policies or the misapplication of resources, the long-term prospect is for adequate food supplies. By "adequate" we mean both an increasing amount of food per capita and an improving nutritional balance in the countries of the world currently deficient in either of these respects. Indeed, within 200 years we anticipate that—if desired—it will be possible to increase world food consumption to the level of the United States today (approximately 2,000 pounds per capita of grain equivalents annually). Our argument will be based upon what can be accomplished with conservative expectations for technological advance, coupled with reasonable management, but with no requirements for unusually good luck or especially fortunate technological breakthroughs, even though some such breakthroughs now seem inevitable. However, we will also assume sufficient economic development (as discussed in Chapter II) so that either the poor can pay for the food they need or it can be financed.

The organization of food production in more advanced societies is currently based upon exceedingly complicated systems that are not easily achieved by poorer countries. These systems include: highly educated and trained farmers, land that has been developed over decades and maintained for high productivity, the availability of large amounts of capital for farm machinery and equipment, sophisticated transportation and storage facilties, marketing organization, manufacturers, processors, agricultural schools, research and extension services, numerous and far-reaching communication networks, an adequate market to buy the food produced and a complex system for delivering and selling the food. The rate at which a similarly complex system can evolve in developing countries depends a good deal on the social, political and economic milieu. In some cultures we find the system has evolved fairly quickly, and in others its progress has been slow and difficult, rarely maintaining the population above the subsistence level and often letting it slide into shortages and famine. It is these anomalies in agricultural development that account to a considerable degree for the great disparities in food production and distribution.

Additional confusion has been created by estimates made, with the best of intentions, by prestigious organizations anxious to dramatize the plight of the few by making it appear to be the curse of many. The Food and Agricultural Organization (FAO) has been a prime example. In 1950 its director, Lord Boyd-Orr, claimed that two-thirds of the world's people went to bed hungry. The noted economist Colin Clark * later showed that Boyd-Orr's successors knew this statement was untrue. It had been based on a simple confusion compounded by inaccurate FAO statistics; nonetheless they were loath to lose the impact its pronouncement had made. (It was this tendency to exaggerate the international food problem that

* In his book *Starvation or Plenty?* (New York: Taplinger Publishing Co., 1970).

provoked *The Economist* in 1952 to describe the FAO as "a permanent institution devoted to proving that there is not enough food to go around.") The FAO later changed its point of view, in its 1969 publication *The State of Food and Agriculture,* and stated that the food problems of the future might well be ones of surplus rather than shortage, the new optimism evidently spurred by the initial results of the Green Revolution.* But in 1970, in its *Third World Food Survey,* the FAO again sounded the alarm, claiming that 60 percent of the population of the developing areas (about 40 percent of the global population) suffered from undernutrition, malnutrition or both. More recently, however, it has softened this statement by estimating that only 10 percent of the world population has an insufficient protein-energy supply. Yet all of these shifts have occurred during a lengthy period in which the per capita food production of the poorer countries has remained approximately constant, perhaps increasing slightly (that is, food production has at least maintained pace with the growing population).

The food production system in the United States today is somewhat analogous to a highly automated manufacturing firm. It is huge but requires relatively few people for its operation and maintenance. (Between 1790 and 1974, farm employment declined from 90 to 4.4 percent of the total labor force.†) Although in principle the American system can be emulated by poorer countries, in practice we expect that, for several decades to come, food for most of the people in the world will come from relatively small farms operated by farmers and their families, comprising from perhaps 20 to 70 percent of regional populations. The task of organizing and training large masses of small landholders to become efficient producers undoubtedly is much more difficult than

---

* The introduction and rapid spread of high-yielding varieties of wheat and rice which took place in the noncommunist developing countries in the mid-1960's.

† U.S. Department of Agriculture, Economic Research Service, *A Chronology of American Agriculture,* rev. ed. (Washington: U.S. Government Printing Office, 1971).

a similar task for small numbers of large landholders. This argument has little relation to whether a nation is socialistic, capitalistic or communal. It is, instead, a matter of the sheer numbers involved, their traditions, their education and the availability of capital and management resources. Moreover, it is obvious that a successful organization for efficient food production implies the need to transfer most of the population from small farming communities to industrial areas, a shift that will have profound social and economic implications.

We can easily understand that the transition from an agricultural to an industrial society will require decades for the more adaptable developing countries, and possibly generations for the others. But surprisingly, perhaps, a strong urge to accomplish this transition is manifested today by most of the developing nations. They appear to have a sound instinct for the path to relative wealth, a willingness to struggle for it, and, in our view, an excellent chance to achieve it.

FUTURE DIRECTIONS IN FOOD PRODUCTION

In making the case for the future of food production, we will discuss three distinct approaches. First, we will consider conventional food produced conventionally. Clearly, this may not be the major method of production in 2176, and most likely whatever replaces it will be more efficient. Therefore, if we can make a reasonable case that after 200 years the world can produce an adequate amount of food for 15 billion people by using today's conventional methods, then clearly an actual solution can be expected to be much better in terms of costs, quantity and quality. This is the sense of the *a fortiori* arguments that we have relied on so much in this book, seeking one conceptual solution to a major issue through a simple, if suboptimal, approach. If this approach can at least be made plausible, then the more likely, actual solution should obviously bring better results.

In the second approach, producing conventional food unconventionally, a number of processes are now in existence, new ones are under development, and undoubtedly others are still to appear. In addition, improvements in productivity can be expected to come from the constant technological efforts that attend such processes. We will stress, as an illustrative and hopeful example, the potential of a recent development known as the "nutrient film technique" (NFT), for growing plants without soil under either partially or fully controlled conditions.

The third approach we will discuss is that of unconventional foods produced unconventionally, a very promising avenue through which it appears likely that palatable nutritious foods can be mass-produced in more or less automated factories. With advanced technology, food would be extracted from almost any organic matter, including wood, leaves, cellulose, petroleum and even urban and agricultural wastes. In retrospect, from the vantage point of the American Quadricentennial, this approach may well appear to have been the easiest way to provide basic food requirements. Even today the required technologies appear to be well within our grasp. The cost of the food produced this way is expected to be substantially less than from conventional agriculture, and the production potential appears essentially unlimited by anything except demand.

Finally, one of the major themes of this chapter is that although instances of famine and malnutrition may continue for the same reasons as in the past—poor weather, societal traditions that are difficult to change, or political choices which are counterproductive—the prospect for an abundant supply of food for future generations is not in any reasonable sense limited by existing physical resources. The world is likely to be much better fed 100 years from now than it is today; after 200 years current American standards, or even better, could very well be the norm. Furthermore, it will become increasingly difficult for bad luck and/or poor management to hold back progress.

The task ahead looks difficult, but it may seem less so looking back from the year 2176. From that vantage point, 20th-century concerns about food may appear merely as a temporary detour of imagined and real troubles on the road to success—troubles that were largely self-imposed. The motivation now exists for increasing per capita food production and providing security against severe annual fluctuations in output. The resources, the technology and the capital all appear to be adequate now and improving steadily. The outcome will be a reflection of mankind's wisdom in choosing sound policies in various sociopolitical arenas; but it is going to be increasingly difficult to choose disastrous ones.

NUTRITIONAL REQUIREMENTS

Nutritional requirements are known to vary according to climate, age, sex, body weight and physical activity. But even when these factors are taken into account, there are still significant differences in the various estimates of minimum calorie and protein needs. For example, the FAO has estimated 1,900 calories per day for a South Asian engaged in minimal activity.* Colin Clark, on the other hand, estimates 1,625 calories per day for similar circumstances—that is, for small-bodied persons working four hours per day in a hot climate. For a larger-bodied person in a cooler climate (for example, North China) working throughout the agricultural year, Clark's minimum requirement is slightly greater than 2,000 per day.†

Minimum protein requirements are known to be affected by caloric intake as well as the quality (fractions of various amino acids) of the protein. When the caloric intake is insufficient, the human body evidently diverts some of the protein to meet the energy deficit. Consequently, the protein deficiencies of the poorest regions of the world have been judged to occur largely as a result of insufficient calories.‡ This in turn causes various deficiency diseases and creates a greater susceptibility to infection.

* United Nations World Food Conference, *Assessment of the World Food Situation Present and Future*, Rome, November 5–16, 1974, p. 66.
† *Starvation or Plenty?*, p. 17.
‡ Michael Latham, "Nutrition and Infection in National Development," *Science*, May 9, 1975.

To obtain sufficient protein from nonmeat sources it is necessary to consume at least two different vegetables (for example, rice and beans) at each meal in amounts that will supply at least the minimum required caloric intake.* Since not all the components of proteins satisfy nutritional requirements equally, the FAO suggests that protein adequacy in a vegetable diet requires an intake of between 52 and 68 grams daily to obtain from 29 to 37 grams of usable protein. The most balanced proteins for human consumption are available from meat, fish and dairy products; the range of usable protein from a vegetable diet varies from 54 to 75 percent, compared to 69 to 95 percent for protein from animal products. Clark's figure for protein is 0.5 gram per kilogram of body weight, or about 25 grams per day for the average adult African or South Asian. Thus his estimate suggests that between one-half and two-thirds kilogram per day per person of grain containing 8 to 13 percent protein is required in Africa and South Asia to meet the minimum needs for both calories and proteins. Using an average of 2,200 calories per day per person, we calculate that 15 billion people would require 4.8 billion metric tons per year † to obtain all of their calories and proteins directly from grains. This would be about three and a half times the current world grain production.

INCREASING FOOD PRODUCTION: MYTHS AND REALITIES

Can all of the world's growing population be fed at least at a subsistence level? Can it be fed better? Various answers have been given to these frequently asked questions. The simple argument often presented is that hunger grows exponentially while agricultural resources are finite and possibly at or near their ultimate limit now. We assert that this argument

---

* No single vegetable provides protein with all the amino acids in the proper proportion for human needs. Two (or more) vegetables can, if selected properly.

† Unmilled weight; normal loss in milling is 10 percent for wheat, 28 percent for rice; we have assumed 20 percent average milling loss.

overlooks or ignores the startling (and exponential) progress in agriculture in the last 100 years that has made agriculture such a dynamic and impressive system in the developed world. The principal engines of this progress have been increasing affluence and advancing technology. In conventional agriculture, these engines can be used to: (a) increase and improve acreage under cultivation, (b) increase yields by better inputs and multiple cropping, (c) increase efficiency of distribution systems and (d) decrease pollution by improved processes and better management.

Will they be sufficient? Let us now examine some of the opposing neo-Malthusian arguments to see whether reasonable rebuttals may be found.

1. *Population growth and rising affluence*

The neo-Malthusian position usually begins with the argument that the primary sources of increasing demand for food are population growth and rising affluence, and that therefore food scarcity will be a recurring problem in the future. However, as we have already pointed out, rising affluence appears today to be a causal factor in slowing population growth and hence is now an ally with, not an enemy to, the cause of such restraint. Second, rising affluence appears to be precisely what is needed to help the world's population avoid malnutrition and famine, for it can provide the education, research, markets and capital for the production of more food of better quality. Thus, as the population growth rate slows down in the developing nations, as even now it appears to be doing, we might expect a gradual increase in food production per capita, an important component of any reasonable definition of the road away from poverty.

It has been argued that Americans should eat less meat and stop fertilizing their lawns and golf courses to make more food and fertilizers available to the poorer countries of the world; but, however noble the intentions, these policies are unlikely to have any measurable impact, much less any long-run significance. Except for short-term fluctuations caused by weather and other temporary economic factors, there is no shortage of food or fertilizers; either can be bought if the funds are available. Furthermore, resorting to such sacrifices in the U.S. does not put food into the mouths of the hungry. Supply and demand still seems to be the basic economic determinant for the flow of agricultural commodities in the world market system. Indeed, it can be argued that the huge grain surpluses that helped tide the world over the 1972–74 shortages were made possible only because the United States and other exporting nations, as meat-eating countries, had acquired large food stocks and had developed a huge grain-producing system (including reserves of cropland) to satisfy the associated demand for grains and to cushion against any lean years. Without that development, the period from 1955 to 1975 might have had some quite different characteristics—namely, much less grain production, much smaller inventories from which to meet international emergency needs, smaller investments in agricultural research, and delayed development of cheaper fertilizers because of lower demands. (Technical advances reduced the cost of nitrogen fertilizer by 50 percent during the 1960's.)

Although prices fluctuated between 1929 and 1972, overall a downward trend occurred in real prices for grain, undoubtedly as a result of the greater production and productivity. The technology that had to be developed at great expense to make this productivity possible is now available, essentially free, to all of the less-developed countries; thus the path at least to developing their own inputs adapted to local conditions is clearly marked. About the only thing that self-restraint in the consumption of meat and fertilizer would do is to add to the propaganda that the rich are taking away from the poor—a position which we argue is in almost every way (except, perhaps, in certain crisis situations) contrary to the facts and counterproductive.

2. *Cropland and water*

Pessimists also argue that additional fertile cropland and water sources are increasingly difficult to come by, that the "best land" is already under cultivation—ignoring the fact that most land had to be developed for it to be considered "best land." As one expert has observed:

> . . . only about one-tenth of the land area of the earth is cropland. If it were still in raw land in its natural state, it would be vastly less productive than it is today. With incentives to improve this land, the capacity of the land would be increased in most parts of the world much more than it has been to date. In this important sense cropland is not the critical limiting factor in expanding food production. . . .
>
> Harsh, raw land is what farmers since time immemorial have started with; what matters most over time, however, are the investments that are made to enhance the productivity of cropland.*

The claims of water scarcity ignore the many ways of obtaining agricultural-quality water such as digging new wells, "harvesting" rainfall, utilizing rivers better, recycling waste water and desalinating seawater. The Ganges River basin, covering parts of four countries—India, Nepal, China and Bangladesh—offers a striking example of an abundant and largely untapped water source. Within India it ranges over 800,000 square kilometers containing a population of about 225 million. Some of the current problems of effective land use and water development in the Ganges Plain arise from the highly seasonal flow of the river and its tributaries. The key to a successful water development project in this region is the storage and beneficial use of a major part of the monsoon flows which now run to the sea. It has been estimated if this potential were developed and some modern agricultural technology utilized, the irrigated areas of the Ganges Plain could produce more than 150 million metric tons of grain, enough to provide a minimum satisfactory diet for 600 million people, the entire population of India. According to this calculation, the value of the potential cereal crops would be about $500 per hectare, 10 times the annual costs of the irri-

---

*Theodore Schultz, quoted in D. Gale Johnson, *World Food Problems and Prospects,* Foreign Affairs Study 20 (Washington: American Enterprise Institute for Public Policy Research, 1975), p. 46.

gation.* Finally, as discussed later, there are many techniques in development for utilizing water more efficiently.

3. *Increased costs of agricultural inputs and increased yields*

It is frequently said that the intensification of agricultural production will lead to higher costs of food production because of rising costs of agricultural inputs. It will be increasingly difficult, according to this view, to obtain higher crop yields—especially in developed countries where the land is already heavily fertilized. One response is to emphasize the fact that production of agriculture inputs is also a dynamic process. Fertilizer, perhaps the most essential input for increasing yields, is an excellent example.

First, although the price of energy strongly affects the cost of fertilizer, there are other important components such as technological advances over time, economies of scale and utilization factors. Some of these are displayed in Table 14,

Table 14. Prices for Urea (expressed in 1974 U.S. dollars; MCF = thousand cubic feet)

	Technology/Plant Size		Utilization (Design Capacity of 1667 Tons/Day)	
	1960 333 Tons/Day	*1974 1667 Tons/Day*	*60% of Capacity*	*90% of Capacity*
Price of:				
Natural Gas	Free	$1/MCF	$1/MCF	$1/MCF
Urea	$164/ton	$116/ton	$155/ton	$120/ton

SOURCE: D. Gale Johnson, *World Food Problems and Prospects,* p. 47, notes 12 and 14.

* Roger Revelle and V. Lakshminarayana, "The Ganges Water Machine," *Science,* May 9, 1975. One hectare equals 2.471 acres.

which shows that with 1974 technology and economies of scale, and even with the price of natural gas at $1 per thousand cubic feet, the gate price * of urea (a principal nitrogenous fertilizer) is considerably cheaper than from older, smaller plants even if the gas was free. In addition, in some developing countries where fertilizer plants often operate at 60 percent or less of design capacity, an increase to nearly 90 percent, which is regularly achieved in developed countries, could lower their costs considerably.

Second, with increased fertilizer, the productivity of the other inputs (water, insecticides, etc.) can also be increased, contributing further to lower unit costs.

Third, productivity can also improve over time as farmers learn to use fertilizers more effectively. In addition, the use of seeds better adapted to fertilized land and the determination of optimum plant density also serve to better yields.†

Fourth, the neo-Malthusian argument glosses over the important matter of unequal responses of soils to specific measures. For example, the estimated incremental yield from the addition of one ton of nitrogen to India's depleted soil would be about 10 to 12 tons of wheat or rice, much greater than that of soils already improved.

Finally, it wouldn't matter if the argument were correct in the long run if the per capita income increased faster than the cost of food. In that case people could afford to pay more for their food (which they will do anyway to improve its taste and social desirability‡).

4. Climate and ecological stress

Because the world currently lacks the buffer of large international grain reserves, fears are often expressed about pos-

---

* Price of fertilizer as it leaves the factory.

† D. Gale Johnson, *World Food Problems and Prospects,* pp. 46–47.

‡ Just as what is considered "proper clothes" has little to do with the minimum required for modesty and to protect one from weather conditions, so what is considered a "proper diet"—that is, socially acceptable and desirable—has little to do with nutrition and much more to do with social standards, style and personal taste.

sible climatic changes. It is true that the results of speculation about long-term changes in the weather are complex and uncertain, involving cyclical versus random theories of weather patterns. If weather is randomly variable, then in any given year some areas will naturally have more favorable weather than others. If weather also follows a cyclical pattern, and in particular if it is now in a cooling trend, as some observers believe, it appears that the impact on crops will be mixed. For example, corn and soybeans at lower latitudes would be hurt by a shorter growing season; in Asian rice-growing areas, a major disaster would be caused if the monsoon failed. But if it turns out that the world is entering a long-term cooling period, but only very gradually, agricultural technology offers many alternatives that could be phased in, such as controlled-environment agriculture, more widely adaptive varieties and synthetic foods. But this, of course, adds to our argument that the sooner LDC's achieve a high level of affluence and technological sophistication the better, since it is exactly these resources and capabilities which would enable them to deal with such negative developments. Poor and technologically unsophisticated people have no such capability.

The claim that severe ecological stress is caused by intensive agricultural activity is associated with much confusion that needs research and clarification. The main questions apparently are related to whether the runoff after application of chemical fertilizers and pesticides causes significant water contamination, what the short- and long-term effects of this might be, and what countermeasures are available. A study of the water quality in Midwest streams suggests that fertilizers have not been shown to be the cause of eutrophication of bodies of water and finds no evidence that the heavy application of fertilizers endangers human health.* The Federal Water Pollution Control Administration, which has kept an annual census of fish kills since June 1960, has reported that of the number of fish reported killed, only 2.5 percent were attributed to the use of pesticides.

Criticisms of past abuses in the application of chemicals

---

* George H. Enfield, "Water Quality in Midwest Streams," paper presented at the Midwest Fertilizer Conference, Chicago, February 17, 1970.

to control pests have already shifted research and development programs toward more environmentally acceptable insecticides, herbicides, fungicides and rodenticides.* The best strategy claimed for controlling most pests is "integrated pest control," which has as its goal the maintenance of potential pest populations below the level at which they cause serious health hazards or economic damage. This strategy involves the coordinated use and management of many technologies, including preventive measures, resistant varieties, pesticides, biological agents, proper cultural practices, crop rotation, sanitation and specialized chemicals such as attractants and growth regulators. It has been estimated that annual losses caused by pests could be reduced—perhaps by 30 to 50 percent—by making better use of technologies now available. Eventually, this could mean an increase of 10 to 15 percent in the world food supply without bringing any new land into production. Still, integrated control is a complex high-technology approach which will require much time and effort to achieve large-scale worldwide use. During the period of transition to better controls, it does not appear likely that the world faces an extreme threat from the use of current pesticides.

5. *Government priorities*

It is often argued that misplaced government priorities in the less-developed countries have emphasized industrialization rather than focusing on the agricultural sector as the initial engine of growth. This argument, especially as to misplaced priorities, seems to us to have a fair degree of validity for some of the developing nations. For example, the Indian government, after initial success with the Green Revolution, switched its emphasis from agriculture to industry and became excessively vulnerable to the 1972–74 food crisis. In this connection, we should note that with few exceptions the developed

* Committee on Agricultural Production Efficiency, National Research Council, *Agricultural Production Efficiency* (Washington: National Academy of Sciences, 1975), p. 168.

countries industrialized only after a secure agricultural base had been established.

Agricultural self-sufficiency is obviously important to economic health and growth. It reduces the danger of malnutrition and averts severe strains on foreign exchange. A nation with stockpiled reserves or excess food production capacity is less vulnerable to natural disasters and their economic consequences. Still, most developed countries have for some years been net importers of food and have managed quite well. It is the less-developed countries which need to assure their food production. The recent food crisis might have helped in reorienting government programs in these countries to more appropriate policies. Although the World Food Conference did not result in any spectacular new institutional arrangements or intergovernmental programs, it did serve to publicize two important issues related to food production: reserves and self-sufficiency.

6. *Long-run scarcity and triage*

The final and most frightening claim of some neo-Malthusians is that the world is entering so severe a period of international scarcity of major agricultural goods that mankind may have to come to grips with the decision of who shall eat and who shall not (the *triage* decision *), a decision presumably to be made by the major grain-exporting nations. This view assumes that world food production soon will reach an inadequate limiting level which cannot be overcome. Even though food aid has decreased over the past ten years, the available evidence clearly suggests that it is highly unlikely

---

* Triage refers to a World War I system for sorting the wounded into three survival categories: (1) those who would survive without help; (2) those who would probably die anyway; and (3) those to whom medical help was likely to make the difference between survival and death. The limited medical resources were then concentrated on the third category. A triage concept in food aid evidently visualizes writing off the "hopelessly" needy nations. While we agree that the emphasis has to be on self-help, and therefore acknowledge an occasional need for "hard decisions," we deny any need to make decisions that are really comparable to the triage system.

that the United States or any of the other grain-exporting countries would consciously accept mass starvation in any nation without giving some assistance—almost certainly when "food surpluses" are available—probably at the cost of some belt-tightening if necessary. The question then is: Will serious belt-tightening ever be necessary?

The major counterargument to the triage concept is that even in the short run, but especially in the long run, agriculture's inherent flexibility and dynamism, together with the expected gradual approach toward population stability, will effectively defuse the threat of an inevitable long-term global food scarcity. This is not to say that nations or governments cannot contribute to calamities through mismanagement, callousness or lack of foresight, or that there cannot be bad luck, but it is to deny, emphatically, that the problems are beyond solution. Indeed, it is the major purpose of this chapter to make the opposite case: that, given reasonable attention, food problems should ease rather than grow with time.

SCENARIOS FOR THE NEXT 200 YEARS

In ascending order of sophistication, the following are several technological avenues to a future of abundant food production:

1. The increased use of relatively conventional techniques employing current technology with modest future improvement.
2. The application to conventional agriculture of newer technologies that are now under development but may require a decade or two to be phased into mass production.
3. The use of successful unconventional technologies which are promising today but require further development and testing.
4. The widespread adaptation of dietary tastes and habits to inexpensive food produced by high-technology factories in the long term.

A practical fifth approach would combine the above four by using relatively conventional techniques in the near term and high technology or "exotic" methods over the longer term, with some changing of tastes being phased in gradually as they are required or desired. This fifth case provides a broad basis for a reasonably optimistic scenario in which the long-term increases in food production and/or adaptations of tastes are more likely to be evolutionary than revolutionary.

In attempting to estimate the production increases that the world might expect from relatively conventional agriculture as well as from more "exotic" technologies, our major purpose is to provide a perspective for the future in which food demand can be effectively—perhaps even abundantly—met.

1. *Conventional agriculture*

A. EXPANDING TILLABLE ACREAGE

Of the world's 1.1 to 1.4 billion hectares of arable land, farmers today harvest some 700 million hectares. The balance is in pasturage and other uses. Excluding Greenland and Antarctica, the world has 13.15 billion hectares of land, of which the FAO estimates 3.19 billion to be potentially arable. Thus the potential farm acreage is over four times that now being harvested. Table 15 depicts a few of the principal sources of additional land and the major requirements to make them productive. The average cost of opening new land in previously unsettled areas has been variously estimated from $218 * to $1,150 per hectare.† Whatever figure is chosen, it seems clear that such costs should be no great deterrent in a world of growing affluence, even if they should run as high as $2,000 per hectare within some of the regions listed in Table 15.

---

* Paul Ehrlich *et al., Human Ecology, Problems and Solutions* (San Francisco: W. H. Freeman and Company, 1973), p. 90.

† President's Science Advisory Panel on the World Food Supply, "The World Food Problem" (Washington: U.S. Government Printing Office, 1967), cited in Donella H. Meadows *et al., The Limits to Growth* (New York: Universe Books, 1972), p. 48.

Table 15. Some Sources of New Agricultural Land

Region	Amount (hectares)	Requirements
Latin America—Principally Brazil	450 million	Advances in tropical soil research—especially the alleviation of the leaching of nutrients by heavy tropical rains—in order to improve the existing low soil fertility.
Principally the Peruvian and Chilean seacoasts	50 million	Low-cost water—probably from desalination of seawater. This arid area has the advantage of constant, ideal growing temperatures (68°–75°F.), day and night, year round.
United States	100 million	Anticipation of sufficiently high prices to justify the investment required.
Sub-Saharan Africa	500–700 million	200 million hectares: eradication of the tsetse fly; estimated to cost a total of $20 billion over 20 years. 300 million hectares: irrigation. An additional 200 million hectares now exist in sparsely populated regions.

B. MULTIPLE CROPPING

The equivalent of additional land area can be gained wherever there are opportunities to grow more than one crop per year. The developing countries generally have better opportunities for "multicropping" since most are located in tropical and semitropical areas with longer growing seasons. With multicropping the total 3.19 billion hectares of potentially arable land could be made equivalent to approximately 6.6 billion hectares, almost 10 times that harvested today, though approximately three-quarters of this additional potential would require some irrigation for multicropping to be feasible.*

* The World Food Problem: A Report of the President's Science Committee, Vol. II: Report of the Panel on the World Food Supply (Washington: U.S. Government Printing Office, 1967), p. 434.

C. YIELD

Increased yields per unit of land farmed probably offer the quickest opportunity for increased food production via conventional agriculture, and a major key is the adoption of high-yielding varieties (HYVs) of grain. The potential of HYVs has many facets:

1. An improved response to fertilizer.
2. Additional possibilities for multicropping.
3. Opportunities to increase the protein quantity and quality per pound of grain.
4. Alleviation of the threat of disease generally attendant in wide-scale monoculture by crossing many varieties of the same grain to build in a broad spectrum of genetic resistance.
5. More productive varieties over the full range of growing conditions, varying from no fertilizer and very limited water to ideal conditions.
6. Innovations such as triticale, a cross between wheat and rye combining the high-yield potential of wheat with the inherent disease resistance and hardiness of rye.

The longer-term outlook for HYVs is very favorable for the developing world; but for near-term benefits, government assistance is needed to marshal the resources and carry out the policies to enable farmers to exploit the HYV potential effectively. The great range of wheat and corn yields among various nations indicates the real possibilities for near-term improvement.

The potential for expanding the use of HYVs is made clearer when it is understood that:

1. The use of HYVs has been heavily concentrated in relatively few countries and even there in many cases only on the better-irrigated land in selected regions.
2. Most farmers using HYVs have failed to adopt the entire recommended package of inputs, such as adequate fertilizers, water, insect and disease controls. For example, at the end of the period of initial widespread introduction of

HYVs (1966–70), only 12 percent of the Indian HYV farmers were fully following recommendations; yet the use of HYV's was responsible for approximately 60 percent of the overall increase in wheat production and 75 percent of the increase in rice production in the decade between 1960–63 and 1970–73.*

3. The vigorous response of HYVs to fertilizers determined in test plots, when compared to the relatively low use of fertilizers on HYVs by farmers, suggests that the potential yield is much higher than has been achieved (especially in the depleted soils of many less-developed countries).

4. With the projected increase in fertilizer production capacity over the next five years, adequate supplies should be available by 1980 to meet most of the world demand.

How much do all these potential conventional changes portend for food production over the long term? The following are some rough estimates:

	Conservative	Optimistic
1. Increased agricultural land harvested	factor of 2.5	4
2. Multicropping	factor of 1.5	2
3. Average yield per crop: Improved use of		
fertilizer	factor of 1.5	2
irrigation	factor of 1.5	2
HYVs	factor of 2	2.5
Other inputs	factor of 1.2	1.4
Multiplicative totals	factor of 20	110

These potential increases in production include the possibility of opening new tropical lands which lend themselves to both multicropping and the entire input package of high-yielding varieties. (Our later estimate that grain requirements will increase by a factor of 11 over 200 years should be well within

* Joseph W. Willett (of the Economic Research Service, U.S. Department of Agriculture), "The Ability of the Developing Countries to Meet Their Own Agricultural Needs in the 1980's," a speech given at the Canadian Agricultural Economic Society, Quebec, August 6, 1974.

our conservative estimate of an increase in production by a factor of 20 from purely conventional means.)

2. *Unconventional or currently "exotic" agriculture*

In following the second and third technological avenues, progress in some unconventional techniques continues and is assumed to be reasonably—but not outstandingly—successful. It is clear that a technological advance does not necessarily have to be exotic to be dramatic. For example, the nutrient film technique (see Figure 8), a rather novel and

Figure 8. Nutrient Film Technique

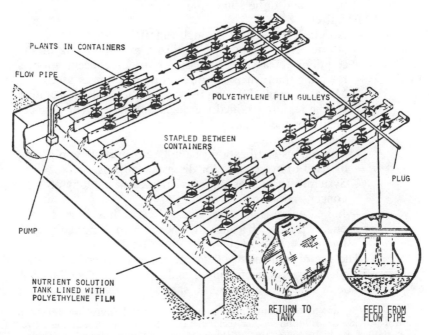

SOURCE: A. J. Cooper, "Soil? Who Needs It?," *Vegetable Grower,* August 1974, p. 18.

simple variation of hydroponics, is rapidly coming into use today.* This technique of growing crops was conceived in the 1960's at the Glasshouse Crops Research Institute in England and is in practice in some 20 countries today, primarily for high cash-value vegetables and flowers. The NFT method has the following characteristics:

1. Capital and operating costs are low; only a waterproof material, such as polyethylene, is required for gulleys. The system does not require extensive, rigid, water-tight tanks or expensive root-support media, as do other kinds of hydroponics.
2. Water:
   —Recirculation and the configuration of the gulleys eliminate loss from drainage and evaporation.
   —Storage requirements are minimal since plants thrive in a thin film of nutrient solution (a one-millimeter film has been found to be sufficient).
3. Fertilizer·
   —No nutrients are lost through runoff.
   —A low concentration of fertilizer may be used in the solution; yet a wider range of nutrient concentration is tolerable than when a solid rooting medium is used.
   —Mistakes made in composition of the nutrient solution can be rapidly rectified via quick adjustment (or replacement) of the solution.
4. Soil-borne diseases:
   —Continuous sterilization of the liquid in its flow pipe can be used to overcome root disease problems.
   —Systemic fungicides and insecticides at nonphytotoxic † concentrations can be used.
   —Increased resistance to virus diseases has been experienced, possibly because the root system is not subject to the abrasions encountered with soil culture.
5. The use of triangular gulleys, acting as a watershed, avoids the leaching effect of rainfall and permits outdoor farming. Rocky or saline soils pose no special problems.

---

* We place a strong emphasis on NFT here not because we believe it will provide the solution we are seeking, but because it is one of the newer variations of hydroponics that might be developed into part of a solution. Also, we believe the use of a specific illustration for the *a fortiori* argument will make the point more vividly.

† *Nonphytotoxic* means nonpoisonous to plants.

6. Elimination of drying-out cycles increases average growth rates.
7. Temperature control of the nutrient solution enables longer growth periods in both colder and warmer climates.
8. The shallow stream of nutrient solution in the plastic gulley allows a single thick, continuous root mat to form, providing a very stable support for plants.

As with most new techniques, there are still some uncertainties: In some instances, root death has occurred, lowering yields; however, precautions taken in early 1975 to prevent root death are claimed to have been successful so far. Little is known about the need for sterilizing the nutrient film, although if necessary this can be done easily at small cost. There is only limited experience with its use, and most of this has been for certain high-cash crops. Its applicability to the principal grains appears feasible but has yet to be demonstrated. Still, if one looks at NFT from the standpoint of a developing country's small farmer, the potential benefits (as seen in the listing of its characteristics) are dramatic, particularly in view of greater availability of credit due to shorter time between crops.

NFT is far from its full development, but the process is spreading rapidly. Its successful application to the cultivation of outdoor grass for grazing or turf lends hope to the possibility of its use for growing rice and wheat at competitive costs. Capital requirements may be lowered if a cheaper alternative to polyethylene, such as a cellulose or a silicone-based material, is developed for the gulleys. Experiments are now being planned to grow cereal grains in shallow, wide, rigid gulleys on a layer of absorbent material saturated with nutrient solution and able to hold seeds in place.

We suggest, but only as an *a fortiori* argument, that the world could produce all of its cereal grain needs by some form of hydroponics or other soilless controlled growth * by

---

* Conventional hydroponics requires the use of a solid rooting medium which introduces high capital-cost components. True hydroponics entails the growing of food without any solid rooting medium. The NFT development greatly enhances the possibility of relatively low capital-cost, soilless food production.

the year 2176. We chose this alternative for a variety of reasons:

1. Agricultural technology to date has tended to increasingly modify nature's way of growing: the use of special seeds, chemical fertilizers, pesticides, herbicides and irrigation; the alteration of foods genetically to suit needs; and a whole host of methods and techniques for planting, cultivating and harvesting which deviate from nature's pattern. It is to be expected that this modification can be continued much further.

2. The input and loss factors can be much lower in hydroponics than in conventional agriculture. Potentially, it is a nonpolluting, high-productivity, controlled-environment agricultural system.

3. Hydroponics can use relatively inexpensive arid land or desert areas where the large amount of sunshine is beneficial for plant growth and makes possible several crops per year.

4. Although the standard hydroponics approach to date has been high in capital costs—anywhere from $20,000 to $80,000 per acre, depending on the complexity of the installation *—we expect that technological advances, economies of scale, conservation of water and nutrients, the sheer size of world income, and alternate uses for land can make wide-scale hydroponics feasible and competitive during the next century, especially because of its potential for obtaining four or more crops per year.

Since the world, with an average GNP per capita of $1,300, currently produces grain at a normal price of about $100 per ton, a world 200 years from now with a projected GNP per capita of $20,000 could undoubtedly afford grain at even $500 a ton, five times the current price and our highest estimate for the cost of producing grain by large-scale hydroponic techniques after 100 years or more of research and development. We expect, of course, that actual production costs would be much less—probably even less than today's $100 per ton. Assuming present U.S. consumption rates, and with three grain crops annually, each yielding 12 metric tons per hectare, 15 billion people in 2176 would require crops

---

* These estimates are based upon recent Israeli experiences. It is possible, of course, to make much greater investments.

covering about 2 million square miles. Actually, we would expect a hydroponics-type operation by then to better current field records (wheat approximately 13 metric tons per hectare; corn about 19 metric tons per hectare for a single crop). Six relatively unused areas—the Sahara Desert, the Amazon basin, the Gobi Desert, Saudi Arabia, Australia and the seacoasts of Chile and Peru—offer some 7.5 million square miles of excellent opportunities for large-scale controlled-growth operations where maximum sunshine is available. These lands alone, although not suitable today for conventional agriculture, potentially could produce more than three times the food requirements estimated above for the world in 2176. There remain, of course, problems of political feasibility and reliability.

To sum up, hydroponic techniques have been shown capable of growing crops with less water, fertilizer and other inputs than needed in conventional agriculture, and of growing them unblemished and free of disease or insect attacks. We believe it is plausible to assert that after 200 years of experience to improve these techniques, it will be possible to grow grains at today's yields per acre at costs not more than five times today's (in constant 1975 dollars). To buttress this argument still further, we note that in 1967 a prestigious summer study team at the Oak Ridge National Laboratories concluded that wheat could be grown by conventional methods in an optimally designed nuclear-powered industrial complex for somewhere between $40 and $100 per ton. None of this required any new breakthroughs in technology, and 100 percent of the water was to be furnished by a nuclear-powered desalting process. Even if these estimates were optimistic by a factor of two or three, they still would provide another *a fortiori* argument for the feasibility of feeding very large world populations.

Clearly, with the economic growth projected in Chapter II, almost everybody in 2176 would be able to afford to pay five times the current grain prices. In this example affluence alone creates a context in which really new solutions are made available. Actually, we expect the price of food in real terms to go down, not up. But we hedge this expectation by emphasizing that affluent people can afford expensive solutions, and that expensive solutions will be available if for some reason our optimism turns out not to have been justified.

Thus it is possible to argue that the world's principal food requirements can be produced by unconventional means at tolerable costs on land nearly worthless now. Even more importantly, we can assert that in reality the world is likely to find a much better solution, one that we cannot comprehend in the present context. However, because it is relevant to our topic, we will speculate on a few of the exotic future possibilities currently being discussed.

3. High-technology possibilities for the future

A new approach that might be technologically feasible for supplying food within a decade or two is the production of single-cell protein (SCP).* This high-protein food can be grown in a petroleum-based medium or by the conversion of cellulose from trash, paper, wood or agricultural wastes to glucose, which in turn can be transformed by microbial action to SCP. It appears to be commercially possible to produce SCP suitable for animal feed on a large scale by this process by the mid-1980's. Shortly thereafter, an improved product, suitable for human consumption, is expected to be practical.

Within a decade there are likely to be 10 to 15 SCP plants throughout the world, half in Europe and each with a capacity of about 100,000 tons a year.† It has been estimated that the cost of production of SCP from municipal waste would be less than half the cost of the soybean meal now widely used; thus an early potential of SCP is its use as a low-cost supplement to eradicate protein deficiencies from human diets. It should be noted that the above techniques eliminate almost all problems of land use, climate, pollution and farm runoff.

---

* SCP is "complete," containing all eight essential amino acids. Its crude protein content is high—44 to 51 percent, compared to 32 and 42 percent for soybeans. Some current production of SCP is now used as a livestock feed supplement.

† "Single-Cell Protein Comes of Age," *New Scientist,* November 28, 1974, p. 639.

Genetic innovations also hold promise. For the medium term, the production of grains with a better balance of amino acids appears nearly certain because of: (a) the breeding of new varieties, (b) the fortification of grain grown from traditional varieties, and (c) the potential for new plants from "wide crossing" (for example, triticale). For the long term, it appears that the opportunities offered by current research on cell and tissue culture are more than merely interesting speculation. Tissue culture offers the possibility of transferring desirable genetic potential among widely divergent species as well as among similar plant species. Cell culture (protoplast hybridization) offers the possibility of creating new plants via the fusing of different nuclei of two species within the same cell membrane. To date cells with unfused nuclei of two species within the cell membrane have been formed in the laboratory for soybeans with corn, barley, peas or rapeseed, as well as numerous other vegetables. Once the problem of growing fused nuclei is solved, if it is, then this technique could permit a wide range of new plants incorporating many desired characteristics, such as increased protein, disease resistance, higher yield and nitrogen fixation.*

4. *Grain for the next two centuries*

As indicated earlier, our reasonably optimistic scenario is based on conventional agriculture gradually and partially giving way to unconventional and finally exotic methods, as well as upon a gradual change in dietary habits if this becomes desirable. Figure 9 depicts this scenario for grain production (or its equivalent) over the next 200 years. The lower boundary of the figure represents minimum nutritional requirements while the upper represents our view of a more realistic supply of grain equivalents, depending on both nutritive and "aesthetic" factors. The early part of the 21st century is

* August E. Kehr (of the Agriculture Research Service, U.S. Department of Agriculture), "New Developments in Plant Cell and Tissue Culture," a talk to the Third International Congress of Plant Tissue and Cell Culture, University of Leicester, England, July 21–26, 1974.

Figure 9. A Reasonably Optimistic Scenario for Equivalent Grain Production, 1976–2176, for Feeding the World's Population

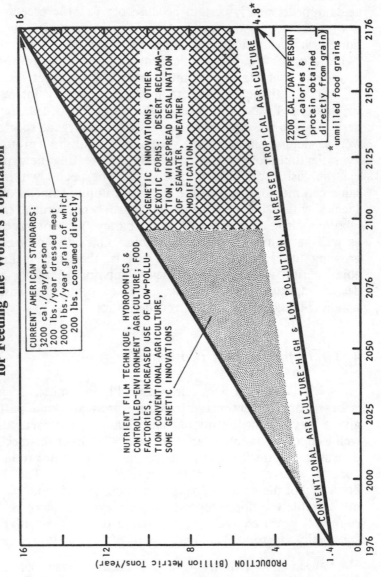

marked by the advent of controlled-environment agriculture, while the 22nd century may see increasingly widespread use of exotic and/or high-technology means of producing food.

By the year 2176 man's daily diet may include nutrients from foods such as single-cell protein, "super cereal," and synthetic foods which would be considered exotic if available today, but which might be common by then. The factors that determine long-term changes in man's diet are economy, health, taste and convenience. Although food habits are usually difficult to change quickly, they do change and people do gravitate toward palatable foods that are cheaper or more nutritious. And if they don't, it will most likely be because they are so rich and food is so abundant that there is no economic need to worry about nutritional values (as is often the case today).

The potential for use of synthetic foods in 2176 appears greater in light of such developments as the recent rapid increase in meat analogues made from soybeans. This "meatless meat" lends itself to large-scale food preparation; it is cheaper; and it provides more usable protein than animal meat. (But it is far from the cheapest protein available.) Sales of this synthetic reached $10 million in 1973, and are expected to exceed $1 billion by 1980, replacing 20 percent of the natural meats in processed foods.*

For nutritive fortification of food, the single-cell protein offers great promise, especially in those areas of the world where there is a severe protein deficiency. Even today fortified foods are taken for granted (for example, iodized salt, enriched breakfast cereals). Thus it should not be difficult to expect changes in diets if the economic considerations are desirable and the cultural or social mores are not too rigid—not in a year, or in five years, but with economic or nutritional benefits it should be quite possible in two to five decades. Within the span of our scenario, we consider changes in diet a virtual certainty.

* E. B. Weiss, *Marketing to the New Society* (Chicago: Grain Communications, Inc., 1973), p. 32.

THE SPECIAL PROBLEM OF INDIA

When one examines the world food situation and potential severe shortages, attention is immediately turned to the South Asian subcontinent and especially to India. With a population approaching 600 million, projected to reach 1 billion by the year 2000, India has lived with the threat of famine for centuries. Currently, the Indian population represents roughly half of the world's food problem.

To a large extent the government of India seems to have exacerbated the problem with misplaced priorities. Since its independence India has emphasized industrialization (with capital-intensive industries such as steel yet to become profitable) and more recently national defense and development of nuclear energy, all of which have diverted resources that could have been applied to the agricultural sector. India's defense expenditure is the largest item in its budget, taking one-third of the government budget in 1972–73. Agriculture, on the other hand, declined over the period 1971–74 from $1.1 billion to $850 million. Desperately needed irrigation facilities and fertilizer production have not been encouraged, and the problem has been compounded by a failure to operate existing fertilizer plants at more than 60 percent of design capacity. Perhaps equally important have been the unfavorable terms of trade to which farmers have been subjected, demonstrated especially in the relatively high fertilizer prices set by the government.* In addition, India's food procurement and distribution system is buffeted by rapidly shifting governmental policies attended by administrative incompetence and corruption. Attempts to obtain grain from the private sector at prices well below those of the open market, and a

---

* For example, it has been calculated that in 1968–69 the Indian farmer required 5.2 kilograms of rice to purchase 1 kilogram of fertilizer, compared to only 1.35 kilograms for the Japanese farmer and only 1.15 kilograms for the Pakistani farmer (James D. Gavan and John A. Dixon, "India: A Perspective on the Food Situation," *Science*, May 9, 1975, p. 546).

ban on the movement of commercial quantities of wheat to neighboring states, have induced widespread hoarding and smuggling of grain.

To summarize, the lack of priority given the agricultural sector, an absence of a strong agricultural infrastructure, national policies that discourage foreign investment, unrealistic planning, a bureaucracy often bordering on paralysis, lack of competence in the international market, and the tolerance of corruption at all political levels appear to be the principal factors which have hamstrung India's agricultural development.

Does the foregoing imply that India is destined for mass starvation or is perpetually tied to intolerable levels of food imports? Examination of India's agricultural sector shows a considerable potential for greater food output. When compared today with China, Japan or Taiwan, Indian agriculture has a rather low degree of fertilizer use, a rather high ratio of arable land to population and relatively low yields.* Moreover, India is blessed with extensive and fertile river basins. The need for irrigation and development of water resources is one key to greater production since monsoon rainfall occurs only over a four-month period, leaving a large part of the country semi-arid for the remainder of the year. As stated earlier, the development of the Ganges basin could increase grain production by 150 million metric tons or more, a development that alone could meet the increases in minimum nutritional requirements during the next quarter-century.

India's immediate potential for expansion is not a matter of technical feasibility, but depends rather on whether it can undertake the policies and programs needed to use its resources effectively. It appears that only in the Punjab region has much organization for effective production already taken place. An improved approach would appear to require both a decentralization of planning and a change in national emphasis from regulatory to facilitative procedures.† In the short

* *Ibid.*

† For a more complete discussion of this recommendation, see John W. Mellor, *The New Economics of Growth: A Strategy for India and the Developing World,* a Twentieth Century Fund Study (Ithaca, N.Y.: Cornell University Press, 1976), Chapter 3.

run, an increased use of fertilizer is the principal means of raising agricultural output for India, as it is for most nations. For the longer run, increased agricultural output will depend mainly on institutional changes which will encourage such actions as better use of water resources and multicropping, and will create an environment conducive to the efficient use of new technologies.

In response to the urgent need to increase India's food production, its government announced in March 1975 that developmental priorities had shifted to food and energy. When she proclaimed a state of emergency at the time of the Indian political crisis in June 1975, Prime Minister Indira Gandhi introduced a number of measures ostensibly aimed at improving the lot of the peasant. The promised measures included steps to bring down prices, reduce peasant debts and achieve a fairer distribution of land. In addition, the government promised to increase the amount of irrigated land by 19,000 square miles and electric power by 20 percent. The new policies could greatly help to develop India's agricultural potential, but only if the government makes a serious long-term commitment.

It is clear that there are many means for providing ample food for the world during the next 200 years. The availability of resources and a powerful expanding technology leave no doubt as to the potential of both conventional and nonconventional agriculture. In addition, flexibility in dietary habits enhances the prospects for exotic factory foods in the decades ahead. These potentials, however, should not be taken as an invitation to complacency. A tremendous effort will be required to realize them over the long term. More crucial in the short run will be enlightened and intelligent attention to the institutional factors that can enable available resources and technological skills to be utilized fully.

VI

The Near-Term Environment:
Clean Air, Clear Water
and Aesthetic Landscapes

UNTIL RECENTLY, people treated their environment as a free commodity, accepting as natural the gifts it provided of air, heat, water and the disposal of wastes. Now, however, the environment can no longer fulfill these needs for civilization without economic cost and/or environmental degradation. Demand, having increased dramatically during the last 200 years, has exceeded the free supply. As a result, although the environment still provides these resources, they are now limited, no longer free (but not necessarily costly) and/or tainted. Advanced industrialized societies are learning that they have only two options: to restrict their demands or to pay for the environment by keeping it relatively clean and protected.

It is our main thesis that while it will be expensive to develop and maintain a satisfactory environment over the next quarter-century, it will continue to be both economically and technically feasible during the next 200 years, even if the world population and economy grow, as we project, to 15 billion people and a $300 trillion GWP. Our secondary thesis is that with improvement in technology and practice, eventually the costs will go down.

A PERSPECTIVE ON THE CURRENT ISSUES

The environmental issues are politically "up front" these days, in part because they are relatively new but also because some very expensive changes must be made in the way things are done as a result of recent legislation. Moreover, it is never easy to give up old customs and habits. Not only must the cost of meeting reasonable environmental standards on new projects now be internalized, but, in principle, the costs necessary to retrofit factories, buildings, transportation systems and farms to meet new standards must be accepted. Furthermore, these changes are to be accomplished within a few short years. This is a painful commitment. The Council on Environmental Quality estimated that by 1982 the pollution control expenditures for the previous decade would total $325 billion (in 1973 dollars), with an annual expense for operating and maintaining the systems of about $27 billion.* Although these sums seem huge, they constitute only a small fraction of our GNP, which presumably can and will be paid.

How well will such expenditures meet the desired standards? There is a vague impression in some circles that the pollution problem simply cannot be overcome in a growing economy. Indeed, the public sometimes seems astonishingly unaware that even the relatively small efforts made to date have resulted in some progress. For example, one of the authors recently found that a group of high school students he met in Pittsburgh were aware that environmental pollution is a major current issue, but none realized that his own city had already cleaned up its air pollution to a remarkable degree. We have been told by some British colleagues that a similar situation exists among students in London. In both cases the young had been taught—and believed—that the

* Council on Environmental Quality, Fifth Annual Report (Washington: U.S. Government Printing Office, 1974), p. 221. Note that the actual dollar costs—which are increased by delays, litigation, closures, abandonments, inflation and oversights—may be greatly underestimated.

situation was deteriorating steadily. There are other examples of successful reduction of pollution. During the 1950's Los Angeles eliminated backyard incinerators and controlled industrial emissions to reduce the air pollution problem. The Council on Environmental Quality has described the 30-year process involved in the cleaning up of the Willamette River basin; * a similar but even more complex effort took place in Germany's Ruhr Valley.

Japan today is spending about 2 percent of its GNP on antipollution devices, perhaps a greater proportion than any other developed nation. That nation is also in the forefront of creating technology that will keep the environment clean and which could easily become a major Japanese export. The Japanese have experienced especially severe pollution problems because of their high population density and their spectacular economic development during the past 30 years. Rapid development without encumbering environmental controls enabled them to become a wealthy nation in a short time. While they were not necessarily mistaken in this policy, they must now pay the cost of neglected environmental adjustments. But they now have the money and technology needed. Also, one learns through hindsight how things might have been done. So Japan may become a model for many of the less-developed nations: Its past successes and errors should help guide would-be followers toward a more optimal path. For example, one serious error the Japanese made was to overlook the poisonous potential of wastes from heavy metals; mercury poisoning caused a major tragedy in the Minamata and Nigata bays, resulting in more than 100 human deaths in addition to disasters among birds, fish and cats.†

The debate about proper test procedures for avoiding

* Council on Environmental Quality, Fourth Annual Report (Washington: U.S. Government Printing Office, 1973), pp. 44–70. The sharp contrast between the relatively clean environment of modern times and the putrefaction and hazardous conditions during the last century is carefully documented in a fascinating book, *The Good Old Days—They Were Terrible* by Otto L. Bettman (New York: Random House, 1974), which we strongly recommend to those who desire a 100-year perspective on U.S. environmental issues.

† Council on Environmental Quality, Fifth Annual Report, p. 27.

such hazards associated with advancing technology is a complex one. Although everyone who wants to achieve a reasonable balance between potential risks and benefits has access to the appropriate forums, mistakes have been and inevitably will be made—in exercising too much caution as well as in taking too many risks. The evidence suggests that most developing countries understand their option of accepting some pollution in the short or medium term in order to attain more rapid economic growth—and that they will probably have to pay a higher cost eventually for retrofitting with antipollution equipment, presumably after poverty has been much reduced or eliminated. Since current technology can often substantially reduce pollution from new installations at tolerable costs, the future problems of countries now developing may prove less severe than those presently facing more advanced nations.

Nevertheless, the developing nations will have to make many difficult decisions in complex situations. For example, Rio de Janeiro has one of the finest harbors and beaches in the world; the famous Copacabana is enjoyed mostly by tourists, well-to-do Brazilians and visiting businessmen. Therefore, one might question whether the Brazilian government should expend the large sums needed to maintain this beach and harbor rather than use the money to develop the poverty-stricken northeast region. In a similar vein, one might also ask whether the Taj Mahal or Chartres Cathedral should have been built at the expense of the peasants of those times. How is the general long-term benefit to society traded off against the short-term costs to the local poor?

The environmentalist movement deserves credit for helping to create the great interest in this issue, and the accompanying tensions, which have led to major actions by governments—even though these organizations have sometimes allowed their dedication to the cause to overrule their good judgment. Some of the credit also belongs to their predecessors —hunters, outdoor sportsmen and nature lovers—who led a strong movement for environmental preservation and in fact formed the major public constituency of the Sierra Club prior to the mid-1960's.

Entrenched lobbies require strong new counterlobbies to bring about change through legislative action. Thus, without the dedicated efforts of the current environmentalist movement, it is unlikely that Congress would have authorized strong controls over automobile emissions. We believe that some important arbitrary decisions were needed and were made. For example, when Congress in 1970 set the deadline for the automotive industry to produce vehicles with effective emission controls, it would have chosen 1980 if it had relied upon the industry's advice, and in due course that deadline might well have been pushed back to somewhere between 1985 and 1990. In fact, when Congress chose 1975, it chose an arbitrary five-year period, apparently for no compelling reason. (Efforts to track down a more precise reason for this figure have yielded only the observation that it was an obvious number—the fingers of one hand!) In retrospect, this action appears to have been both appropriate and wise, since it served as the spur that caused the industry to move—if not very rapidly. If Congress generally set arbitrary standards and stuck to them, it could prove to be very costly. But the setting of high standards to be met in a short time, which later can be allowed to slip by a year or two, can prove an effective approach without resulting in terribly high costs. Actually, it turned out that Japanese companies were able to design automobiles to meet the U.S. standards before American companies. But the fact that the U.S. manufacturers did not meet the original deadlines hardly makes a strong case for special punishment. Their struggles to comply with this unexpected change in the rules and the losses they have already suffered may be punishment enough. The lack of sympathy by some of the more militant environmentalists, to the point of "total unforgiveness" over the industry's agony, might almost be labeled "bigoted" and probably is counterproductive, as such a stance costs them some support and makes them appear vindictive.

The environmental movement probably also lost supporters because of its relentless attempt to delay the Trans-Alaska Pipeline (TAP), even after the energy crisis had become critical. Environmentalists were successful—and probably justified—in bringing about the review of the original pipeline plans; indeed, substantial and useful modifications resulted. But subsequent delays seemed to reflect little more than excessive zeal and ideological intensity. If during the next several years the Alaskan North Slope and adjoining offshore areas are found to have, say, a 50-billion-barrel oil reserve instead of the 10 billion now conservatively estimated, lengthy delay in the completion of the pipeline, caused in large measure by court proceedings brought by those in extreme opposition, may turn out to have produced a blunder in U.S. policy of historic dimensions. Such a delay could become a classic example of an indulgence of the kind that even a wealthy advanced country cannot afford. And even at 10 billion barrels, the lost years have probably caused a balance-of-payments loss of about $25 billion or more.

In critical times a country needs understanding from its citizenry and flexibility in behavior. This is not to imply that the mere existence of an emergency is sufficient cause for riding roughshod over environmental considerations or legal restraints. But some bending, some temporary compromises, may be necessary. A major weakness of the environmental movement is its apparent need to oppose every major project, often, it would appear, simply as a matter of "principle." Undoubtedly there are some specific reasons for opposition in each case, but to oppose all projects, the good and the bad, is to delay without sufficient cause and at great expense government approval of those programs that are vitally needed. Few of the good things in life come free. Hard choices must be made, and concerned environmentalists must share in the responsibility. In effect, there should be a "cost impact" statement filed by environmental groups of the cost of their intervention; in some instances it might be realized that, in the long run, the real costs of intervening may exceed those of not intervening at all. Otherwise, excesses of the environmentalists—especially in the midst of a recessionary economy—could well create an unfortunate backlash and result in a general public distrust and subsequent rejection of many of the positive contributions the environmental movement has to offer.

SOME CONSEQUENCES OF
ENVIRONMENTAL REGULATION

Because legislation of the last decade has perhaps made it too easy for anyone to interfere with almost any proposed change, the result has been an enormous amount of lobbying, harassment, political initiatives, litigation, abandoned projects and bitterness. It seems obvious that new procedures are needed in order to settle environmental disputes with greater dispatch. The huge costs associated with protracted delays evidently were not contemplated by Congress when it passed the National Environmental Protection Act (NEPA) of 1969. Besides the postponement in building the Trans-Alaska Pipeline, there are many other examples of costly delays caused by objections made by environmentalists. Indeed, it is difficult to find any proposed project related to the important area of new energy supplies that has not been so affected. This applies to coal mining or conversion plants, ocean drilling for oil and gas, oil-shale projects, nuclear power, thermal electric power, transmission lines, pipelines, refineries, petroleum or natural gas storage, and even geothermal power.

Another consequence of the environmental movement, resulting from its hasty rise to prominence and the attendant political power, is that it has been responsible for some disastrous decisions. In retrospect, some of these mistaken judgments may even seem humorous, but it is no laughing matter when they add unnecessary costs to be borne by the already overburdened taxpayers. And there are even tragic examples when millions of people have suffered from ill health or in some instances died because of such a mistake, as exemplified by the DDT case:

Ceylon was one of the first Asiatic countries to ban DDT, with startling results. More than 2 million Ceylonese had malaria in the early 1950's when DDT was first introduced to control malarial mosquitoes. After 10 years of control, malaria had all but been eliminated in Ceylon. The country banned the pesticide in 1964. By 1968 over a million new cases of malaria had appeared. Ceylon rescinded its ban on DDT in 1969.*

Of course every new movement attracts dedicated workers who are relentless in pursuit of their goals and unable to make rational modifications of their positions—perhaps a definition of extremists. Unfortunately, our political process is vunerable to such extremism and serious consequences can result. Perhaps the greatest blooper is that nobly worded section of NEPA which allows any "interested" citizen (often translated as "fanatic") to "intervene" (translate: "harass as much as possible") in "any" environmental impact hearing (and they have, it seems, in *every* one).

The 1970 amendments to the Air Quality Act of 1967 reflect a comprehensive revision of previous pollution control statutes in the United States and are generally considered to constitute the most advanced approach to air quality management in the world today. The latest figures from the Environmental Protection Agency's monitoring programs indicate that these standards are beginning to be met quite generally throughout the United States. A large number of the reporting stations show that particulate and sulfur dioxide standards are being met on the average throughout the year. Automotive-related pollutants such as carbon monoxide and hydrocarbons have been reduced substantially, although these chemicals and the nitrogen oxides are still a problem for many communities. The new auto pollution control devices for the 1975 models and those of later years should help to decrease these pollutants steadily in the near future. It is doubtful whether all air quality standards can be met throughout the country for the indefinite future as the population and industrial and transportation activities change. If they could be, the standards should and probably would be made more stringent. On the other hand, the public is aware of the laws, regional plans have been approved, and action has been taken to limit the emission of pollutants. It is clear that the air is

* Cy A. Adler, *Ecological Fantasies* (New York: Green Eagle Press, 1973), p. 194. See also *The New York Times,* March 16, 1969; Rita Gray Beatty, *The DDT Myth* (New York: The John Day Co., 1973), pp. 12–13.

getting cleaner and that this trend will continue. The frequent emotional charges to the contrary as a general proposition are simply unfounded (see Figure 11). The coming decade will demonstrate the degree to which strong public involvement and major expenditures can succeed in meeting the recent standards for clean air.

The Federal Water Quality Act of 1972 is clearly one of the most far-reaching pieces of environmental legislation. By 1977 all nonpublic stationary sources of water pollutants must employ the best practicable control technology currently available, and public sources must have at least the equivalent of secondary treatment of sewage. By 1983 the best available technology economically achievable must be installed. By 1985 a national goal of *zero pollutant discharge* into navigable waters is to be attained, an impossible goal and thus one clearly destined for modification (or reinterpretation) to more realistic standards. One result will probably be a lot of abuse hurled at the government for "selling out."

The Environmental Protection Agency has accelerated its efforts to obligate funds appropriated by Congress for municipal waste treatment construction. A total of $18 million has been authorized by Congress, and grants reached nearly $3 billion in fiscal year 1975. It is likely that the 1977 requirements will be widely achieved, but the 1983 and 1985 goals imply major process changes in industry, as well as in municipal pollution control, some of which are not yet designed. Probably because of recent huge increases in cost estimates, there appears to be movement toward revision of these goals; in fact, no one has yet defined what "zero pollutant discharge" would mean in practice.

Certainly progress has been made in limiting additional water pollution, and a beginning has been made toward cleaning up the rivers, streams and lakes of this nation. On the other hand, even if the 1985 goals were achieved, most waters of the United States would still be receiving both urban and rural runoff, which injects various quantities of sediment, chemicals, bacteria and even viruses. The degree to which this area-wide pollution (as contrasted to point-source pollution) will be controlled and over what period of time are still among the issues that must be resolved through legislative action and technological progress.

ENVIRONMENTAL ECONOMICS

Every student of elementary economics has learned that, in theory at least, pollution controls should cease when the next dollar spent yields less than a dollar's worth of benefits. In other words, we know conceptually the exact optimal point to which our control activities should be carried. Unfortunately, in practice a serious problem impedes the use of the optimal solution: While we can often reasonably approximate the expenditures required for pollution abatement, there is no clear or accurate way to measure the economic value of most of the benefits (cleaner air, a cleaner lake or a quieter street) or most of the social costs (health hazards, ecological stresses, unsightly landscapes) even in gross terms, let alone to determine marginal choices. This difficulty is so great, in fact, that the concept of an optimal point has little value outside the economics classroom, for in practice the optimal point is usually determined in Congress as well as in the numerous political arenas at other levels.

Somehow out of this maelstrom of environmental struggle, solutions emerge and standards are set which of course are constantly subject to change as the endless search for the optimum goes on. Consequently, the current standards for air and water quality, radioactivity, noise levels and other elements must be considered temporary. Today's rules and regulations, together with voluntary local customs, define the current optimum point; tomorrow's will almost certainly be different. This situation appears chaotic and inefficient to some who are deeply involved and can see many of the blunders along the way. However, a rich country has the advantage of being able to afford temporary mistakes and inefficiencies—to a substantial degree. If, as we expect, after another decade or two the battle will have subsided to a less controversial level of administration of rules and regulations, history may eventually determine that for a democratic society we followed a practical and satisfactory route.

Figure 10. Pollution Control Costs as a Percentage of the Gross National Product

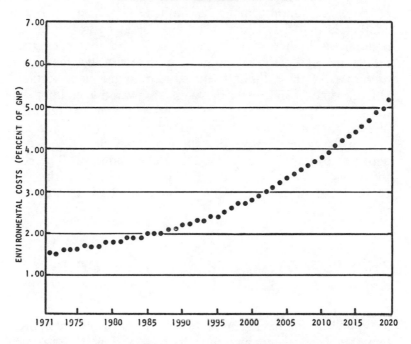

SOURCE: Adapted from S. Fred Singer, "Future Environmental Needs and Costs," in *Economics of a Clean Environment*, a Report of the Proceedings of a Symposium cosponsored by The Mitre Corporation and the American Geophysical Union in McLean, Virginia, published by The Mitre Corporation, McLean, Virginia, July 1974, p. 21.

An important problem to be resolved in the years to come can be seen in Figure 10, which projects increasing costs for pollution control over time as a proportion of GNP—from about 1.5 percent currently to between 5 and 6 percent in 50 years. In other words, if the model is correct, the environmental maintenance costs will be a steadily increasing portion of our GNP and a substantial growing burden on the economy, exceeding the projected defense budget in 2020. However, like all mathematical models, this model is vulnerable to the claim that it provides an oversimplified view of the real world; still we expect that it will prove reasonably accurate for the next few years. One of its potential weaknesses is that it assumes that the reduction of wastes per unit of output as a result of technological improvements is limited to a factor of two; another is that the reduction in abatement costs per unit of pollutant is limited to a factor of two, and that even these results are only gradually attained over several decades. (The usefulness of these limits is questioned in the next section.) On the other hand, we believe that a wealthy country like the United States is going to want very high standards— indeed, that it will want to keep improving them until the cost becomes prohibitive. Substantial funds are likely to be allocated to improving the land and the landscape. The costs for clean air and water appear likely to peak during this century and subsequently diminish—at least as a percentage of the GNP.

TECHNOLOGY: FORCE FOR GOOD OR EVIL?

A currently popular attitude is to blame technology or technologists for having brought on the environmental problems we face today, and thus to try to slow technological advance by halting economic growth. We believe this view to be thoroughly misguided. If technology produced automobiles that pollute the air, it is because pollution was not recognized as a problem which engineers had to consider in their designs. Obviously, technology that produces pollution is generally cheaper, but now that it has been decided that cleaner cars are wanted, less polluting cars will be produced; cars which scarcely pollute at all could even be made. This last option, however, would require several years and much investment. Although technology is responsive to the will of the people, it can seldom respond instantaneously and is never free. If society changes its requirements there will, of course, be added costs to pay, at least during the transition.

Technology cannot end all problems—perhaps not the most important ones—but technology can solve or alleviate almost all pollution problems and it can also create a physical context that makes possible the creation of a better society and culture.

We take the position that nearly every measurable environmental blight or hazard can be corrected by a combination of technology, a reasonable amount of money, sufficient time to make the required changes, and (occasionally or temporarily) some (otherwise undesirable) self-restraint. Many environmentalists tend to rely almost completely on the self-restraint approach, which, we believe, is disturbing to the nation and probably counterproductive to the cause of a cleaner environment. Normally, one cannot change automobile pollution by more than a factor of 2 or 3 by self-restraint, while technological improvement seems likely to yield a factor of 5 to 50. In a few cases it may be reasonable to require the phasing out of an activity or a moratorium on an industry or potential industry, at least until the major objections can be handled. This course of action was followed, for example, for some smelting operations, and it may be deemed advisable for the proposed breeder reactor, perhaps even other nuclear power reactors. In other cases, an appropriate decision requires striking a cost-benefit balance between aesthetics and health or other needs (for example, standards for engine exhausts or the use of pesticides). This involves a political process which during the short run produces aggravation on both sides. However, the aggravation usually subsides as the problems are solved and people's interests shift, as in the case of the Trans-Alaska Pipeline.

The limits-to-growth model—with its conclusion that continued economic growth causes pollution that will inevitably overwhelm us—is undoubtedly incorrect. Our principal argument is that although the fraction of our GNP needed to control pollution may increase over the near term, it is likely to remain a very small part of the whole GNP. Secondly, we conclude that from now on, *if the choice is made,* the air, water and landscapes can become cleaner over time—along with continued economic growth. Whenever more stringent standards are adopted or it is decided that environmental improvements are to be achieved more rapidly, or both, average income will, for a time, be reduced accordingly. But these are political and economic issues whose resolution can be found partly through technological advances and partly through political decisions.

We will discuss two areas in which pollution is a major problem today and which are under intense scrutiny by many organizations for possible technical solutions. These are the automobile engine and the electric power plant. In using these two examples, our purpose is to help provide a better perspective on technology as a resource for future pollution control and to help make persuasive the above conclusions.

The automobile engine: The internal combustion engine undoubtedly now constitutes man's largest remaining source of air pollution. But some progress has already been made toward alleviating this problem and further improvements have been mandated and are scheduled for the near future. Table 16 shows the improvements already achieved and those anticipated; these range between factors of 6 and 20 for re-

Table 16. Automobile Emissions, 1957–67, and under Federal Standards, 1970–75 [in grams per mile] [a]

	Hydro-carbons	Carbon monoxide	Nitrogen oxides [b]
1957–67 autos, averaged	8.7	87	
1970/71 standards	4.1	34	
1972/73/74 standards	3.0	28	[b] 3.1
1975 interim standard			
United States	1.5	15	3.1
California	0.9	9	2.0
Statutory standard	0.41	3.4	0.4

[a] All values are expressed in terms of the 1975 Federal emission test procedure.

[b] The NO_x standard became effective with the 1973 models. California's NO_x standard of 2.0 grams per mile became effective with the 1974 models.

SOURCE: Council on Environmental Quality, Fifth Annual Report.

ducing the emission of various pollutants. But even if the newest standards are met as scheduled, still further improvements based on new engines are possible over the next 10–50 years. These could (and probably will) over that period of time essentially eliminate any significant emission of air pollutants. It is not certain, of course, whether it will take 15, 25 or 50 years to accomplish the desired result, but there is evidence that it can readily be done by the early part of the next century, and quite possibly in this one.

Several technological possibilities point in this direction. One is the use of clean-burning fuels such as natural gas, propane, hydrogen or various alcohols in current (but probably improved) internal combustion engines. Another possibility is to use an improved emission control system, such as the catalytic converter, perhaps in combination with a stratified-charge engine and "cleaner" gasoline (from which most of the sulfur has been removed). These kinds of changes are all near-term possibilities that concentrate on new fuels and minor engine modifications. Over a longer time period, the internal combustion engine may give way to one of several external combustion engines which could burn many of today's fuels with relatively insignificant amounts of pollution. The major potential as seen now is related to the possibilities inherent in (a) a Stirling cycle engine, (b) a Rankine cycle (steam) engine and (c) a Brayton cycle (gas turbine) engine, each of which is under intensive research and development.

Finally, perhaps the most likely medium- or long-term successor to current motor vehicles is the electric automobile. In principle, such vehicles would be simpler, perhaps less expensive, substantially more efficient in energy consumption, practically pollution-free, almost silent in operation, would require much less maintenance or servicing, and would last much longer than today's cars. The major technological problem remaining to be solved is related to providing a sufficient amount of energy storage—the electric equivalent of a tank of gasoline—and several promising options are being actively studied. These are: (1) the use of advanced storage batteries, which might furnish about 10 times the energy (per pound) of current lead batteries; (2) the fuel cell, which can "burn" hydrogen or any of several light hydrocarbon fuels cleanly and efficiently to produce electric power; and (3) the flywheel, which, with recent designs and new high-strength materials, can in principle outperform most of the batteries being considered today. The major constraint now visualized on the use of electric vehicles (assuming a satisfactory solution to the energy storage problem) is the time required for recharging batteries or reenergizing flywheels. Normally this would be done overnight or whenever an hour or more is available. However, continuous driving beyond the range of the stored energy may not be feasible except possibly with an engine based on fuel cells. Even this limitation on driving range is far from certain since a number of concepts have been proposed to circumvent it (for example, a hybrid engine that can combine the advantages of shorter-distance electric drive with a cross-country, gasoline-powered engine—at some additional costs, of course). There appears to be little doubt that an electric automobile will come into widespread use; only the timing appears uncertain, but it is probably much less than 50 years.

Electric power plants: Today the power plants that burn fossil fuels, especially coal, are major targets for air pollution controls. Those burning natural gas pose no significant pollution problems, but because of the competing demands for gas, most fossil-fueled power plants in this country burn coal or oil and therefore need substantial controls. In the near term these controls are expected to be costly—especially since there appear to be shortages at present of low-sulfur coal, and some natural gas and petroleum-fueled plants will be phased out to meet the various goals developed out of Project Independence. However, for the medium and long term, so many options are likely to become available for relatively clean power that timing and phasing appear to be the only major problems. In the United States the basic technology is in hand today, although the design, development and construction time to achieve substantial commercial production may require between 10 and 25 years. Some of the major new options are:

1. Clean-burning synthetic gas made from coal—especially low-BTU gas
   a. from coal conversion plants
   b. from *in situ* gasification of coal
2. Low-sulfur synthetic crude oil or alcohols made from
   a. coal
   b. oil shale
   c. other fuels: tar sands, peat, organic wastes
3. Solar or geothermal electric power
4. Nuclear fission or fusion reactors

All of these options have the potential for a great reduction of air pollution, but the fission reactor is still seen by many as posing unacceptable safety and arms-control hazards. (Later in this chapter we discuss the environmental objections to mining and conversion operations for oil shale and coal that are related mostly to local land use and water requirements. Unfortunately every large industrial venture creates some environmental disturbance.)

By the turn of the century, it appears very likely, the environmental health hazards associated with power plant emissions will be reduced by a factor of 10 or more from the pre-1970 levels. Not only would the use of cleaner fuels diminish pollution, but by the appropriate siting of new power plants, the impact of the residual emissions could also be reduced. For example, offshore locations are now being considered seriously for large energy installations. Finally, in the long term, fusion and solar and/or geothermal energy, rather than fossil fuels, are likely to assume the major burden of clean power production—unless some of the nuclear fission options become sufficiently acceptable and are more economical. After this transition begins, the remaining air pollution from power production can be expected to diminish steadily.

Difficult pollution problems: Various technological options are now being studied or designed for controlling other pollutants. Each of the major problems associated with sewage, solid wastes, agricultural runoff and chemical hazards appears to be reducible in a number of ways based upon good management and/or new technology, and generally by much more than a factor of two, although in some cases solutions may not be practical in the near term (for example, effective handling of the storm runoff in many urban centers, as discussed below).

One of the reasons pollution control encounters such resistance today is that the new regulations often require the retrofitting of existing installations—nearly always a much more costly and difficult task than providing appropriate controls during the initial installation. A second reason is that the time allowed to control the unwanted emissions generally appears too brief to those saddled with the task (and too long to those pressing for results).

Under present circumstances, therefore, certain environmental problems are much more difficult to resolve than others. Thus dealing with the nonpoint sources of water pollution has some particularly nasty aspects—one being the problem of storm runoff from urban areas where sewers and storm drains are now combined, an unfortunate inheritance from earlier times. Since most treatment plants cannot handle the volume of water from sizable storms, they merely divert most of the runoff (and sewage) into the rivers or other receiving waters during these periods. The obvious solution— separation of the sewer and storm drain systems—would be an enormous task that not only could cost more than $100 billion,* but would literally require the excavation of nearly every street in most of the major urban centers—an exceedingly unpleasant prospect. It seems more likely, therefore, that less costly and disrupting partial solutions will be sought, at least over the short or medium term. One such possible solution would be to create a system that can impound the initial runoff from a storm before diverting the rest of the flow; the impounded water, containing a large amount of the accumulated street pollutants, could be treated before being discharged into the rivers.

* One 1974 estimate was $235 billion (*Engineering News Record,* September 12, 1974, p. 17). More recently, the sum of $444 billion was estimated by Vice President Rockefeller's Commission on Water Pollution Control as the required U.S. expenditure (reported in *The New York Times,* September 28, 1974).

Clearly, designing new cities, new power plants, new vehicles and new industries to meet required environmental standards would be relatively less painful or difficult than the agonies of retrofitting the existing system to meet the legislated new standards. These problems are likely to be severe during the next decade or two but should steadily diminish shortly after that.

LAND-USE ISSUES

Land-use environmental issues pose some interesting problems of choice. There is no "right" way of deciding whether it is better (a) to strip-mine for minerals and later restore the land, thereby leaving it in a disturbed condition for as much as a decade or more, or (b) to pay the extra costs (including higher risks to miners) associated with underground mining. Either way or neither may be chosen. A trade-off exists between increased wealth on the one hand and degrees of health, safety and aesthetics on the other, and an appropriate balance between them must be found.

For future political decisions, it might be reasonable for policy-makers to envisage at least three major categories in the relationship between environmental controls and land use. The first would be the most protected regions, such as special wilderness areas, including mountains, national parks, lakes and scenic deserts—areas which, by common consent, would be kept in a state of nearly natural purity. Any noticeable polluting activity would be strictly forbidden or severely controlled. The second category would involve areas in which most people spend most of their time—the residential, industrial, commercial and farming districts; and it is here that the major struggles to define an optimum environment will be and, we believe, properly should be part of the political scene for at least the next decade. The third category would be defined as one in which "junk piles" of one kind or another, for economic or technological reasons, could be tolerated in a few selected regions for greater or lesser periods of time—for example, some strip-mining operators in remote areas until the land is restored, drilling in oil fields until depleted, use of surface pipelines or transmission lines until they are obsolete.

Indeed, in a few cases, it might be undesirable (for example, too costly) to require a complete or equivalent restoration of the original terrain. The citizens of the region might prefer other alternatives to spending $10,000 per acre to restore land formerly valued at perhaps $100 per acre. However, in the last two categories we would generally encourage the current trend: to set legal standards to assure that any major disturbances which are not self-healing would be repaired if practical—more or less gradually and in reasonable consonance with the economics of the local situation. The time periods involved could vary from months to decades, but rarely would be longer. Although it may be galling for any environmentalist to accept our "junk pile" category as necessary, we would argue that it is a normal and required attribute of any industrial society, past, present and future. The time requirements for restoration, or the degree thereof, may be appropriate subjects for continuing debates, but not the principle that such a category is necessary. In a developed country as large as the United States, certain limited areas must be temporarily expendable.

In retrospect, to return to a previous example, it seems strange that the environmental movement fought with such tremendous energy in the battle against the Trans-Alaska Pipeline. How could they ignore the fact that this venture, with such obviously great economic impact, only required the use of much less than .01 percent of the Alaskan area—land generally located in a region so remote that, except for the workers, it would be seen only by a few of the most adventurous tourists? Furthermore, with proper design, the impact on wildlife at most would be negligible and might even prove to be of some small benefit (for example, the pipeline could offer occasional refuge from the Arctic wind). The delay in starting the TAP not only added billions to the original cost, but meant that the American people had to pay about $5 billion annually for several additional years to foreign producers for their fuel requirements.

Perhaps there are some lessons here that will permit more reasonable decisions to be made in the future. Where the land and the environment can readily be restored approximately to their original condition, we would contend that there should be little argument about whether or not strip mining should be approved. Where restoration to the original condition is not feasible but a reasonable aesthetic substitution can be designed, then perhaps the only debate should be in the choice of the form of restoration. A more difficult case would be one in which a particularly arid climate prevents either restoration to nearly original conditions or a pleasing alternative, and here it seems quite proper to expect a major environmental struggle. The eventual decisions, presumably, would result from a combination of (1) the effective arguments about the environmental consequences, (2) the importance of the project to the country, (3) the cost to the country of a temporary immobilization of the natural processes of the area (not all areas can be assigned the same degree of worth) and (4) (as always) the preponderance of political clout among the various lobbying groups.

FUTURE ENVIRONMENTAL PROGRESS

The great surge in the worldwide concern with the environment that began in the 1960's has now not only culminated in a new national consciousness about environmental quality but, aided by the accelerating trends to improve the quality of life that characterize economically advanced nations, has also led to great progress in controlling pollution in Japan, North America and northwestern Europe. Lesser but important advances have occurred in most of the other affluent nations of the world, and also in some of the less affluent. The victory of the environmentalists may not yet be completely apparent because it is still in process (see Figure 11). And in some of the less affluent nations, a parallel victory may (perhaps quite properly) be delayed somewhat until the costs of the associated slower economic development become

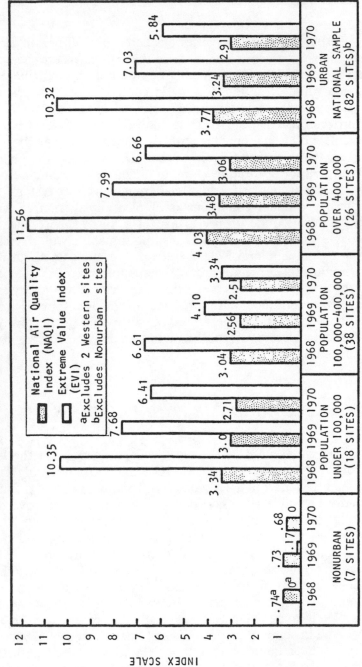

Figure 11. Combined Indices of Air Pollution for Selected National Air Sampling Network (NASN) Sites, National Population-weighted Averages

SOURCE: C. A. Bisselle, S. H. Lubore, and R. P. Pikul, *National Environmental Indices: Air Quality and Outdoor Recreation*, The Mitre Corporation, McLean, Virginia, April, 1972.

acceptable. Even in three of the most dedicated areas—Japan, North America and northwestern Europe—it may take about another 10 years before the full impact of trends toward environmental improvement can be seen.

This interim period will not, however, be one of repose. We expect to witness a constant battle between the more militant environmentalists and those who must suffer the financial impact of the clamor for "too rapid" solutions—especially those obliged to retrofit existing installations at great expense to rectify their past "carelessness," or those who feel that an adoption of costly and unreliable environmental technologies might soon have to be repeated.

Generally, however, we expect progress to occur through a succession of appropriate compromises: protection of the environment where it is practical and useful, and encouragement of economic growth where it is relatively productive and the environmental disturbance is believed less important (as with oil from Alaska). Battles will be fought continually, and there will be many setbacks. New offshore leases for oil drilling or increased strip mining of coal will be defeats in the eyes of some people, but victories or reasonable compromises for others. We expect that most victories will be won by the moderate majority who are willing to pay reasonable costs (both directly and indirectly) to achieve clean air and water, without carrying any policy to extremes. In particular, we believe most people are willing to tolerate small amounts of aesthetic and environmental damage in areas that are important for national security, economic stability or further economic growth, as long as most of the populated areas are being steadily improved and the recreational areas enlarged. Their objective will not be the impossible one of zero environmental damage or no change, but rather to accept the bad with the good in changes which improve the overall quality of life by reasonable standards—including social stability and economic growth, where feasible.

We expect that with the passage of time there will be fewer struggles over life-and-death or critical health decisions and severe economic damage, but instead efforts will be increasingly focused on aesthetic or quality-of-life issues—

perhaps even relatively marginal ones. Only fanatics will feel personally defeated (or see a disaster for mankind) each time a power plant is sited, an oil tract leased or a pipeline built. The majority will learn that new power plants are much cleaner and safer than the ones of the 1960's; that drilling for oil can be done in new ways that reduce by 90 percent or more the danger of spillage and contamination of beaches and marine life; and that pipelines can be built aesthetically with only temporary scarring over small areas. Indeed, this will constitute progress, and for their part in it the environmentalists and others who fought the early battles are to be thanked. Many mistakes and setbacks will certainly occur, as a result of overzealous programs or excessive political pressure. But probably by 10 or 15 years from now, almost certainly by the year 2000, it is very likely that we will be able to look back with great pride on our accomplishments. We will breathe clean air, drink directly from rivers and enjoy pleasing landscapes.

VII

The Difficult Long-Term Environment: Maintaining Earth's Fragile Envelope

WE NOW COME TO some of the most misunderstood but, at the same time, important and dramatic environmental issues. If it subsequently turns out that "progress"—as exemplified by science, technology and industrialization—is judged to have been a mistake, the most likely reason for such a retroactive judgment would be that mankind precipitated a major catastrophe or inadvertently triggered some inexorable disastrous process that passed a point of no return. The most obvious example, of course, would be a large-scale and indiscriminate nuclear war. Another would be an irreversible cooling of the earth leading to a relatively rapid emergence of a new ice age. The converse may be even more likely—the heating of the earth and melting of the ice caps—but in our opinion this would not be an overwhelming catastrophe that would tip the balance against progress. Or a portion of the ozone layer could be destroyed, or perhaps large parts of the ocean overloaded with excessive toxic waste. (Both of these also would presumably be limited catastrophes, comparable to many historical events.) Some scientist might accidentally release a mutated virus into the environment which would cause a disastrous epidemic, or accidentally an equally dangerous virulent agent might be transported from Mars or Venus to the earth. Conceptually, there are probably many other scientific innovations or new technological processes that might appear so quickly that those exposed could neither adjust to the phenomenon nor negate it in time to avert a major or total disaster. In any case, various kinds of limited difficulties or local disasters are probably inevitable. But most people have been willing to accept such risks as one of the many costs of progress—an attitude that is not expected to change quickly.

TECHNOLOGY AND THE FAUSTIAN BARGAIN

Thus science and technology—which in Western civilization removed poverty, illiteracy, hunger, frequent and severe disease, and short life spans for the majority of people and created for them instead relative affluence, improved health and medical care, longer life expectancy and a sense of increasing power—now appear to some groups to raise a general threat to the continuation of our civilization. Yet civilization has made a commitment to science, technology and industry— one that might indeed be called a "Faustian bargain." For, as we remember, Faust (in Goethe's play) bought magical (that is, secular) knowledge and powers that he was compelled to use and then perforce he had to proceed to the next experience, the next project—or be forever damned. And that illustration provides a good analogy with some formulations (not ours) of the current predicament. We do agree that mankind is involved in a process that probably cannot voluntarily and safely be stopped, or prematurely slowed down significantly, even if there are good arguments for doing so. But we maintain that on balance and with some exceptions (for example, nuclear proliferation), the arguments are heavily against deliberate policies to halt or slow down the basic long-term technological trend, even if it could be done with safety. Indeed, we would prefer to accelerate some aspects of this trend, while being prudent and generally watchful in order to prevent or reduce the impact of the baneful possibilities.

Those who suggest stopping or slowing technological progress face several problems. The foremost difficulty is the sheer political, economic and technical practicality of launching an effective campaign of this sort against the existing active opposition and/or apathy. While the zero-growth advocates and their followers may be satisfied to stop at this point, most others are not. Populations grow, and their aspirations cry out for satisfaction; prudence and foresight require that a high priority be assigned to creating an economic surplus and developing technological "muscles" and flexibility. New pressures arise regularly, impelling various "backward" groups to modernize in order to get their share of the available material rewards. Even the most advanced societies find moral as well as practical and selfish reasons for maintaining or accelerating their current momentum. Any serious attempt to frustrate these expectations or desires is likely to fail and/or create disastrous counterreactions. Some may argue that the people struggling for affluence have been brainwashed, that they are giving up "everything" for "nothing," but we believe they are responding reasonably to such objective pressures as overpopulation, national security and local poverty as well as such obvious aspirations as the revolution of rising expectations and/or the more or less clearly formulated image of what seems to be a highly desirable postindustrial society. Thus—extending our Faustian analogy—any concerted attempt to stop or even slow "progress" appreciably (that is, to be satisfied with the moment) is catastrophe-prone. At the minimum, it would probably require the creation of extraordinarily repressive governments or movements—and probably a repressive international system.

Most of the current no-growth advocates argue for a redistribution of resources as opposed to continued growth as a means of improving the current quality of life. But we have argued that many of these "reformers" do not mean what they say. They already have a high standard of living and do not see any real future gain for themselves if others improve their economic standards—although they may not recognize these as their true feelings. It appears to be true, as we have already indicated, that many in the upper middle class are "spending more and enjoying it less"; also there are many other legitimate and illegitimate sources of their opposition to growth. But whatever the reasoning of the "haves" may be, the "have-nots" would like to achieve a great deal more of the affluence they see before considering giving up their ambitions, and they are likely to be hostile to those who try to stop them—even if there is a good cause for doing so, and in their (and our) view the case is neither good nor plausible.

Indeed, we believe that our optimistic conclusions, set forth in previous chapters, on the outlook for energy, raw materials, food and near-term environmental issues are responsible and reasonable. But we do have our ambiguities and caveats, our fears and apprehensions about other aspects of progress—though they are not of the sort likely to be persuasive to the poor or even to most of the wealthy. Nevertheless, there are issues on which we share some of the uncertainties and failure of nerve afflicting so many of the doomsday prophets—not to the same extent or in the same way, but we do have a basic empathy with some of their arguments and concerns.

The biggest difference between us is in our conclusion that it is both safer and more rewarding to move forward with caution and prudence on the present course than to try to stop or even to slow down generally. But we are not fully confident that the results of moving ahead, even with care and wisdom, will necessarily prove to be without danger; we are only convinced that the odds favor this course. Indeed, we would estimate the odds at five to one or better that all the serious long-term problems will be successfully dealt with in due course—and at a cost that is acceptable in most people's judgments. We can only offer our best intuitive conclusion, but we do not believe any other practical policy has a better chance for avoiding great tragedy. In other words, we are optimistic about the long term; we believe that in time society will be able to cope with any technological problems—and we are confident that there will be sufficient time, though not always enough to avoid all trouble.

TECHNOLOGICAL INNOVATION: MISTAKES OF OMISSION AND COMMISSION

It is often suggested that adequate technology assessment (TA) studies should be required for any technical innovation before proceeding with commercial applications—that the burden of proof be placed on the people who want the innovation. It sounds reasonable to say that it is up to the innovator to prove that his innovation is safe, but there are some difficulties in this position. If as a general matter high standards of justification were set and enforced, many important projects would not get off the ground. Full and definitive TA studies of complex projects and phenomena are often simply not feasible. We have never seen an *a priori* analysis that would justify the conclusion: "Let's go ahead with the project; we understand the innovation and all of its first-, second- and third-order effects quite well. There can be no excessive danger or difficulties."

Indeed, many times the people looking for second-, third- and even fourth-order effects have often seriously erred about the first; in any case, they usually cannot establish the others with any certainty. For example, most of the limits-to-growth studies discussed in earlier chapters have many first-order facts wrong—a revealing sample of how difficult the problem is.

None of the above is meant as an argument against doing TA studies. On the contrary, in many cases much will be learned from such studies. But one cannot expect them to be complete and reliable, and placing too great a requirement on innovators doing such studies can simply be an expensive way of doing less; it entails all the problems and disutilities of excessive caution and of slowing down innovation in a poorly designed—and often capricious—manner.

The two basic kinds of innovative mistakes are those of commission and of omission. The first is illustrated by the case of DDT, discussed in the previous chapter, and by the cyclamate episode. In 1969, the U.S. Food and Drug Administration banned cyclamates (a widely used substitute for sugar in diet food and soft drinks) because rats that were fed heavy doses during most of their lives developed bladder cancer. It has now been revealed, however, that the original research that led to this finding did not permit any firm conclusions to be drawn about cyclamates since they were tested in combination with other chemicals. In addition, subsequent studies have failed to corroborate the original findings. Not only may this abrupt and premature ban have deprived numerous persons suffering from diabetes and hypertension of a medical benefit, but it also cost the food and soft drink industries an estimated $120 million. In this case the mistake of commission swamped the potential cost of a mistake of omission. In choosing between avoiding a clear danger by doing something and avoiding a less clear—though potentially much greater—danger by deciding not to do something, society usually does prefer the former.

The mistake of omission can be illustrated by considering what might happen today if a firm tried to get aspirin accepted as a new product. It is known that even a small amount of aspirin can create stomach or intestinal bleeding, and in some persons larger amounts can cause ulcers or other serious side effects. Furthermore, we still know very little about how aspirin operates. Thus one could argue rather persuasively that if a pharmaceutical company tried to introduce aspirin now it would fail to pass the standards. And yet, because of its effectiveness as a cure or palliative for so many ailments, it is probably one of the most useful drugs available. Indeed, there is now a good deal of argument that the FDA is causing more harm by excessively slowing down the introduction of new remedies than it would if the rules were relaxed a bit.*

As another example, let us assume that the U.S. authorities had made a TA study of the automobile in 1890. Assume also that this study came up with an accurate estimate that its use would result eventually in more than 50,000 people a year being killed and maybe a million injured. It seems clear that

* See "FDA Rapped for Delay on New Drugs," *Science*, September 12, 1975, p. 864, reporting a study by two University of Rochester pharmacology professors on this issue.

if this study had been persuasive, the automobile would never have been approved. Of course, some now say that it never should have been. But we would argue that society is clearly willing to live with this cost, large and horrible as it is. In Bermuda, which restricts drivers to 20 miles an hour, there are almost no fatal accidents except with cyclists. On Army bases, which restrict speed to 15 miles an hour, fatal accidents are unknown. Similar speed limits could be introduced in the United States if they were wanted, but the majority of Americans apparently prefer 50,000 deaths a year to such drastic restrictions on their driving speeds. In fact, the recent nation-wide reduction to a maximum speed of 55 miles an hour to save gasoline clearly is saving thousands of lives a year, but there is little pressure to go further in this direction.

Another problem with technology assessments is that even a good TA would not have made a satisfactory prediction of the impact of the automobile—that is, on the one hand predicting the accident rate and related first-order difficulties, and on the other what society would be willing to accept. And it is even less likely that the TA would have foreseen accurately many of the secondary impacts of the automobile on society (just to take a small example, recall the influence of the automobile on social and sex mores in the 1920's and 1930's, or the role of the U.S. automobile industry in helping to win World War II).

This is precisely the question that corners us: Every technology assessment study depends on having reasonable data, theory and criteria available, and all are unreliable and quite limited in practice. Perhaps 100 or 200 years from now man will both analyze and control his future much better than at present; thus it seems plausible that there may be fewer problems of misunderstood or inappropriate innovation two centuries from now. And especially if man has become dispersed throughout the solar system in independently survivable colonies, there would be a much smaller possibility of doomsday. Moreover, if such a disaster were to occur on earth, it probably would be through politics or bureaucratic mistakes associated with war, rather than inexorable or accidental physical processes leading to total catastrophe.

It is easy and even tempting to many people simply to ignore the costs and moral issues associated with mistakes of omission. Indeed, most people might prefer being responsible for a mistake of omission than one of commission, even if the latter were much smaller. This is particularly true, as we have pointed out, if one has been raised in an upper-middle-class environment and has achieved a comfortable status. But most of the world is not satisfied with the economic status quo. It is important for these people to move forward; they are willing to accept great costs if necessary and to take great risks as well in order to improve their economic status. They want aspirins and automobiles, whatever uncertainties and terrible costs may be associated with them. On the other hand, the major pressures to retard economic development and technological progress in many parts of the world are for safety—safety from the environment, safety from the possibility of outside intervention, safety from internal political unrest, and safety from accidental disturbance of natural balances in the forces of nature.

Some years ago, after nuclear testing began in the Pacific, the debate arose about the acceptability of subjecting people to the threat that these tests could cause bone cancer or leukemia. The main question was whether this possibility was sufficiently large to justify suspending further testing. Almost everybody at that time accepted the assumption that every megaton of fission yield would probably cause 1,000 new cases of bone cancer or leukemia worldwide. Because this increase might not actually be detectable in the incidence of these diseases, many people argued that the harm was negligible. Others argued that no one would test the bomb with even one person on the island if it meant killing this person. What then gave us the right to continue testing just because the deaths would be anonymous? It would appear that people are more willing to accept deaths which are not traceable to specific causes, but only when they cannot clearly identify the victims ahead of time—and thereby possibly prevent those deaths.

It is simply a truism that most activities in our society have a finite chance of resulting in some death. For example, it was once the rule of thumb that, on the average, every $1 million worth of construction resulted in the death of one worker; this appalling ratio has decreased dramatically until now it must be something like one worker per $100 million in construction. But obviously this expectation does not stop us from putting up buildings, even of the most frivolous kind. The same principle is involved in an example cited earlier—society's unwillingness to lower the death rate in traffic accidents by reducing speed limits. It is not a sufficient answer that in the case of the automobile one voluntarily accepts the risks to which he is subjected. There are many people who would like to curb the automobile but who nevertheless run the same risk of accident as those who oppose curbs. In our view, there is nothing intrinsically immoral about society subjecting its citizens to this risk when a majority have evidently concluded that the benefits outweigh the risks and the risk is of a more or less customary sort.

Another important issue arises when the damages are spread out over time—an issue that was long misunderstood partly because of a misleading theory of the English biologist John Haldane. According to his theory, any negative genetic mutation was bad, but minor mutations could ultimately cause more damage than lethal mutations. The argument went as follows: Assume a fixed population. Assume that a parent with a defective gene passes it to one of his children. Thus every defective gene, if it does not result in premature death, is transmitted to an individual in the next generation. If the gene is lethal, it results in immediate death in the next generation and the matter is finished; there is no further inheritance. If the gene is not lethal but has a tendency to cause colds, then this gene can be passed on for many, many generations until eventually it will cause a cold in the bearer at a time when catching a cold tips the scales against the bearer and causes him to die. Then, of course, the gene would no longer be passed along in the future. Notice what happened here. The lethal gene caused an immediate death and was finished. But not only did the less lethal gene also cause death eventually and with mathematical certainty, but along the way it resulted in much damage, giving many people colds over many generations. Therefore, according to Haldane's theory, if anything, the nonlethal mutated gene caused more damage than the lethal mutation. This is certainly mathematically correct, but it ignores such issues as time-discounting and rate of occurrence, both of which should be added to the analysis when the damage is spread over many generations. It is difficult for most people to understand this concept because they often interpret it to mean that the damage is more tolerable because it is our grandchildren, not we, who will bear it; an inference which appears to be the height of irresponsibility. As a result, many scientists have come to the improper conclusion that damage spread out over time is just as bad as damage which occurs in one generation.

But consider the following counterexamples: Imagine that society must choose between four situations: (1) 100 percent of the next generation would be killed; (2) 10 percent of the next 10 generations would be killed; (3) 1 percent of the next 100 generations would be killed; and (4) a tenth of a percent of the next 1,000 generations would be killed. In the first case, one has an end of history—everybody is dead. In the last case, great damage occurs, yet it is scarcely apparent because it is spread out over such a long period of time and among so many people. Clearly the first choice is intolerable; the fourth, while tragic and nasty, could certainly be better tolerated under most circumstances—indeed, in many situations similar to the fourth case, it would not be possible to measure the damage or prove that it existed. Any analysis of the difference between the first and fourth situations must take account of this spread over time, even though the total number of people killed is exactly the same.

This example is applicable to many of the environmental problems we should consider, such as the disposal of radioactive wastes and various toxic chemicals, both of which entail the remote possibility of an accident to some unknown group of people in the distant future. It also applies to many of the issues involving genetic damage of one sort or another, in which the injury may be shared by many generations or be inflicted on future generations.

One last point in this connection is almost frivolous and

we would hesitate to mention it if it did not come up so often. If there is a constant probability of some random event occurring, then no matter how small the probability, sooner or later the event will occur. This is an accurate but insignificant observation because the underlying assumptions and conditions practically never happen. It is similar to noting that exponential growth will not continue indefinitely because of the finite character of the earth, solar system or galaxy. Since we know that in reality exponential processes cannot be sustained, the question is simply what causes such curves to turn over, when this is likely to occur and what happens when they do. Similarly, what about the argument that mankind must be disaster-prone because so many of its activities carry with them some small probability of causing catastrophes? One reply is that conditions are changing with extraordinary rapidity and the problems associated with present activities may have little or no validity in the long term. In fact, this may be particularly true of such things as genetic damage caused by radiation or chemical pollution—or by pollution generally. It seems quite probable that, within a century or so, man will be able to prevent such damage, and that calculations of accumulated damage 10 to 100 generations from now will probably turn out to be irrelevant. In fact, it is a major theme of this chapter that most predictions of damage hundreds of years from now tend to be incorrect because they ignore the curative possibilities inherent in technological and economic progress. Of course, this reasoning would not apply to a world in which technological and economic progress were halted, but we do not consider that a likely possibility.

THE DIFFICULT ISSUES: POSSIBILITIES FOR CATASTROPHE

Let us now, in the remainder of this chapter, discuss briefly some of the specific issues which concern us all, neo-Malthusians as well as technology-and-growth advocates. We do not expect to settle any of these issues—only to formulate and illustrate some of the concerns. Some of the possibilities set forth are probably very real; in any case, no one can say now that certain events would *not* occur. But at the same time no one can show, in a rigorous and documented way, that they will be as important and dangerous as some of the publicists and experts claim—or even that they will exist (as opposed to being potential matters of concern to any prudent individual). Their "realities" are largely unknown quantities, particularly given the fact that these problems are almost all in the future and that future progress might very well remove most of the dangers or costs. And while some would argue that we should choose the "safe" no-growth strategy now, they overlook the enormous costs and risks involved in slowing down or making innovations more difficult.

We will begin with perhaps the most discussed issue of all—the dangers of unrestrained exponential growth. The literature is filled with predictions of the sensational consequences that could result from such continued growth. For example, a 3 percent annual growth in energy consumption could liberate enough heat to cause the oceans to boil after about 350 years. A less extravagant but still rigid calculation assumes a stable world population in the year 2100 of 20 billion, each consuming an average of three times as much energy as the average U.S. citizen consumes today—which, with today's technology, would release heat roughly equal to 1 percent of the solar energy at the earth's surface (about 10 times that projected in Chapter III). Initial calculations indicate that the average global temperature would increase 4 to 6 degrees Fahrenheit and the average temperature at the poles might increase as much as 20 degrees Fahrenheit. The Arctic Ocean ice pack might permanently melt, but this condition would not markedly increase the level of the oceans since the Arctic Ocean ice is a floating mass. If the Greenland and Arctic ice caps also dissolved over a period of centuries, substantially raising the level of the oceans, this would hardly mean the end of human society. Major shifts might be forced in agricultural areas and in coastal cities. On the other hand, a warmer average temperature might bring into production huge agricultural areas in Canada and Siberia. No one knows whether desert areas such as the Sahara or the Australian outback would increase or decrease in size. In any case, energy use at such a rate, if feasible at all, is more than a century away. Most importantly, however, these calculations ignore the likely increase in the efficiency of the generation, conversion and use of energy a century or two from now, which, according to our conservative estimates in Chapter III, would reduce the heating by a factor of four—and to the extent that various forms of solar energy are used, the heat generated would be even less. Once these factors are taken into account in the analysis, the likelihood of any of the dire events discussed above just about disappears.

Paradoxically, some scientists have indicated that the earth will tend to cool in the near future; in fact, some have warned of an oncoming glacial period. It is tempting to speculate that a very sophisticated approach to the future climate would permit mankind to balance natural forces with his own activities to maintain indefinitely the global heat balance and the earth's average temperature; but it is necessary to improve substantially the simulations and calculations of natural heat-balance changes as well as the effects from man's activities in order to achieve sufficient understanding of these phenomena. And there would seem to be plenty of time to do this—and even to take corrective action if necessary.

Of primary importance to mankind is the maintenance of reasonable proportions in the chemical constituents of the biosphere—especially of the atmosphere. The oxygen content of the atmosphere has been balanced for over a billion years through various factors: production by photosynthesis and consumption both by the oxidation of minerals exposed through weathering and by the oxidation of carbon through decomposition of plants. Recently, concern has been expressed that this oxygen balance is a delicate one—for instance, that a large spill of a hypothetical biocidal chemical or some new disease might kill enough green plant life to cause a small drop in the production rate of oxygen. The consequent lowered concentration might permit larger amounts of lethal ultraviolet light to reach the earth's surface, further stifling photosynthesis. Such a cycle might continue until there was very little oxygen left in the atmosphere and thus very little life left on earth. On the other hand, many plants are protected against lethal ultraviolet rays, and it is hard to imagine a biocidal chemical—or even a new biological disease—spreading to such an extent as to rival the expansion of the glaciers, which caused no noticeable change in the oxygen concentration of the atmosphere. Thus concern over the oxygen cycle seems premature, if valid at all.

The atmosphere's carbon dioxide content, however, will remain a closely watched potential threat for some time. Since roughly 1850, a rapidly increasing use of fossil carbons in the combustion of petroleum, natural gas and coal has led to a steadily increasing concentration of carbon dioxide (CO_2) in the atmosphere. This increase in CO_2 conceivably has one main effect—the trapping of long-wave infrared radiation from the surface of the earth, which tends to increase the temperature of the atmosphere. The observed increase in average global temperature of about 2 degrees Fahrenheit between 1850 and 1940 was attributed to this cause. However, since 1940 the average global temperature has decreased about half a degree Fahrenheit—a decrease attributed to the presence of soot in the atmosphere from industrial emissions, even though these emissions have been falling in recent years. It is very likely that the CO_2 concentration of the atmosphere will increase about 15 percent by the year 2000. This might cause an increase in the average global temperature of 1 to 2 degrees Fahrenheit. It has been calculated that a *doubling* of the CO_2 content would lead to an increase in average temperature of 4 to 6 degrees Fahrenheit, but it seems unlikely now that the carbon dioxide content will ever double unless mankind wants it to happen. Consequences of such increases in concentration cannot be reliably predicted today; in 50 years or so, such predictions might be routine. In any event, a carbon dioxide catastrophe does not appear to be imminent.

Another claim of possible long-term damage is related to the use of nitrogen fertilizers. There is evidence that the heavy application of chemical fertilizers to the soil, while increasing total crop production, leads to lower efficiency in the utilization of soil nutrients. The noted environmental scientist Dr.

Barry Commoner believes that nitrate fertilizer fails to rebuild the humus in the soil. He argues that the excess nitrate is leached from the earth, washed to the rivers, and ultimately to the lakes and oceans where it stimulates eutrophication. And, whether or not this is the cause, the eutrophication or clogging of lakes by overgrowth of algae is undoubtedly a problem in the waterways of most industrialized countries. In addition, Dr. Commoner suggests that nitrate and, in some cases, bacterial-produced nitrites can lead to poisoning of humans, particularly infants, and that excessive nitrates do get into water supplies and food.

For these reasons, Commoner believes that the present stress on nitrogen fertilizer has already produced important environmental hazards and carries the risk of serious medical dangers. He considers corrective measures urgent, and in his view, this would mean the limitation of the use of nitrogen fertilizers in agriculture, as well as the control of automotive emissions of oxides of nitrogen. The problem of automotive emissions may be solved by advanced engines or improved fuels. But if agricultural yields were decreased by limits placed on the use of nitrogenous fertilizers, there could be severe effects on food supplies for the world's population. Most agricultural scientists seem to disagree with Dr. Commoner's arguments and conclusions. Again, there is no immediate threat to life itself, but certainly the nitrogen cycle should be researched and in any case bears watching. Even if his arguments were found to be correct, and no technological correction were possible, we believe that the world would accept a small increase in the death rate and the other attendant problems rather than suffer the consequences of a catastrophic decrease in food production.

Regarding the highly toxic chemical compounds containing metals such as mercury, lead and arsenic, it appears to be clear that dangerous concentrations of these elements can be controlled. For instance, the mercury scare of the early 1970's led to stringent control of the release of mercury into waterways, and at present there appears to be little significant danger from that element to the general population. Similarly, the other toxic chemicals almost certainly can be adequately controlled whenever they appear to be posing a threat to the general health and welfare.

One of the primary roles of the atmosphere is to shield life on earth from the deadly ultraviolet rays of the sun. Most of this protection is afforded by the ozone, a gas formed by the interaction of sunlight and oxygen. Ozone happens to absorb ultraviolet light, thereby preventing most of the ultraviolet rays from penetrating to the earth's surface. We now know much more about ozone and upper-atmosphere reactions thanks to the debate over the supersonic transport (SST) and its effects on the stratosphere. The Department of Transportation and the National Academy of Sciences have recently published extensive reports containing the latest scientific evaluation and analysis of upper-atmosphere conditions and reactions. Both indicate that the main threat to the ozone layer from a fleet of SST's would be from the nitrogen oxides produced by the high-temperature reaction of atmospheric oxygen and nitrogen in the turbine engines; water vapor, sulfur dioxide and particulates formed by the engines may also interact with the ozone layer. Even so, it is doubtful that an SST fleet in daily operation throughout the world would have a noticeable cumulative effect. Certainly, once more, careful monitoring is in order to determine if there might be a problem.

The investigations produced a new problem, however. Scientists at Harvard suddenly realized that freon, used widely in aerosol sprays, seems likely to rise slowly but surely from the surface of the earth into the stratosphere, where it may be split by sunlight, releasing free chlorine. The chlorine can react with the ozone, leading to some depletion of the protective layer. Calculations seem to show that the amount of freon already released into the lower atmosphere will contribute to a decrease in the ozone concentration during the next several decades. The question then is, at what point will the decreased ozone allow sufficient ultraviolet light to reach the earth and cause a significant threat to plant, animal and human life? Again, the answer is still unknown. In certain circumstances, sunlight can cause skin cancer. Adding to the complexity of the situation is the fact that higher than normal amounts of freon have been detected in the snows of Antarctica, suggesting that some of the freon is frozen out once it is brought to the South Pole by atmospheric circulation. Certainly the freon problem represents another case for extensive monitoring and analysis—a program now under way.

Another potential threat to the ozone layer and to the heat balance of the earth are clouds produced by high-altitude aircraft, both regular and supersonic. Some measurements have indicated an increase in cloudiness over the earth already. Besides interacting with the ozone, possibly a minor effect, clouds have two effects on the heat balance of the earth: They reflect solar radiation, and they decrease the outgoing terrestrial radiation at the top of the atmosphere. The first effect lowers the temperature of the earth's surface; the second raises it. Current calculations indicate that a 1 percent change in skycover would have a negligible effect on the temperature of the earth's surface, if the clouds now reflect half of the earth's outgoing radiation. Additional calculations are in progress.

Another threat, and one that could conceivably be of the sudden-death variety, is related to possible genetic changes. For example: very recently, scientists at the Stanford University School of Medicine were able to combine genetic information from two different sources into a single biologically functional DNA molecule. In other words, they successfully carried out some rather advanced and potentially very powerful genetic engineering and manipulation. In fact, they were able to combine part of the genes of a bacterium with the genes from a toad. They called the results "chimeras" because conceptually they were similar to the mythological chimera, a creature with the head of a lion, the body of a goat and the tail of a serpent. These research workers (and others) were so alarmed by their own success that they formed a group in the National Academy of Science that sought voluntary deferral of potentially hazardous experiments involving recombinant DNA molecules. For instance, one might be able to develop a bacterium which could produce a disease with no known antibody, thereby causing a catastrophic threat to life. This research is continuing under rigorous standards for public and environmental safety. It is an area fraught with both potential benefits and potential harm, and very careful research would appear to be justifiable on balance. But it is also a grey area—and the question arises as to who should be balancing potential effects and making decisions. Because of the dangers involved, some have suggested that future research of this kind be carried on in earth-orbiting laboratories, when these become feasible, or in other highly controlled and isolated environments.

The reader can see, even from the limited number of issues presented above, that concern and prudence are indeed warranted. The more one is involved in such studies, the more one tends to develop a sense of the "fragility" of the environment, but it is also worth noting that this sense can be misleading. Man has already experienced many disasters and strains in the earth's history. In fact, it is less than 10,000 years since the last ice age. Furthermore, man's impact normally is much less than that of natural forces and processes. Finally, both the environment and most ecological systems must be tough and largely self-correcting or self-healing; otherwise, neither would have survived to date.

It may yet turn out that future man will marvel at the paradoxical combination of hubris and modesty of 20th-century man, who, at the same time, so exaggerated his ability to do damage and so underestimated his own ability to adapt to or solve such problems. Or it could be that future man, if he exists, will wonder at the recklessness and callousness of 20th-century scientists and governments.

VIII

From Present to Future: The Problems of Transition to a Postindustrial Society

WE HAVE A DIFFICULT TASK in this chapter. At this point, hopefully, the reader is at least aware of our various arguments that any limits to growth are more likely to arise from psychological, cultural or social limits to demand, or from incompetency, bad luck and/or monopolistic practices interfering with supply, rather than from fundamental physical limits on available resources. Thus, as we imply by the title of this chapter, most of our basic concerns about the long-term future should not be on the technological issues already discussed (with the exception of long-term environmental problems) but on the issues on which mankind is more likely to make wrong decisions, in part because they are not understood and in part because they are genuinely uncertain and/or intractable. Even with excellent leadership and good luck, the outcomes can vary enormously.

BASIC CURRENT DIRECTIONS AND CONTEXT

It seems to us that we can best focus our discussion by introducing what we call the basic, long-term "multifold trend" of Western culture. This is a set of interacting trends, many of which go back almost 1,000 years, which together seem to us to represent the most basic tendencies in the evolution of Western culture—and, especially since World War II, in much of the rest of the world.

Examining what have been thought of as the largely desirable aspects of this trend gives us a reasonably good idea of what has been meant by the term "progress" in the last 200–300 years. It is interesting to realize that at most times in the last 1,000 years elites in various Western subcultures would have been horrified at many of the developments that were to take place in the "next 200 years." While there is some reason to believe that this will be less true of our generation, it would be surprising if the rule did not hold for us—almost certainly for some developments, perhaps for most. However, what we call the "topping out" phenomenon may limit the kinds of change we in the United States would find most objectionable—that is, in certain areas (crime, violence, drugs, promiscuity, etc.) we expect a reversal of past tendencies to begin very soon.

The basic elements of this multifold trend are outlined below. The reader will note that some of these points have emerged in our discussion, in earlier chapters, of the various issues facing the world.

1. Declining role of traditional and "intuitive" (that is, common sense) behavior and increasing role of explicit, manipulative rationality and social engineering applied to social, political, cultural and economic issues as well as to shaping and exploiting the material world. Increasing importance of theoretical and academic formulations and knowledge as opposed to experience and on-the-job training. Also, and perhaps inevitably, increasing problems of ritualistic or pseudo-rationality and educated incapacity, as well as various reactions against rationality.

2. Increasingly sensate (that is, empirical, this-worldly, secular, humanistic, pragmatic, manipulative, explicitly rational, utilitarian, contractual and hedonistic) culture; recently an almost complete decline of the sacred and morally binding, and a relative erosion of widely accepted taboos and totems; some current signs of limited "romantic," mystic, transcendental or religious counterreactions.

3. Accumulation of scientific and technical knowledge; increasing use of this knowledge as man's most basic resource and a resultant increasing independence of geography and limited local resources.

4. Increasing affluence and (recently) increasing leisure and a revolution of "rising entitlements" as well as rising expectations; both the rich and the poor tend to get richer, almost everywhere.

5. The rise of bourgeois, bureaucratic, technocratic and "meritocratic" elites and specialists; growth of impersonal organizations and institutions; lessened dependence on familial and communal institutions.

6. Institutionalization of economic development and technological change, especially investment, research and development, innovation, and technological and institutional diffusion; recently an increasingly conscious emphasis on synergisms and serendipities; even more recently, a loss of nerve and growing opposition among upper-middle-class elites to so much "forced" rapid change, but much less opposition by various traditionalist groups in non-Western societies.

7. Worldwide industrialization and modernization; also growing concept and realization of a world ecumene (but ecumene not community, "world city" not "global village," and "world market" not "marketplace")—that is, impersonal and businesslike interactions as opposed to the close human ties implied by the words "community," "village" and "marketplace"; but also a growing, if still fragile, sense of "world public opinion" and of shared responsibility for all human beings.

8. Increasing capability—both private and national—for violence and destruction; growing tolerance for terrorists and politically motivated violence and those who support such activities.

9. Population growth—now explosive but tapering off; economic growth also explosive but may increase even more before tapering off.

10. Urbanization and recently suburbanization and urban sprawl; soon the growth of megalopoli—that is, increas-

ing movement to urban-suburban areas as opposed to rural; decreasing peak densities within these areas; partial merging and overlap of once separate urban areas.

11. Decreasing importance of primary and (recently) secondary occupations and goals; soon a shift from tertiary to quaternary occupations and goals; eventual emergence of postindustrial economy, institutions and culture.

12. Recent emergence of superindustrial economy and resultant dominating character of its impact on the social and physical environment.

13. Increasing literacy and role of mass formal education; recently the "knowledge industry" and increasing numbers and role of intellectuals and of decision-making and attitudes based on secondhand knowledge (for example, books, lectures and staff reports) as opposed to direct personal experience.

14. Future-oriented thinking, discussion and planning; recently some improvement in methodologies and tools—also some retrogression in the general level of discussion (even by futurologists).

15. Increasing universality of the multifold trend—but an increasingly felt need for national, ethnic, communal or other group differentiation and identification.

16. For 1,000 years, a more or less increasing tempo of change in all of the above; but perhaps a slowing down in next two or three decades—at least in some areas.

Listing the elements separately leads us into some arbitrary and artificial distinctions and categories, but one could think of this multifold trend as a single entity, the various elements overlapping, reinforcing and changing each other. Every element is both a driving force and a consequence (although some should be viewed more as one than the other). While the multifold trend as presented is more applicable to Western culture than to the world as a whole, it is becoming increasingly universal.

We have already emphasized that we do not expect the road to the year 2000, much less 2176, to be smooth. There

are lots of wiggles and reversals in the basic trends. Our studies
have identified almost 70 separate problems which we call the
"1985 Technological Crises" (see Table 17); we expect that

Table 17. 1985 Technological Crises

By 1985 the following areas are likely to give rise to special technological
dangers:

1. Intrinsically dangerous technology
2. Gradual worldwide and/or national contamination or degradation of the environment
3. Spectacular and/or multinational contamination or degradation of the environment
4. Dangerous internal political issues
5. Upsetting international consequences
6. Dangerous personal choices
7. Bizarre issues

1. Intrinsically dangerous technology

   a. Modern means of mass destruction
   b. Nuclear reactors—fission or fusion
   c. Nuclear explosives, high-speed gas centrifuges, etc.
   d. Research missiles, satellite launchers, commercial aircraft, etc.
   e. Biological and chemical "progress"
   f. Molecular biology and genetics
   g. "Mind control"
   h. New techniques for insurgency, criminality, terror or ordinary violence
   i. New techniques for counterinsurgency or imposition of order
   j. New serendipities and synergisms

2. Gradual worldwide and/or national contamination or degradation of the environment

   a. Radioactive debris from various peaceful nuclear uses
   b. Possible greenhouse or other effects from increased CO_2 in the atmosphere, new ice age because of dust in stratosphere, damage to ozone layer, etc.
   c. Other special dangerous wastes—methyl mercury, PCB, etc.
   d. Waste heat
   e. Other less dangerous but environment degrading wastes such as debris and garbage
   f. Noise, ugliness and other annoying by-products of many modern activities
   g. Excessive urbanization
   h. Excessive overcrowding
   i. Excessive tourism
   j. Insecticides, fertilizers, growth "chemicals," food additives, plastic containers, etc.

Table 17. (continued)

3. Spectacular and/or multinational contamination or degradation of the environment

   a. Nuclear war
   b. Nuclear testing
   c. Bacteriological and chemical war or accident
   d. Artificial moons
   e. Supersonic transportation (shock waves)
   f. Weather control
   g. Big "geomorphological" projects
   h. Million-ton tankers (Torrey Canyon was only 111,825 tons) and million-pound planes
   i. Other enterprise or mechanism of "excessive" size

4. Dangerous internal political issues

   a. Computerized records
   b. Other computerized surveillance
   c. Other advanced techniques for surveillance
   d. Excessively degradable (or unreliably reassuring) centralized capabilities
   e. Improved knowledge of and techniques for agitprop and other means of creating disturbances
   f. Improved knowledge of, and techniques for, preventing disturbances
   g. Complex or critical governmental issues leading to either "technocracy" or "Caesarism"
   h. Nuclear weapons affecting internal politics
   i. Excessively illusioned attitudes
   j. Other dangerous attitudes

5. Upsetting international consequences

   a. Both new and "traditional" demonstration effects
   b. Technological obsolescence of "unskilled" labor
   c. New synthetics—e.g., coffee, oil, etc.
   d. Forced modernization
   e. Growing guilt feelings by many in wealthy nations—particularly among the alienated or young
   f. Inexpensive and widely available "realistic" communications and physical travel
   g. Accelerated "brain drains"
   h. Cheap (synthetic?) food
   i. Cheap education
   j. Control and exploitation of the oceans, space, moon

6. Dangerous personal choices

   a. Sex determination
   b. Other genetic engineering
   c. Psychedelic and mood-affecting drugs

Table 17. (continued)

---

d. Electronic stimulation of pleasure centers
e. Other methods of sensual satisfaction
f. Excessive permissiveness and indulgence
g. Dropping out and other alienation
h. Excessive narcissism or other self-regard
i. Super-cosmetology
j. Lengthy hibernation

7. Bizarre issues

   a. Generational changes—e.g., extended longevity
   b. Mechanically dependent humans—e.g., pacemakers
   c. Life and death for an individual—e.g., artificial kidneys, etc.
   d. New forms of humanity—e.g., "live" computers
   e. "Forcible" birth control for "impossible" groups
   f. Other external controls or influence on what should be a personal or even institutionally private choice
   g. Life and death or other control of "outlaw" societies which have not yet committed any traditional crime
   h. Even the continuation of the nation-state system
   i. Controlling and limiting change and innovation
   j. Radical ecological changes on a planetary scale
   k. Interplanetary contamination

some of these will be dealt with well, but many will not be. The future may well hold in store not only the familiar "four horsemen" (war, famine, plague and civil disorder), but more modern catastrophes as well. A useful analogy can be made between the first half of the 20th century and our present situation. If anyone in 1910 had used the period 1890–1910 as a baseline and applied current techniques to make projections for the next 50 years and restricted himself to economic and technological variables, he would have made quite accurate long-term predictions (that is, as of 1960), though he might have been off for much of the intervening period. Events such as two world wars, the Great Depression, bloody revolutions and many economic and technological innovations first caused lags in the curve of development and then produced a "catching up" phenomenon. The forces behind technological and economic growth had a surprising staying power and intensity that enabled them to make up in prosperous years for deviations from basic trends in troubled ones. This suggests that the trends disclosed during the period 1890–1910 were relatively basic, and that much of the rest of the first half of the 20th century was "aberrant"—a position we would accept.

We are not arguing that this basic trend in economics and technological variables will continue indefinitely—quite the contrary, as we have seen in the S-shaped curves we have projected for population and economic growth. But we do believe it will continue, even if it is with the "topping out" and other modifications indicated.

It is most useful at this point to concentrate first on the next decade or two, for which we have a fairly good concept of what might happen, and then treat the later years in more general terms. The short-term projection given below essentially assumes a satisfactory recovery from the current recession, a relatively successful control of inflation and a reasonably stable world political order. And, as always, it also assumes that there is no catastrophe sufficiently large to change drastically the basic multifold trend. Looking, therefore, at just the next two decades, we would assume the period would be marked by the following features:

1. A basic change will occur in the character of the two fundamental curves of world population and GWP over time. Both curves should pass through a point of inflection (the population curve may have already passed through this point), so that from then on the metaphor of (worldwide) exponential growth will be increasingly misleading.

2. Barring extreme mismanagement or bad luck, the period 1976–85 should be characterized by the highest average rate of world economic growth in history, perhaps 6 percent, though by 1985 or soon thereafter the slowdown of the upper half of the distorted S-shaped curve should begin to be felt. At least for a while, an increasing emphasis is likely to be placed on monetary problems, commodity issues (including food, energy and resources) and neo-Malthusian concerns—and, of course, some possibility exists of a renewed depression. Some of the more significant themes of this decade seem likely to be:

   a. The demographic or GWP transition of #1 above.

   b. An unprecedented period, worldwide, of economic

growth, world peace, capital movements, world trade, tourism, etc.—but as in the previous *Belle Epoque* (1901–13) also a period of anarchistic movements, terrorism, *fin de siecle* feelings and many "tolerated" excesses.

c. The relatively full emergence of the superindustrial economy (which is also an emerging postindustrial economy).

d. A decade or two of technological crises (and of technological solutions).

e. The end of the post–World War II system politically, economically and financially.

f. A decade of institutional crisos (and of new developments and institutions to cope with these crises).

g. A (troubled?) period of value/attitude transitions.

h. The continued emergence of East Asia on the Asian and world stages—but with Japan more likely than China to play the most crucial role, at least for a time.

i. Nuclear proliferation (mostly clandestine and particularly—or solely—in the Third World).

j. The opening up of new sources of energy and other resources.

3. An increasingly multipolar political world which should result in a steady and nearly complete erosion of World War II politics (Cold War; distinction among World War II victors, losers and neutrals; colonization/decolonization issues; etc.), with the following possible consequences and developments:

a. More than 20 large nations that can be ranked in 1985 by GNP as follows (in billions of 1975 dollars and with an estimated range of plus-or-minus 20 percent around the indicated levels):

$2,500 United States
1,200 Japan and U.S.S.R.
  600 France and West Germany
  450 China
  250 Canada, Italy, United Kingdom
  150 Brazil, India, Mexico, East Germany, Poland, and perhaps Iran
   75 Netherlands, Sweden, Belgium, Australia, Argentina, Saudi Arabia and Switzerland

b. Rise of Japan as an economic, financial and technological superstate (and soon afterward as a political or military superpower also).

c. Full re-emergence of both Germanys (but with some critical political disabilities remaining).

d. Emergence of France as the largest national economy (at least in terms of nominal "purchasing power" or GNP) in Western Europe.

e. U.S.-Soviet strategic equality or possibly Soviet strategic superiority, accompanied by a relative decline of both in power, prestige and influence.

f. Possible Europe-wide security arrangements; possibly also a growing "Finlandization" of Europe, or other tendency for Europeans to be excessively conciliatory to the Soviets.

g. Some degree of settlement or normalization of national relations between the two sides of the divided nations of Korea and Germany, but the persistence of a high degree of separate national identity and a refusal, on one or both sides, to recognize such separation in permanent legal and moral terms.

h. A continued feeling that nuclear war, or even large conventional war, is unthinkable (the divided countries, India/Pakistan, and Arab/Israel could be exceptions, though even these confrontations may seem increasingly stable), but low-level violence, both official and unofficial, persists or even increases.

i. An evolving European Economic Community (with perhaps a new role for France as the leading nation of the community); also a possible breakup of the current EEC.

j. Possible creation of an East European EEC; most likely a growing independence of East European nations, perhaps even an explosive weakening of Soviet control.

k. The creation, at least ad hoc and perhaps even self-consciously, of an economically dynamic Pacific TIA * —perhaps similarly for a Western Europe-North Africa-Middle East-Central Africa TIA.

* Trading Investment Area—a group of countries who send and receive at least half their foreign trade and investments to and from each other.

l. Between 5 and 10 clandestine nuclear powers by the late 1980's (among the possibilities: Israel, Taiwan, South Korea, Pakistan, Iran, Egypt, Libya, Saudi Arabia, Brazil and Argentina).

m. Many other new possibilities: new alliances, new arms races, a politically unified Europe, an intensely isolationist and/or nationalist U.S., a deeply troubled and perhaps inwardly oriented U.S.S.R., and a unified and aggressive communist Indochina, a communist Italy or Portugal, a left- or right-wing Japan, a business-oriented, revisionist China, new trouble spots and confrontations, a Persian Gulf dominated by Iran.

4. This economic and technological ecumene will set a context for further development of a unified but multipolar, partially competitive, mostly global and technological economy characterized by:

a. A general understanding of the process and techniques for sustained economic development; also a worldwide capability for modern industry and technology and the development (erratic and incomplete but still largely effective) of the necessary domestic and international institutions to sustain such economic growth.

b. A worldwide Green Revolution (including new technologies) and enormous expansion in availability of energy and mineral resources, but, for the next few years, real difficulties in furnishing food, energy and fertilizer to the poor at a reliably low price. By the end of the period, or even sooner, there should be, as a result of technological progress and huge investment (including the intensive exploitation of the Arctic regions, oceans and many other currently unexploited areas), a surplus (as compared to today) of energy, resources and commodities.

c. Despite much hostility, a continuing, even growing importance of multinational corporations as innovators and diffusers of economic activity and as engines of rapid growth.

d. A great development of indexed contracts and financial instruments and perhaps a renewed role for gold in the international monetary system (the latter mainly as a store of value and perhaps as *numeraire*). The

SDR (special drawing rights) will also be developed as a world currency, but will almost certainly fail to achieve full acceptance. General recognition of inflation and "poverty of affluence" as basic and primary problems that compete with the need for full employment and mitigate the downside of the business cycle.

e. Some development of "futurology ideologies" and the reinvigoration of the concept of "progress," as opposed to "limits to growth" and "gap" ideologies, but these will also thrive in some quarters.

f. Sustained growth in international trade, communications, travel, investment, etc., and high (3-15 percent) GNP growth almost everywhere, especially in the "six dynamic areas" (Japan, "little neo-Sinic cultures," * Eastern Europe, southern Europe, part of Latin America,† most OPEC countries).

g. Increasing worldwide unity in technology, private industry, commercial and financial institutions, but relatively little unity in international legal and political institutions.

h. Increasing problems of unemployment in less-developed countries and labor shortages in developed countries; some partial solutions such as development of both official and unofficial institutions to move the labor to the work and the work to the labor; also two-way "brain drains."

i. Full emergence and partial solution or adaptation to many aspects of the 1985 technological crises.

j. But little or no overall long-term catastrophes with environment, pollution or the scarcity of resources, though many temporary crises will occur and doubtless some regional catastrophes (particularly with respect to food or pollution). Some thalidomide-type catastrophes. Many false alarms—for example, the banning of cyclamates.

---

* South Korea, Taiwan, Hong Kong, Singapore, perhaps North Korea and both Vietnams, and, if there are not sizable political and security problems, Thailand and Malaysia (respectively 10 percent and 35 percent ethnic Chinese).

† Brazil, Mexico, Colombia and perhaps others.

5. Some acceleration, continuation and selective topping out of the multifold trend of Western culture:

    a. Particularly among upper-middle-class elites in the "Atlantic Protestant culture" there should be a continued erosion of the traditional societal levers, a search for meaning and purpose, some cultural confusion, ideological polarization, social conflict, growth of discretionary behavior, etc.

    b. Increasingly revisionist communism, capitalism and Christianity in Europe and the Western Hemisphere, a continued crisis of liberalism, some persistence and even a new eruption of the counterculture

    c. Populist, conservative, backlash, or "counterreformation" movements.

    d. Increasing problem worldwide of educated incapacity —that is, illusioned, irrelevant, ideological or other impractical argumentation and attitude among intellectual elites, accompanied by greater emphasis on feelings and emotions among some of these.

    e. Further reaction to emerging postindustrial economies in developed nations (with about 25 percent of world's population) and in enclaves elsewhere, including:

        1) "New" political milieus: continued great influence of "humanist left" in at least the high culture of developed nations (but particularly in the U.S. and the northwest tier of Europe), and also a conservative reaction and even a large conservative counterreformation in universities and the high culture.

        2) Emergence of "mosaic cultures" (at least in U.S.) incorporating esoteric, deviant, communal and experimental life-styles. Some increase in anarchistic behavior and movements. Further ideological and political development, as well as continued erosion, of the counterculture.

        3) Possible successful synthesis between old and new, especially in France, Switzerland, Japan, Singapore and some of the "Atlantic Protestant" areas.

        4) Other developments of postindustrial societal institutions and postindustrial cultures.

6. A relatively anarchic but also relatively orderly and unified world, but with new issues of domestic and international stability:

  a. Much greater attention to basic human and emotional needs—for example, to the Chinese Communist guarantees (adequate food, clothing, shelter, health care, education, retirement and funeral expenses) and to Abraham H. Maslow's hierarchy of values and life goals (different emphases and priorities relative to one's affluence and state of safety).

  b. Continuing growth in both desirable and undesirable discretionary behavior; corresponding worldwide "law and order" issues—possible unconventional or even bizarre use of terror, violence, subversion, unilateral changes in international rules.

  c. Possibility of some bizarre ad hoc countermeasures.

  d. Some trend toward separatist and regionalist movements in many formerly stable nation-states as well as postwar decolonized states.

7. Emergence of many new technologies in such areas as energy sources, transportation, pollution control, food production, communications, genetics, other biological and related sciences; and, perhaps equally important, fantastic increase in the capability of information-processing systems and automation.

8. Initial, but not necessarily successful, moves toward a huge expansion into outer space. Much should be learned about the likely possibilities for outer space—and if these turn out to be favorable, a basis laid for perhaps an explosive exploitation and colonization in the 21st century.

9. Other important (both significant and insignificant) surprises and turning points.

10. Last, the world will no longer be thought of as being divided into a rich OECD world composed mostly of Japan and Western cultures, a communist world, and a Third World. Instead, the Comecon and OECD worlds and such areas as the little neo-Sinic cultures and some of the Persian Gulf countries will probably be lumped together as a highly developed world. Communist Asia will be considered a rapidly developing and quite successful

culture, even though nominally with a relatively low GNP per capita (about $1,000 by the year 2000). There will be a relatively successful portion (about half) of the Third World which should attain about $2,000 per capita by the year 2000 and a still desperately poor group, mostly concentrated in the Indian subcontinent but including limited parts of Latin America and Africa, which could (with reasonable policies) average about $200 per capita by the year 2000.

THE EROSION OF TRADITIONAL SOCIETAL LEVERS

It is clear that the world of the immediate future will be confusing, complex and very difficult to cope with. Among the features cited in this short-term projection that concern us most—and one to be considered a central issue for the transition, and possibly for the long term as well—is the erosion of the traditional societal levers and their replacement by other values, both transient and relatively permanent. It is primarily the upper middle class which has begun to experience this erosion at this point; perhaps three-fourths of the American people still share most traditional values. We believe, however, that the erosion may eventually affect the rest of society. Most importantly, we do not believe that America will perform adequately if the children of the upper classes remain unsocialized: Too much productive capacity will be lost, and too much damage will be done by them. But if we are correct and traditional values cannot be restored, then Americans will have to import, invent and inculcate new values. It is optimistic to believe that this can be done easily and consciously. Values are not ordinarily created *ex nihilo* or by speeches, but are formed, like nations, by blood and history and by slow evolution and growth. To the extent that it can be done, however, we should encourage the evolution of American values in certain directions. Some of these new values emerged in the early 1960's in many prestige universities and elsewhere, and while they were largely submerged during the middle and late 1960's, we believe that they can be revived. Indeed, the current "transition" and/or search for meaning and purpose seems likely to encourage them—particularly in the upper and upper middle class (that is, the high culture).

First among the possibilities is the graceful acceptance of affluence. Americans are going to be enormously wealthy, so they must learn how to spend their wealth without becoming satiated, disappointed or fashionably antimaterialistic. They have to learn to take certain everyday affairs seriously (without becoming obsessed with them) in order to avoid boredom, and to compensate for the fact that they no longer have life and death struggles to engage their emotions. They have to learn to be gentlemen and ladies who pass their time doing difficult—if not useful—things well.

Perhaps such a life sounds unbearably petty, but this is the result of not having to fight barbarians, Nazis, famine or disease or to conquer the frontier. Conflicts like these may have added flavor to life, but most people have always claimed that they would rather not have to fight for survival. In any event, hopefully such things are largely behind us, though doubtless some threats will remain and even grow if they are ignored too much. In their relative absence, Americans must be like the Athenians, who loved gymnastics. If there was a war, they performed gymnastics to stay fit in order to fight. If there was peace, they had more time for gymnastics. Unfortunately, Americans tend to be more like the Spartans and Romans, who got into shape to fight anticipated wars, but tended toward sloth in peacetime and prosperity. We must learn the virtues of family life and conversation and social interaction with our friends. Epicurean (in both the Greek and the modern senses) values will be vital to many if Americans are to spend their leisure time at home without killing everyone in sight because of overfamiliarity and boredom.

A primary problem will lie with government. If the developed world comes to seem relatively safe and affluent and if most of the remaining issues are regarded as conditions which may evolve over time but not as problems to be dealt with immediately, then governing may become an uncharis-

matic, low-morale profession. There may be no great programs
or crusades to attract people, but it will be just as necessary
then as it is now to recruit intellectually capable individuals
into government service. America will be a mature nation at
last, and will have accepted the democratic ideal as far as is
practical. Externally, some may choose to go adventuring in
outer space or to the bottom of the sea, but most will be
satisfied to watch everyone become richer and seemingly
safer—and enjoy these adventures vicariously.

If government is to continue in such an environment, a
class of people will have to be developed who serve because
they know it is necessary to do so. Their model will be the
English civil service, their goal will be maintenance and their
motto will be the epigram of William, Prince of Orange: "It
is not necessary to hope in order to act, nor succeed in order
to persevere." Such men will most resemble the stoics who ran
the Roman Empire for hundreds of years out of a sense of
duty, while the rest of the populace pursued their private interests. There is, in fact, a group in the United States who
already have these characteristics—that is, many military offi-
cers, who are expected to separate themselves from their families, risk their lives and perform menial tasks in peacetime and
who accept their duty like the soldiers they are.

The Founding Fathers believed that a democracy was impossible where the people lacked the republican virtues, by
which they meant moderation, self-discipline and modesty.
We have attempted to suggest some of the rationale behind
this position and how those virtues may be regained.

HOW SAFE WILL THE WORLD BE?

We have used such words as "relatively" and "apparent"
in discussing our future safety. How realistic is this "apparent"
safety? It should be understood that this impression of safety,
whether correct or not, can be powerful and overwhelming—
at least as related to most kinds of military threats that
might have been taken seriously in another era. Thus the

Australian government recently announced that its defense planning would be based on the assumption that no serious confrontation or crisis was likely to arise in the next decade. To accept this assumption, one must believe that 13.5 million people would not be challenged in their occupation of a continent-sized area with abundant resources and would not need to defend their possession of these scarce resources. Indeed, much of the developed world generally thinks in terms of "free security," and little connection is made between defense efforts and feelings of security. Ask any citizen of Canada or the United Kingdom (or of many other nations) if he would feel safer if the national defense budget were doubled or in greater danger if it was halved. In most cases the answer would be no to both questions.

Plausible as the Australian position may be, it has at least one serious defect. Such policies almost always lead to a further concept of "safe for the next ten years" as measured from a moving present. This allows for mobilization, if there is a serious perceived deterioration in international affairs, but by then there would almost certainly be great resistance to recognizing such deterioration and to reacting appropriately. Equally serious is the fact that the policy leaves the country almost completely unprepared for sudden changes in the security situation. It also encourages an almost reckless degree of complacency and carelessness.

It should be clear that it would be quite easy to write scenarios for the late 1980's and the 1990's in which the world degenerates into a kind of jungle—or in which some movement like communism suddenly takes on renewed vitality and dynamism—and for some of these scenarios there is no need to wait for the late 1980's. It would take us too far afield to describe the various possibilities for the weakening of the Western nations on the one hand and for the emergence of dangerous challenges on the other. We will content ourselves here only with the observation that it is unlikely that the history of large-scale international violence will be terminated simply because the world will have passed through the population and GWP inflection points—even though these two events do have many stabilizing aspects and do make conceivable and plausible (perhaps too plausible) an unprecedented degree of commitment to the status quo and peaceful evolution.

TRANSITIONAL PROBLEMS OF MORALE, ATTITUDES AND THE QUALITY OF LIFE

In the transition to postindustrial society, a vast group of intellectuals will be created as the need for expertise increases (and for self-serving reasons as well). These intellectuals may suffer from the most intense anomie of all social groups. In becoming a mass profession, they open themselves to sharper criticism as a group because their average standards necessarily decline, their contacts with outsiders wither, they become less self-conscious as a stratum but more actively self-serving, and they make clear their belief that they should wield social power. As this group's social status declines and its numbers rise, various segments will be organized, sometimes as an agency of government or other social institutions. Thus a key new form of social conflict becomes institutionalized. At the same time society faces a momentous political and social choice regarding the degree to which scholarship will be fragmented and autonomous or unified and harnessed to the tasks of other institutions. If one considers the acceptance of the zero economic growth thesis currently put forward by some groups, together with a willingness to organize and harness scholarship, one can imagine a trend over several centuries toward an essentially Confucian meritocratic social order dominated by self-serving and self-justifying—even if also communal and paternalistic—university-trained mandarins and bureaucracies.

We should also note that, just as the auspicious trends carrying us from feudal to industrial to postindustrial society have generated various new and pressing problems, so some of the projected auspicious trends of postindustrial society will certainly generate their own forms of dissatisfaction. For instance, some writers allege that a leisure revolution is likely to occur in the United States. Professionals and managerial workers have good reason to be skeptical about the growing leisure of postindustrial society, but it is at least imaginable that substantial proportions of the population will eventually work a three-day week and not "moonlight" during their four nonworking days. If so, the intense boredom that afflicted the aristocracy of the 18th and 19th centuries could return with a vengeance—but probably less as a mass phenomenon than as one which afflicts various self-conscious elites.

In the emerging postindustrial society the scale of industry expands to the point where the TVA becomes a middle-sized project, and the scope expands to include most of a continent if not the world. The coexistence of this phenomenon, which we call the "superindustrial society," with the postindustrial society, creates fundamental threats to the environmental stability and to recreational uses of the environment. The side effects of the huge scale and scope of modern industry are, of course, exacerbated by rising population—less of a long-run problem than is commonly supposed, but for the present it can cause severe difficulties in certain parts of the world such as India and China. As already stated, we do not believe the world in general or the United States in particular will suffer from long-term shortages of energy or resources, or that continued superindustrial development is inconsistent with a clean environment. Nor does population growth in the United States need to create overcrowding of living areas in any strong sense—as we have already demonstrated in our demographic discussions. However, superindustrial society does imply the following: difficult transitions to new sources of energy and other resources, and the necessity of new regulations and vast new expenditures to maintain a clean environment, to prevent the almost complete disappearance of wilderness areas in the United States and the overuse of existing recreational facilities to the point where the continued existence of some will be endangered.

Thus it could be said that to a great extent the problems of modern society, and particularly those affecting the quality of life, derive not from major social failures but from major social successes; for as we have seen, the most pervasive and deeply rooted problems can result from the successful transition from pre-industrial to industrial to superindustrial and postindustrial societies. This is why the discussion of quality of life takes for granted the successful performance of traditional governmental functions and the maintenance of high per capita income. Quality of life now usually refers to a set of problems that are overwhelmingly the consequences of success: anomie resulting from successful promotion of social mobility; blue-collar "blues" resulting from the successful transition out of the class structure and struggles of early industrial society; pollution resulting from successful rapid growth; perverse outbreaks of the martial spirit as a result of a generally peaceful world and the imposition of peaceful values; and intense concern with recreation and leisure issues because so many have nothing more important to be intensely concerned about. Other "failures of success" are listed in Table 18. It seems to us that recognition of the fact that today's

Table 18. Some Failures of Success

We have	*But we also have*
1. Affluence	1. No need to wait for possessions or most of what we desire, hence relatively little need for self-discipline. As a result people are at the same time overly concerned with satisfying their material wants and satiated, bored and petulant when they do and furious if they do not receive what they want immediately.
2. Continuous economic growth, technological improvements	2. Impossible demands made on the government: Steady growth uninterrupted by business cycles is required as a matter of course; unrealistically high growth rates are demanded; all groups in society must grow economically at the same rate so that no one is left behind. Improvements in technology encourage unrealistic expectations elsewhere.
3. Mass consumption	3. Aesthetic and commercial standards are determined by the tastes of the masses.
4. Economic security, little real poverty	4. Emphasis on relative poverty, hence a desire for radical egalitarianism.

Table 18.   (continued)

We have	But we also have
5. Physical safety, good health, longevity	5. A neurotic concern with avoiding pain and death. Alternatively, the lack of genuine danger and risks leads to the creation of artificial and often meaningless risks for the sake of thrills.
6. Government "for the people"	6. No realization that there are goals higher than the welfare of the people—e.g., the glory of God, national honor, great projects and achievements.
7. The belief that human beings and human life are sacred and the only absolute	7. The belief that nothing is more important than human life, hence that nothing is worth dying (or killing) for. Loss of aristocratic and uplifting ideals and of various distinctions between superior and inferior performance and individuals.
8. Rationalism and the elimination of superstition	8. The loss of tradition, patriotism, faith: everything which cannot be justified by reason cannot be justified.
9. Meritocracy	9. No sudden rises to power. Everyone must show his worth by working his way up the bureaucracy—and by bureaucratic and meritocratic techniques. Explanation and rationalization become more important than achievement and success. Further, by the time they get to the top, people have lost much spirit. Hence fewer young, idiosyncratic hotheads at the top to shake things up. Also, no respect for experience which does not constantly prove its worth by meritocratic and bureaucratic criteria.
10. An open, classless society	10. No sense of one's proper place in society. In traditional societies, if you are born an aristocrat, you die an aristocrat. Now, when you rise upward, you don't know when to stop striving. Thus, you have ceaseless struggles for more money and power—or ceaseless struggles against any distinctions of class or privilege—earned or unearned.

problems arise, not from centuries of human failure and rapaciousness, but as the result of extraordinary and multiple successes in attaining the goals mankind has cherished most is bound to have a positive and healthy effect on social morale.

We referred in Chapter I to the quaternary activities which we assume will be most prevalent and important in a mature postindustrial society, but did not give a very clear or specific picture of postindustrial life. We were, in fact, deliberately vague and eclectic because we simply do not know what the United States or other nations will look like in 2176, even if trends do develop as we have projected. We do have some ideas of what may happen in the near term, though, and more important, we have strong fears concerning that near term and the emerging transition to a postindustrial society.

Consider, for example, certain South Pacific islands which, to many outsiders, seemed to be almost a Garden of Eden; in this idyllic economy, many of the necessities of life—perhaps all—came virtually free. On such islands anthropologists invariably found elaborate structures of taboos, totems and rituals. But what outwardly was an earthly paradise was, in some ways, internally a psychological hell, at least by current standards. One is tempted to argue, perhaps too quickly, that there is something in the human psyche which requires that the absence of objective external pressures be balanced by internal psychological structures and goals. Whether we accept this simple formulation or not, it may be a clue to one major set of issues. Actually, we argue that some cultures adapt more easily to affluence and safety than others. Indeed, we would hazard a guess that the "Atlantic Protestant culture" is one that has relative difficulty in adapting to wealth and safety, while the French and Chinese cultures do so more easily.

John Maynard Keynes, in his famous essay "Economic Possibilities For Our Grandchildren," provides us with some interesting insights into this problem:

> I draw the conclusion that, assuming no important wars and no important increase in population, the economic problem may be solved, or be at least within sight of solution, within a hundred years. This means that the economic problem is not —if we look into the future—the permanent problem of the human race. . . .
>
> I see us free, therefore, to return to some of the most sure and certain principles of religion and traditional virtue—that avarice is a vice, that the exaction of usury is a misdemeanour,

and the love of money is detestable, that those walk most truly in the paths of virtue and sane wisdom who take least thought for the morrow. We shall once more value ends above means and prefer the good to the useful. We shall honour those who can teach us how to pluck the hour and the day virtuously and well. The delightful people who are capable of taking direct enjoyment in things, the lilies of the field who toil not, neither do they spin.

But beware! *The time for all this is not yet.* For at least another hundred years we must pretend to ourselves and to everyone that fair is foul and foul is fair; for foul is useful and fair is not. Avarice and usury and precaution must be our gods for a little longer still. For only they can lead us out of the tunnel of economic necessity into daylight.*

Keynes's perceptions may be somewhat romantic—we do not feel that the future belongs to the kind of "flower children" he describes, who in effect (in our terms) "drop out" of contact with most external reality—but we do believe that there will be strong trends in the direction he indicates. And we would like to endorse—in fact, emphasize strongly—the thought of his last paragraph.

We would argue that many of the problems one found in Sweden, Holland, the United States, and to a lesser degree in Canada and Australia in the late 1960's and early 1970's were products of the premature introduction to upper-middle-class elites of some of the characteristics of postindustrial culture. It should be noted that in many ways the country most severely affected was Holland—an interesting phenomenon because Holland had no Vietnam, no race problem, no problem of poverty. Indeed, even its pollution is mostly imported.

We can clarify one kind of transitional problem by considering an image of the United States in the year 2000. At that point it should have about 250 million citizens, of which 50 percent will probably be in the labor force—perhaps 100 to 125 million workers. If we assume the lesser figure of 100 million jobs, it is likely that only about 25 million people will be needed in the so-called primary and secondary industries

* John Maynard Keynes, "Economic Possibilities for Our Grandchildren" (1930), in *Essays in Persuasion* (New York: W. W. Norton, 1973), pp. 365–66, 371–72. Italics added.

—that is, only a fourth of the labor force will man the production-oriented part of the economy. The other three-fourths will be in service industries, some in tertiary services (that is, helping goods-oriented industries) and the rest in quaternary services (doing things judged worth doing for their own sake). It is difficult to estimate productivity in the quaternary activities, particularly in the government sector, and if current trends continue, it could be said that a considerable number of these service workers will simply be receiving disguised subsidies or welfare. That is, the jobs they will be doing will be meaningless in terms of product to society, though they may enjoy doing them; the jobs will merely be an accepted way of transferring income to such people. The salaries they receive will be counted as part of the GNP, but it will be increasingly difficult, in many cases, to associate this portion of the GNP with any kind of increase in benefit to others.

HOW LIKELY ARE DEMOCRACY AND WORLD GOVERNMENT?

Considering the difficulty of discussing changing values and life-styles, what can be predicted about the political systems that will govern in the next 200 years? This is as difficult to project confidently as is the issue of life-styles and values. Moreover, politics will both influence and be influenced by life-styles. For whatever it is worth, we offer some conjectures.

Many countries will be relatively or at least nominally democratic, though some democracies will probably be more authoritarian than truly parliamentary. The reason is not the universal superiority of either the democratic or authoritarian types of government; rather, it is that an affluent, technological world almost has to be—at least initially—somewhat cosmopolitan, secular, pacifistic, relativistic and perhaps hedonistic.

In deeply religious communities there is a strong tendency for the government to be conducted by a theocracy which in effect speaks to God or mediates His wishes. Heroic cultures are often governed by a great leader, an aristocracy or an oligarchy of talent, wealth or military skill. But secular-humanist cultures are not willing to legitimize any of these types of government. Their method of making a government legitimate is by social contract and the manifest consent of the governed, or by a mandate of history which clearly yields acceptable results to the governed (by their criteria).

This need for legitimization by explicit real, or pro forma, elections applies to both real and pseudo-democracies (such as many of today's "people's republics"), to relatively paternalistic, authoritarian governments (as in southern Europe, Latin America and Southeast Asia), or to a dictatorship more or less maintained by naked force (as frequently found in Africa and to a lesser extent in Latin America). In this respect, authoritarian should not be confused with totalitarian or dictatorial governments. In authoritarian states, there is a comparatively high level of legality and usually some lip service to parliamentary representation, including a need for something like genuine elections—if only in a validating and public relations role. Particularly if man is to experience a century of relative peace, and no great inflations or depressions, we can plausibly, but not certainly, assume that even more governments will be democratic than at present.

It should be noted that in the last 200–300 years stable democratic government developed primarily in what we decribe as the Atlantic Protestant cultural area and Switzerland. In all other parts of the world, democracy still seems to be relatively fragile. Clearly, though, it has also attained strength in Israel, France, West Germany and Japan; and to a lesser degree in Italy, Colombia, Venezuela, Singapore, Hong Kong, Costa Rica, Malaysia and perhaps Mexico and the Philippines. But it should be noted that there are almost no other authentic democracies in the other approximately 125 nations of the world. Thus one cannot think of democracy as a movement that clearly dominates other forms of government, particularly if democracy is put under serious strains or if the people and leaders cannot act with a modicum of democratic self-restraint and a firm and informed sense of political and financial responsibility.

It is also likely that there will be many functional organizations which will deal with the various international issues that will arise in the 21st century. Many of the most effective organizations will probably be of an ad hoc nature, but some of them will be part of larger international organizations such as the United Nations.

Many people believe that as more functions are undertaken by international organizations, there will be an almost inevitable growth toward world federal government. But unless the functions are performed with superb efficiency and effectiveness, this kind of evolution by peaceful development rarely proceeds very far without involving considerable violence. It is clear that the requirements of preserving peace and the problems of arms control, the environment and economic relations, as well as many law and order issues, all create great pressures toward peaceful evolution to world federal government. Yet we remain skeptical. One reason for skepticism arises from thinking about the likely answer of the Japanese, Soviets, Europeans and North Americans to the following questions:

1. Are you willing to turn your lives and interests, and those of your families and communities, over to a government based upon the principle of one man, one vote—that is, to a government dominated by the Chinese and the Indians?

2. Would you be willing to turn your lives and interests over to a government based upon the principle of one state, one vote—that is, to a government largely controlled by the small Latin American, Asian and African nation-states?

Clearly, the answer to these two questions will be a very strong negative, as would also be the reply to a suggestion for a bicameral legislature with two branches organized according to the above two principles. We can imagine a world legislature based upon one dollar, one vote (dominated by the United States and Japan)—or on other realistic, if inadequate, measures of actual power and influence. But it is more difficult to imagine such a government emerging peacefully, or being very strong if it did evolve peacefully. There are many ways to create a political consensus; but none of these methods makes it easy to imagine a real world government evolving by purely peaceful means.

IX

The Tasks Ahead

WE WOULD LIKE TO HAVE been able in this book to be completely optimistic, to present a view of the future which argues that while struggle, dedication and intelligence may be required, mankind will resolve all of its problems if only a reasonable effort is made—and even that man's dream of an egalitarian utopia on earth may soon come close to realization. Unfortunately, no such assurances have ever been possible; nor are they now. In particular, we believe that large income gaps between nations could persist for centuries, even though there will be some tendency to narrow. Moreover, our discussion of the long-term environment had to be so uncertain and inconclusive that it may have left many readers with considerably lowered morale after our predominantly optimistic presentation of such issues as growth, energy, food and resources in the previous chapters. Our own attitude is certainly basically positive—and we do not believe that the persistence of income gaps is necessarily either tragic or immoral—but our picture of one aspect of current reality, as set forth in Chapter VII, does make us apprehensive. We are not among those who are pleased or take any satisfaction in finding out that great tragedy, even doomsday, is indeed possible—or at least not to be ruled out—and that various degrees of catastrophe are still possible even in the face of man's best efforts. Such possibilities have always been present, but now they seem to arise as much from man's activities—that is, from what we call the Faustian bargain—as from nature. On the other hand, it is clear that our basic image of the future emerges as bright, and since this image is based on careful analysis and projection—and takes as full account of negative possibilities as we can—it should go far to reassure those who are excessively apprehensive.

It is also equally clear that we would perform an enormous disservice to all, including the poor, by raising expectations or defining what is a relatively normal, healthy and near-permanent condition as a serious moral problem which has to be solved. What most people everywhere want is visible, even rapid improvement in their economic status and living standards, and not a closing of the gap. They would love to double their income in 15-20 years (thus going from poor to middle class), and they are generally shocked to hear that this is indeed a possible and practical goal (which it is in most poor countries—or would be with reasonable government policies—although, of course, much less can be accomplished in 5 or 10 years).

THE FIRST TASK: A REALISTIC IMAGE OF THE FUTURE

Projecting a persuasive image of a desirable and practical future is extremely important to high morale, to dynamism, to consensus and in general to help the wheels of society turn smoothly. But we also want to emphasize that we at Hudson are only interested in improving morale after we are ourselves convinced of the truth of our message. To us, the virtue of the image of the future presented here is not that it may prove useful (though we are highly pleased that this may be so), but rather that our forecast of the future may prove accurate, or at least about the most plausible image one can develop now. If we could not realistically justify an optimistic image, we would be quite willing to portray a negative one, arguing that it is our business to call the shots as we see them. Furthermore, such a negative image, if persuasive and realistic, might help elites to mobilize to face real problems (as opposed to unrealistic negative images, which tend to raise false issues, create unnecessary controversy and divert resources and attention from practical solutions). Actually, we believe that it is almost always easier, except in the direst emergencies, to mobilize society around a positive rather than a negative image. It is also our view that if the negative image is largely inaccurate and morale-eroding as well, it could be destructive if widely disseminated. This might be especially true if it dominates the educational curriculum—as indeed the limits-to-growth view has in a surprisingly large portion of the Atlantic Protestant culture and Japan.

It is also worth noting that it is not true, as many people contend, that what might be called the "max-min strategy" would require taking a limits-to-growth perspective. In such a strategy one examines the worst that can reasonably be expected to happen with each policy and then picks the policy that limits one's risks—that is, of all the policies available, the one with the least damaging of the possible outcomes. We would argue that, in reality, almost the opposite may be true. It is not our postindustrial perspective which would force enormous repression on individual countries and which would consciously continue, in a dangerous way, absolute world poverty. Indeed, it is the limits-to-growth position which creates low morale, destroys assurance, undermines the legitimacy of governments everywhere, erodes personal and group commitment to constructive activities and encourages obstructiveness to reasonable policies and hopes. Thus the effects of this position increase enormously the costs of creating the resources needed for expansion, make more likely misleading debate and misformulation of the issues, and make less likely constructive and creative lives. Ultimately the position even increases the potential for the kinds of disasters which most of its advocates are trying to avoid.

Clearly, the first task is to gain acceptance of a more reasonable view of the future, one that opens possibilities rather than forecloses them. We believe that current prophets of peril are making forecasts that could indeed be self-fulfilling, if only in the short run. For if enough people were really convinced that growth should be halted, and if they acted on that conviction, then billions of others might be deprived of any realistic hope of gaining the opportunities now enjoyed by the more fortunate. Indeed, lacking the incentives that have guided them and their forebears, they too might soon despair, bereft of both ambition and goals, and irresponsible activist leaders might assume power. We believe that eventually—when the postindustrial economy has arrived—much of the industrial imperative and its appurtenances will erode or expire; but to weaken it prematurely, before it has run its natural course, would be to impose unnecessary trauma and suffering and make even more difficult the full exploitation of the many opportunities now available.

OVERCOMING THE KNOWN PROBLEMS OF THE NEAR TERM

Next among the tasks ahead is to find the appropriate means for dealing with the problems of the present and the immediate future. While our scenario for America and the world is generally optimistic for the long term, we do recognize the real possibilities of serious anomalies, dislocations and crises in the short term, any one of which could greatly complicate the process of getting from here to there. Among these potential difficulties are regional overpopulation, retarded economic growth, energy shortfalls, raw materials shortages, local famines, short-run but intense pollution, environmetal surprises and (most fearful of all) large-scale thermonuclear war. While we offer no solutions that will guarantee the avoidance of these problems, we do believe that acceptance of our position presents the best hope of both reducing the possibility of their occurrence and mitigating the consequences if any do occur.

1. Population

Recent data show that the rate of population growth is declining in almost all the developed countries, and that birth rates are also declining in many less-developed countries. These trends have led us (and U.N. population experts) to plausible projections that a maximum will very soon be reached in the rate of growth of world population and that in less than 200 years the number of people on earth will become more or less stable. Nevertheless, there are now—and may continue to be—areas where population increase is about as rapid as economic growth, and this does cause a severe drain on resources needed for development.

However, increased population is not necessarily a *cause* of slower growth, even though correlations can often be found between high population growth rate and low development. The stronger case is that, under current conditions, with economic development there is almost always an associated decline in birth rate. As two Stanford researchers have stated: "From a broad look at the whole world, we conclude that mortality is a function of modernization and development, that truly low levels of mortality are rarely found in the least-developed countries, and that declining natality is found in precisely those LDC's which have made the social and economic progress apparently required for a significant mortality decline." *

Thus the primary response to rapid population growth is not necessarily an antinatalist program, even though such programs can be useful and sometimes have a significant impact, as was the case in post–World War II Japan. A contrary example is just as impressive: In the United States the total fertility rate declined from seven children per woman in 1800 to fewer than two per woman in 1970, *without benefit of an antinatalist program.* (Ironically, it is just at the end of this strong trend that movements for such programs have begun

---

* Frank Wm. Oechsli and Dudley Kirk, "Modernization and Demographic Transition in Latin America and the Caribbean," *Economic Development and Cultural Change,* April 1975, p. 395.

to attract attention.) It seems clear that what is needed for the most part—to truly affect population growth—is economic development in those areas where birth rates are still very high.

2. *Economic growth*

When we come to the question of economic development we find something quite strange indeed: a surprising lack of awareness of the progress that has been made. For example, in 1960 the United Nations set a goal for the Decade of Development of 5 percent growth for the less-developed countries. It was not expected that the goal would be met; it was one of those unrealistic rhetorical goals that one strives for but does not actually expect to attain. Yet the goal was actually exceeded by 10 percent—the less-developed countries achieved an average of 5.5 percent growth—and this impressive feat was not celebrated anywhere. Instead, people began explaining with great ingenuity and desperate eagerness why the Decade of Development had almost totally failed. One issue involved the fact that the poorer two-thirds of the LDC's had achieved only 3.9 percent growth, but the critics failed to realize that even 3.9 percent was actually closer to the goal than it had been anticipated the noncoping nations would achieve; indeed, most had expected that the poor would get poorer, not richer (which they did at rates that would have been judged to be quite high by pre–World War II standards).

We believe that the prospects are good and getting better for the coping nations, and that these are the developing countries that will help drive the world's economic growth in the 21st century. For the noncoping nations, the immediate prospects are not so good, but our projection is that over the long term they, too, will gradually join the ranks of the coping nations. We further believe that the key to accelerating this process is not primarily exploitable natural resources or economic aid or population-control assistance, but instead training, education, innovation, savings and investment, institutional change and what Joseph Schumpeter called "creative destruction." We agree with Simon Kuznets that: "purely technological and economic factors allow sufficient margins, in most underdeveloped countries, to permit substantial and sustained economic growth, even with a significant rise in population growth—at least for the proximate future of two or three decades. The difficulties and the problems lie in the limited capacity of the institutions of the underdeveloped countries—political, legal, cultural and economic—to channel activity so as to exploit the advantages of economic backwardness." * It does not help these countries to erect artificial problems and blocks—or to discourage their commitment and morale. It is precisely the advantages associated with the income gap, as we emphasized in Chapter II, that constitute the great opportunity for the world's poor nations. Thus the task ahead, for America and the developed world, is to help raise the capacity of these nations' institutions to exploit the gap whose very existence can accelerate their growth. Closing that gap will not occur soon—in fact, for a time it may even widen —but meanwhile the doubling or tripling of the income of the poorest that does take place will be a substantial and welcome development for peasants and workers and most businessmen, even if Western intellectual and governmental establishments downplay or ignore this achievement in favor of rhetorical remarks about the inequities of the gap.

3. *Energy*

Long-term energy prospects—resting on sources that are inexhaustible—are very good; but the recent oil embargo showed how vulnerable the world may be in the short term. In these circumstances the task ahead in energy is twofold: the development of alternate energy sources and the achievement of a degree of energy independence.

We have spoken of energy sources as "current," "transitional" and "eternal." Much is still available in the current inventory, especially in coal, but well-intentioned yet wrong-

* Simon Kuznets, "Population and Economic Growth," *Proceedings of the American Philosophical Society*, June 22, 1967, p. 190.

headed policies may keep this energy source from being developed. Price ceilings on hydrocarbons may for a time help restrain inflation, at least as measured by government indices; but they will also encourage the misuse of these fuels, increase dependence on imports and remove incentives to develop alternative sources. Some may temporarily benefit from lower prices, but the eventual cost could be embargo vulnerability, crippling energy shortages and skyrocketing prices. Price floors on hydrocarbons, on the other hand—if set sufficiently high—could slow their use and provide the needed incentive to realize the potential of other energy sources. Encouragement is also needed for transitional sources, particularly synthetic fuels and fission power. In this case, though, high risks and many problems may make government assistance necessary. This can occur in many forms, including grants of government land, tax benefits and accelerated depreciation. Federal assistance will also be necessary for the early exploitation of eternal sources. Here the important task will be to support multiple paths of research and development and to avoid prematurely allocating excessive resources to initially attractive—but far from proven—technologies. (Many argue that this is the case in the current liquid metal fast breeder [LMFBR] type of nuclear power reactor.) We realize that all this represents a considerable intervention by the government in the free market system; but we believe that such intervention is justified—in large part to enable the free market system to better allocate society's resources and to prevent excessive dependence on external sources.

A reasonable corollary to the above is the achievement of a degree of energy autarky—or at least short-term independence. It is fashionable today—as it has been for much of this century, especially since World War II—to preach the value and necessity of global interdependence. But in many matters interdependence increases both the likelihood of sharing bad fortune and the opportunity of being held hostage. Nations cannot "stop the world and get off," but they can seek to follow a course of interdependence that emphasizes constructive cooperation and system toughness rather than potentially destructive dependence and system vulnerability. In terms of energy sources, this is not an argument for *total* independence, which is normally too expensive an alternative in any calculation of opportunity costs; but it is a plea for a degree of autarky sufficient to protect against the threat of energy blackmail or accidental or deliberate slowdown in delivery.*

4. Raw materials

Here the alarm seems genuinely misplaced. Sources of most raw materials are great and, with new discoveries, are growing. (Mining of ocean nodules will vastly increase the supply of several metals considered vital to industry today.) Before these sources are exhausted—if this ever occurs—we anticipate that extraction from high-grade rock and from the ocean itself will be economically feasible; and it is also possible that extraterrestrial mining will provide new, and practically inexhaustible, sources in the distant future. We also anticipate that with the passage from super- to postindustrial economies, the trend to reduced per capita use of raw materials, already visible today in several metals, will continue and accelerate, thus further reducing pressures on supplies.

For those materials which are vital and in short supply in the near term, initial efforts will focus on recycling, conservation and substitution. Most metals that have been mined still exist today, but in some manufactured form. Recycling—which for the most part has only barely begun—can make them usable again. Where supplies are short and recycling is too difficult or too expensive, increased prices will spur efforts toward conservation and the search for synthetics and substitutes. Finally, for those few cases where all the above

---

* This argument runs counter to the major conclusions of the Club of Rome's second report—Mihajlo Mesarovic and Eduard Pestel, *Mankind at the Turning Point* (New York: Reader's Digest Press, 1974)—which emphasizes the importance of global interdependence and stresses the necessity of solving problems in a "global context" by "global concerted action." We believe this goes in exactly the wrong direction, and that the organic interdependence it suggests would ensure that a dislocation anywhere would be a dislocation everywhere. We prefer redundancy, flexibility and a degree of "disconnectedness." If India, for example, goes under, we want to be able to help save her, not go down with her.

approaches prove inadequate, research and development will have to find ways of replacing the processes and devices using the scarce materials, and the old tools and methods will then be relegated to the museums of the future as the relics of a bygone age.

The near-term tasks ahead are: to accelerate the exploration for and exploitation of raw materials and to restore confidence (hopefully justified) in the safety of investment and contracts in the developing nations, whose economies need the stimulus this exploitation will provide; to reach agreements (*de facto* or *de jure*) on the exploration and development of the resources of the world's oceans (it is hoped these agreements will promote constructive cooperation, but at the least they should allow development to proceed at a reasonable pace); and to accumulate stockpiles of vital materials, for that will protect against many eventualities that could otherwise prove destructive.

5. *Food*

Our discussion has emphasized that it is not the *production* of food that is critical—the world has adequate land, water and fertilizer now available to feed its present numbers; rather, it is the inadequate *distribution* of food that accounts for malnutrition, hunger and famine in parts of the world. Regional famine is therefore primarily a problem of public policy and resource allocation. In practice, this can be reduced to the simple proposition that adequate food is available to those who can produce it, who can pay for it, or who can get somebody else to pay for or finance it.

There are thus two urgent tasks which must be undertaken to reduce the likelihood of severe regional or nationwide famines. The first is to create a margin of safety by building stockpiles that can be drawn upon in periods of emergency created by poor harvests and natural catastrophes, as well as by gross errors in national policy. However, it is important to recognize that it is the surplus-food-producing nations of the world (the United States, Canada, Australia and to a lesser extent Argentina) that will have to build these stockpiles, not some international consortium created by the good will of nations whose hearts are full but whose contributions are small. Advocating such international cooperation is often merely a "cop-out," useful more to soothe consciences than to fill stomachs.

The second urgent task is that of achieving vital institutional reforms that will enable food-hungry nations to improve their own agricultural sectors. This should be done as much to increase their GNP's as to provide more food for home consumption. Too often, developing nations—in their haste to industrialize—have emphasized manufacturing at the expense of agriculture in their plans. Yet history shows that, with only a few exceptions, the path to economic growth has been across fields of wheat, not tracks of steel. What is required in the chronically food-short countries are policies that allocate resources to the development of agricultural technology, provide inputs and incentives to farmers to increase production, and create an agricultural infrastructure (including transportation, irrigation, education, storage facilities and sources of credit). These tasks require the assistance and cooperation of the developed nations, but in the final analysis it is each developing nation which must recognize that its first priority is to find ways of producing food and income for its people.

6. Pollution

Much has been done and much still needs to be done to clean both our air and water. The accomplishment grew out of the fact that enough people in enough places discovered that the air and water were deteriorating and that they could afford to do something about it. Thus industries and other groups who had never paid much attention to their impact upon the air and water suddenly found they had to, and could, do so. There has been a growing recognition that air and water are scarce and belong to the public, and that one must pay to use them, just as one pays for raw materials or labor or building space. Moreover, one must operate in ways which protect them. The task ahead is simply to persuade those who use the air and water that they must pay the costs to clean what they have fouled. While it is normally efficient economically to make such payments equal to the costs, it might be better, in principle, to make penalties higher, perhaps twice as high as the actual cost of clean-up, thus not only encouraging steps to prevent fouling in the first place but eliminating any suggestion that the government is going easy on the polluters.

The problem of pollution in the less-developed countries is more difficult. Many in these countries prefer pollution to poverty, and there is some justification to their claim that they should not have to bear a burden not borne by the developed nations when they industrialized. Even if they can afford it, it may be hard to convince nations who are struggling to improve their own circumstances to use their limited resources on expensive or sophisticated antipollution programs. Several points should be made. First, the sacrifice the less-developed countries would make to control pollution is less in many cases than the developed world has had to make in undoing years of lack of attention to the environment. Second, new technologies are regularly being designed which will either make pollution control unnecessary or create situations where the gains in permitting pollution will be small but the losses large. Finally, it is often possible to design plants or programs to permit pollution controls to be added at reasonable costs at a later time, when resources are more abundant. These are choices which each developing nation must make for itself.

7. *Thermonuclear war*

It is true—though not often acknowledged—that even two enormously destructive wars did not appreciably slow the accelerating pace of industrial growth in this century. Nevertheless, one can hardly be so confident that the world could similarly overcome the effects of a war involving the widespread use of nuclear weapons, particularly if they were employed in their most destructive modes (that is, more against civilian than military targets). As we contemplate the tasks ahead, this is probably the single biggest danger.

It is ironic that today—in the atmosphere of Soviet-American détente—there is less concern about thermonuclear war than there was only five years ago, while at the same time, in nations on every continent developments are taking place that could, conceivably within two decades, quadruple the current number of nuclear powers and make atomic weapons almost as common in the world's arsenals as battlefield tanks were in World War II. The greatest concern is, of course, a war which would see the massive and almost uncontrolled unleashing of the nuclear arsenals of the great powers; fortunately the present leadership of each superpower is aware of the enormous destruction such an exchange would cause, and this awareness in itself exercises a very strong restraint. However, even a very small nuclear war could do an extraordinary amount of damage.

The task ahead in dealing with this problem is difficult and complex. Clearly part of it is to try to prevent further nuclear proliferation, but just as clearly such an effort is not alone sufficient, for if this policy fails—as we must realistically consider it might—then to what policy do we fall back? The answer is that while making every effort to slow and halt the pace of nuclear proliferation, we must also begin preparations now to make as certain as possible that a world of more nuclear powers will be even less likely to witness their use, and that if such use occurs, it will not only be an extremely costly failure to the user but will provide a very strong cautionary example to other potential users.

We can only outline the beginning of a program here. One might start by *decreasing* rather than increasing the potential utility of nuclear weapons. Gradually—allowing time for necessary adjustments to be made—nations could decouple themselves from arrangements under which a nuclear "first use" response might be expected in a wide range of contingencies, until finally the United States, and most of the other nuclear nations, were in agreement that the only valid purpose of nuclear weapons is to negate the use of nuclear weapons. Equally, this country must insure—in arrangement with other nuclear nations—that any other use of such weapons will be met with instant and proportionate retaliation. In effect, this would be a resort to the Biblical injunction of an eye for an eye, a tooth for a tooth—the *lex talionis* of primitive tribal law, where the measure of retaliation implies not only "at least," but also "at most." In addition, nations should threaten first to excommunicate and then bring to justice any nuclear offender where it is practical to do so. In a sense, they would be adopting the same peacekeeping attitude as the U.N., which rarely asks who was right but only tries to stop the violence. The primitive tribe has learned that this cannot usually be done unless the damage has been evened out.

By clearly enunciating and living up to these rules, the principle would be established that there is no provocation, no matter how terrible—short only of a nuclear provocation —that justifies use of nuclear weapons, and that any nation initiating such use would not only be cut off from all communication and intercourse with other nations but would immediately be the recipient of at least an equal attack. Achievement of such an agreed disutility for nuclear weapons would admittedly be very difficult, but we believe it is a much more practical approach than would appear at first sight. If made credible, such a policy would eliminate the principal reason for nations to possess nuclear weapons and thus remove or reduce the incentive to acquire them. No other alternative seems likely to slow the pace of proliferation or reduce the danger of living in a nuclear-armed world as much.

It should be noted that the basis for the view of a world without thermonuclear war is the concept that for most countries the best path to wealth, safety and power is through internal development and not through war. It is a great virtue of the postindustrial economy that there are very few conditions under which war pays—or even seems to pay—as opposed to the situation that has applied during much of the pre-industrial and industrial eras. It is true that in a very wealthy society the motive for serious conflict is likely to be other than an economic one, but it is also possible that economic satisfaction might result in much diminished conflict or even fewer occasions for conflict. It is therefore conceivable, though not inevitable, that a postindustrial society may be relatively free from violence and war.

COPING WITH THE UNKNOWN PROBLEMS OF THE LONG TERM

Man's intellectual and physical resources must also be devoted to the task of monitoring and overcoming potentially catastrophic long-term environmental problems. Our first focus is here on earth, where we need to map the full terrain of possibilities, extrapolating from the known to the unknown— and still leaving room for possibilities beyond our extrapolations. To help in this effort, we would recommend the worldwide creation of a number of public and private institutions with various specific purposes, but all with an overall mission of the systematic and intense study of far-fetched and improbable phenomena, but phenomena which would be extremely important were they to occur. In effect, these institutions would together constitute an articulate lobby and an "early warning system" for long-term environmental problems.* It is only fair to warn the public that anyone who studies such phenomena full time is almost certain to exaggerate their likelihood, impact and dangers. To do so is simply human nature. We do want the people making these studies to conduct them with an almost fanatic intensity, since such fanaticism can be very useful in sustaining interest, drive and even creativity. But we do not want this fanaticism to be carried over into judgments on public policy. Our "fanatics" can alert us to the problems and perhaps eventually to their solutions, and they can put enormous effort into the study of both, but we also recognize that this kind of fanaticism, while useful in research and study, can be a disservice if it dominates public discourse.

The first purpose of this early warning system should be to alert the technological and scientific community, govern-

---

* These could be adjuncts to—and participants in—GEMS (the Global Environmental Monitoring System), created as part of Project Earthwatch by UNEP (United Nations Environment Program). See Clayton E. Jensen, Dail W. Brown and John A. Mirabito, "Earthwatch," *Science,* October 31, 1975, pp. 432–38.

ments and other relevant elites. We are not suggesting, of course, that these scientists be restricted from public communication, but we do believe that the general public is usually not in a good position to make early judgments on technical matters. If the experts do not soon reach a consensus, then the public must make its own judgment; and sometimes even if the experts and elites do reach a near-consensus, the public may choose to differ from them.

Our view is that such a system could evolve into a quite effective one. People are now beginning to understand these issues better, including the need for both "whistle-blowing" and concerned but responsible opposition. Often the problem is that there are well-developed biases which can lead to an almost automatic "cover-up" and a protection of vested interests and the status quo. But just as frequently—and this seems to be especially the case today—there is a kind of mindless "opposition for the sake of opposition," nurtured by institutions whose prestige gives them an aura of authority in the public mind. Yet even this kind of opposition is not intolerable and is probably worth the insurance it gives us—since its spokesmen are likely to be right at least as often as they are wrong. (Because these institutions *are* prestigious, people will listen longer and give more credence to their periodic cries of "wolf," but still be attentive when the wolf really *is* there.) Thus society can afford to have cyclamates needlessly banned, without great tragedy, even though such an action should be avoided if the evidence does not justify it. Yet it is also important to understand that overreacting can eventually cause a serious loss of credibility.

On balance, we are confident that the task of monitoring and early warning—if sufficiently supported—could give us the very high probability of acquiring an assessment of long-term environmental problems that is credible and timely enough to permit effective remedial action. But we also believe that it is important to look beyond the earth, to outer space. The imperatives of our current earthbound problems and the constraints of worldwide stagflation have lowered the priority given to activity outside our atmospheric envelope. We point out that the economic growth we project will make available

enormous resources for such activity (1 percent of our projected GWP in 2176 will be a staggering $3 trillion—60 per-
cent of today's GWP and about 1,000 times larger than the
current U.S. space program). It could even turn out that a
capability for self-supporting existence in space would make
possible the continuation of earth's civilization and the resusci-
tation of human life on the planet following an irreversible
tragedy of the kind sketched in Chapter VII. We estimate the
probability of such a calamity as too small, by itself, to justify
such an effort. Nonetheless, its potential disutility is so enormous that a concerted international effort to create extraterrestrial self-sustaining communities, in concert with other space
objectives, would probably be well warranted. In short, what
we are proposing is a dual-purpose lifeboat for spaceship
earth.

THINKING ABOUT THE POSTINDUSTRIAL ERA

We cannot forecast here what the nature, development and
organization of life and society in the postindustrial era will
be, even though we do believe that these are the *real* issues
of the future, far surpassing in their significance—and in their
difficulty—the more tractable issues we have dealt with earlier
in this volume. People often talk about consciously choosing
their future, but historically it is clear that only rarely has such
choice actually been available—and then usually under an
authoritarian political leader such as Augustus, Tokugawa,
Napoleon or Lenin. All of these leaders did make deliberate
choices which set the courses of nations for a century or more.
But the main concern of the future is negotiating the trip from
here to there, and for this reason it is the short- and medium-
term issues which tend to attract the most attention. One
might like to be able to choose the future, but probably the
best we can do is to influence the path by which we reach it.

Yet it is interesting—and in some ways useful—to set
down the likely changes that our descendants will both create

and confront. They do give us an outline of the possible shape of things to come, and in this way prepare and forewarn us as we contemplate the journey.

It seems very likely that many subtle and sophisticated questions will arise as mankind—increasingly relieved of the burdens of simple sustenance and richer in technological capabilities and economic resources—continues its inexorable march across new frontiers. Indeed, some such questions are already arising.

The fundamental physiological and psychological aspects of human life are being altered today, and will be changed further tomorrow. Most of the great diseases of the past have been all but eliminated (smallpox, for example, will soon be a memory almost as distant as scurvy and beriberi), and death increasingly will be mainly the result of either accident or the simple wearing out of vital organs (here, too, new opportunities for life extension are arising through the rapidly growing science of organ replacement and soon of organ regeneration). As man progresses further in genetic research, he will move closer to the time when he will be able to influence the design of his offspring, perhaps even produce them ectogenetically. Man can now alter his mental state with drugs, and over time even influence his personality. Will man, within 200 years, be able to condition his mind to increase his ability to learn, to communicate, to create, and will he have the power to affect others similarly, perhaps without their knowing it?

How will all of these potential changes, many of which are quite likely, affect human beings for whom work—in the post-industrial era—will be an activity of relatively short duration, and of a primarily self-serving nature? It is almost impossible to imagine such an existence. But already there are available electromechanical devices that effect enormous savings of labor, and the next generation of such devices—spurred by the computer revolution—will probably free man from the need to manage them, except for the preselection of appropriate computer programs. What kind of a life will a genetically engineered, vital-organ-replaceable, mental-state-adjustable, computer-robot-assisted human being want to live? Will he find satisfaction in the postindustrial era? Will he seek even more to test himself in the combat of sport, the risk of adventure or the challenge of exploration? Or will he be able and prefer to experience all of this—and more—through artificial stimulation?

And what of social organization in this postindustrial era? Will people group as child-rearing families, in service-providing communities, under national banners? Or will these human beings of dramatically different makeup seek greatly altered institutions? It seems clear that there will be many more people and that most will have the means to obtain more in terms of goods and possessions than they can today. But will these goods be distributed as they are now, acquired with finite resources through billions of interacting calculations of marginal utility? Politics, Harold Lasswell once wrote in a famous definition, is "competition for scarce values." In a world of great abundance for almost all, but greater abundance for some than others, will the same competition still obtain? And in that world of greatly advanced communication and transportation, will we still see each other as being so different?

The postindustrial world we foresee will be one of increased abundance, and thus hopefully of reduced competition; it will be one of greater travel and contact, and thus possibly one of diminished differences among its peoples. But it will also be one of enormous power to direct and manipulate both man and nature; and thus its great issues will still be the very questions that confront us now, though enlarged in range and magnitude: Who will direct and manipulate, and to what ends?

Appendix:
Two Kinds of Issues
Facing Mankind

EIGHT BASICALLY UNCERTAIN ISSUES

These are the real issues of the future. Their general nature is sometimes clear; the exact shape they will take, the degree of danger and problems involved and their likely resolution are unclear.

1. Effects of U.S. superindustrial economy on environment, society and culture of the U.S. and the world.
2. Effects of U.S. postindustrial economy on environment, society and culture of the U.S. and the world.
3. Parallel developments in other countries.
4. Political, institutional, international-security and arms-control issues.
5. Possible damage to earth because of complicated, complex and subtle ecological and environmental effects.
6. Issues relating to quality of life, attitudes, values, morals and morale for different nations and groups.
7. Images of the future and the likely problems and opportunities created by these images.
8. Degree and effects of bad luck and bad management.

EIGHT BASICALLY SOLVABLE ISSUES

These issues are at the center of current controversies and are thus very troublesome for the present and the immediate future. However, a surprisingly broad consensus concerning their nature and possible solution is probably attainable. Thus, the current debate is very misleading and drains off energies which could better be devoted to the real issues listed above. At the same time much current discussion discourages practical steps by assuming that they will be ineffective. If this potential consensus could be articulated and demonstrated, then the issues below could be addressed with greater effectiveness and, at the same time, more attention could be directed to the real issues.

1. Likelihood of population and GWP transition being caused more by "natural" limitation of demand than forced limitation of supply.
2. Overall demographic, land-use and income issues.
3. Agricultural and related food issues.
4. Energy issues.
5. Other resource issues.
6. Issues associated with clean air, clean water and aesthetic landscapes.
7. Partial images of the future, including images of the likely emergence of both the super- and the postindustrial economies.
8. An important and exciting role for space.

Selected Readings

Beckerman, Wilfred. *In Defence of Economic Growth.* London: Jonathan Cape, 1974.

Bell, Daniel. *The End of Ideology.* Glencoe, Illinois: The Free Press, 1960.

———— (ed.). *Toward the Year 2000.* Boston: Houghton Mifflin, 1968.

Brown, Lester R. *Seeds of Change.* Published for the Overseas Development Council. New York: Praeger Publishers, 1970.

————. *In the Human Interest.* New York: W. W. Norton, 1974.

————. *By Bread Alone.* Published for the Overseas Development Council. New York: Praeger Publishers, 1974.

Carson, Rachel. *Silent Spring.* New York: Alfred A. Knopf, 1962.

Chen, Kan. *Growth Policy: Population, Environment, and Beyond.* Ann Arbor: University of Michigan Press, 1974.

Clark, Colin. *The Conditions of Economic Progress.* 3rd. ed. New York: St. Martin's Press, 1957.

————. *Starvation or Plenty?* New York: Taplinger Publishing Co., 1970.

Cole, H. S. D., *et al.* (eds.). *Models of Doom: A Critique of the Limits to Growth.* New York: Universe Books, 1973.

Commoner, Barry (ed.). *Energy and Human Welfare: A Critical Analysis.* New York: Macmillan, 1975.

Daly, Herman E. (ed.). *Toward a Steady State Economy.* San Francisco: W. H. Freeman, 1973.

Drucker, Peter F. *The Age of Discontinuity.* New York: Harper & Row, 1969.

Ehrlich, Paul R. *The Population Bomb.* New York: Ballantine Books, 1968.

————. *The End of Affluence.* New York: Ballantine Books, 1974.

Ellul, Jacques. *The Technological Society.* New York: Alfred A. Knopf, 1964.

Felix, Fremont. *World Markets of Tomorrow: Economic Growth, Population Trends, Electricity and Energy, Quality of Life.* New York: Harper & Row, 1972.

Forrester, Jay W. *World Dynamics.* Cambridge, Mass.: Wright-Allen Press, 1971.

Grayson, Melvin, and Shepard, Thomas, Jr. *The Disaster Lobby.* Chicago: Follett Publishing Co., 1973.

Heilbroner, Robert. *An Inquiry into the Human Prospect.* New York: W. W. Norton, 1972.

Hicken, Victor. *The World Is Coming to an End!* New Rochelle, N.Y.: Arlington House, 1975.

Kuznets, Simon S. *Economic Growth and Structure.* New York: W. W. Norton, 1965.

————. *Economic Growth of Nations.* Cambridge, Mass.: Belknap Press of Harvard University Press, 1971.

Lorenz, Konrad. *Civilized Man's Deadly Sins.* New York: Harcourt Brace and Jovanovich, 1974.

Lukacs, John A. *The Passing of the Modern Age.* New York: Harper & Row, 1970.

McDonald, Forrest. *The Phaeton Ride: The Crisis of American Success.* Garden City, N.Y.: Doubleday, 1974.

Maddox, John. *The Doomsday Syndrome.* New York: McGraw-Hill, 1972.

Meadows, Donella H. and Dennis L.; Randers, Jorgen; and Behrens, William, W., III. *The Limits to Growth.* New York: Universe Books, 1972.

Mesarovic, Mihajlo, and Pestel, Eduard. *Mankind at the Turning Point.* New York: E. P. Dutton/Reader's Digest Press, 1974.

Mishan, Ezra J. *The Costs of Economic Growth.* New York: Praeger Publishers, 1967.

————. *Technology and Growth: The Price We Pay.* New York: Praeger Publishers, 1969.

Nordhaus, William. *Is Growth Obsolete?* New Haven, Conn.: Cowles Foundation for Research in Economics, October 7, 1971

Olson, Mancur, and Landsberg, Hans H. (eds.). *The No-Growth Society*. London: Woburn Press, 1975.

Oltmans, Willem L. (ed.). *On Growth*. New York: G. P. Putnam's Sons, 1974.

Rostow, Walt W. *The Stages of Economic Growth: A Non-Communist Manifesto*. Cambridge, England, and New York: Cambridge University Press, 1960.

Schmalz, Anton B. (ed.). *Energy: Today's Choices, Tomorrow's Opportunities*. New York: World Future Society, 1974.

Schrag, Peter. *The End of the American Future*. New York: Simon & Schuster, 1972.

Schumacher, Ernst F. *Small Is Beautiful: A Study of Economics As If People Mattered*. New York· Harper & Row, 1973,

Vacca, Roberto. *The Coming Dark Age*. Garden City, N.Y.: Doubleday, 1973.

Watt, Kenneth E. F. *The Titanic Effect*. Stamford, Conn.: Sinauer Assoc., 1974.

Weintraub, Andrew; Schwartz, Eli; and Aronson, Richard J. (eds.). *The Economic Growth Controversy*. White Plains, N.Y.: International Arts & Sciences Press, 1974.

Index

Hudson Institute
Prospects for Mankind
Advisory Board

Harry B. Adams
Associate Dean
The Divinity School
Yale University

John Adams
National Resources
    Defense Council

Walter Annenberg
President
The Annenberg School of
    Communications

Robert Berks
Sculptor/Environmental Planner

Lewis M. Branscomb
Vice President and Chief Scientist
International Business Machines
    Corporation

Diane J. Brokaw
The President Ford Committee

Douglass Cater
Director
Aspen Institute

Richard M. Clurman
Time Magazine

William Drayton, Jr.
Associate
McKinsey & Company, Inc.

Rene Dubos
Professor Emeritus
The Rockefeller University

Freeman J. Dyson
Professor
Institute for Advanced Study
Princeton

Frances Farenthold
Attorney-at-Law
Houston

George Farenthold
Managing Partner
Total Oil and Gas Ltd.

James Finn
Editor
Worldview

Herbert I. Fusfeld
Director of Research
Kennecott Copper Corporation

MacRoy Gasque
Vice President and Director, Health
    Affairs
Olin Corporation

Neal Gilliatt
Vice Chairman
The Interpublic Group

Robert W. Gilmore
President
Center for War/Peace Studies

William T. Golden
Treasurer & Director
American Association for the
    Advancement of Science

R. E. Gomory
Vice President and Director of
    Research
International Business Machines
    Corporation

James P. Grant
President
Overseas Development Council

Arthur Gray, Jr.
Chairman
Tallasi Management Company

Eric Hoffer
San Francisco, California

Ernest F. Hollings
United States Senator
South Carolina

Sidney Hook
Professor Emeritus
Department of Philosophy
New York University

Franklin M. Jarman
Chairman
Genesco

Bruce Jacobi
President
Corland Corporation

John G. Keane
President
Managing Change Incorporated

William W. Kellogg
Senior Scientist
Laboratory of Atmospheric Science
National Center for Atmospheric
    Research

Franklin A. Lindsay
Chairman
Itek Corporation

Mack Lipkin
Professor of Family Practice
Professor of Psychiatry (Medicine)
University of Oregon

Bayless Manning
President
The Council on Foreign Relations

Lloyd N. Morrisett
President
The John & Mary R. Markle
    Foundation

Robert Nathan
Robert Nathan Associates, Inc.

Gerald K. O'Neill
Professor of Physics
Princeton University

Herbert Passin
Chairman
Sociology Department
Columbia University

Frances Petersmeyer
Bronxville, New York

Wesley Posvar
Chancellor
University of Pittsburgh

Roger Revelle
Director
Center for Population Studies
Harvard University

W. F. Rockwell, Jr.
Chairman
Rockwell International

Melvin Roman
Department of Psychiatry
Albert Einstein College of Medicine

Daniel Rose
Partner, Rose Associates

Arthur Ross
Vice Chairman and Managing
    Director
Central National Corporation

Leo Rosten
Author, Social Sciences

Bayard Rustin
President
A. Philip Randolph Institute

Wolfgang Sannwald
Chairman and Publisher
MBA Communications, Inc.

Dore Schary
Writer/Director/Producer

Harry Schwartz
Distinguished Professor
State University of New York
    College at New Paltz

Frederick Seitz
President
The Rockefeller University

Eleanor Bernert Sheldon
President
Social Science Research Council

William W. Simmons
President
W. W. Simmons, Inc.

Walmer E. Strope
Senior Operations Analyst
Stanford Research Institute

Frank N. Trager
Director of Studies
National Strategy Information
    Center, Inc.

Frederick K. Trask
Payson & Trask

Paul Weidlinger
Weidlinger Associates

Victor Weisskopf
Department of Physics
Massachusetts Institute of
    Technology

Adam Yarmolinsky
Ralph Waldo Emerson Professor
University of Massachusetts

Charles A. Zraket
Senior Vice President
The Mitre Corporation

Membership on the board does not imply full agreement with this study or the views of the Hudson Institute or members of its staff.